To my father,
. . . *for teaching me to love achievement.*
To my mother,
. . . *for showing me how to be a woman.*
And to Steven,
. . . *for loving the whole package.*

THE
TYPE E*
WOMAN

HOW TO OVERCOME THE STRESS OF BEING EVERYTHING TO EVERYBODY

by

Harriet B. Braiker, Ph.D.

A SIGNET BOOK

NEW AMERICAN LIBRARY

SIGNET TRADEMARK REG. U.S. PAT. OFF. AND FOREIGN COUNTRIES
REGISTERED TRADEMARK—MARCA REGISTRADA
HECHO EN CHICAGO, U.S.A.

SIGNET, SIGNET CLASSIC, MENTOR, ONYX, PLUME, MERIDIAN and NAL BOOKS are published by NAL PENGUIN INC., 1633 Broadway, New York, New York 10019

First Signet Printing, October, 1987

4 5 6 7 8 9

PRINTED IN THE UNITED STATES OF AMERICA

WHAT DO THEY ALL WANT OF YOU?

Your boss—asking you to perform better and better at work.

Your mate—asking you to soothe his ego and stimulate his senses.

Your children—asking you to do everything for them that they say other kids' mothers do.

And most of all, yourself—demanding that you satisfy them all.

What it all adds up to is that it's too much to juggle—unless you get a handle on what you can humanly do and what you can choose not to do. This is the book that shows you how—so as not to risk losing it all instead of having it all!

"Clarifies to women why they are more prone than men to anxiety, guilt, fatigue, irritability, and depression." —A.L.A. BOOKLIST

HARRIET B. BRAIKER is a practicing Los Angeles clinical psychologist and management consultant with wide experience with working women suffering stress. Dr. Braiker (a recovering Type E woman) and her husband (a recovering Type A man) live in Malibu, California.

Contents

Introduction

IN August 1984, *Working Woman* magazine published as its cover story an article I wrote about women and stress. In that article I attempted to differentiate the typical highachieving woman who shows signs of chronic physiological and psychological arousal—stress—from the prototypical hard-driving, aggressive Type A man. And I proposed that overstressed, high-achieving women might better think of themselves as caught in the trap of trying to be *E*verything to *E*verybody: Type E.

The picture I presented was a psychological collage of the stressed women with whom I have worked professionally as a psychotherapist and corporate management consultant, as well as of my own life experience and that of many of my women friends and colleagues. I was not prepared for the astounding tidal wave of response that the concept received. I was literally inundated with telephone calls and mail from all over the country.

"Someone," they all seemed to be saying, "is finally talking about *me!*"

I knew I had hit a nerve and a pretty raw one at that.

Since the first article on Type E stress appeared, my own understanding of women under stress has increased manifold. Women continue to call or write to tell me how much they identify with the concept of Type E stress, and to express their own thoughts and feelings about their stress problems. Many women have become regular patients of my psychotherapy practice as a result of my article, either by self-referral or by referral of their doctors whom they consulted because of stress-related health problems.

The response wasn't restricted to individuals seeking help. Many women—and men, too—in top corporate positions as directors of training and development or human resources have solicited my services as a management consultant to address the issue of women's stress in the corporate environment.

Women's professional and business groups, including Women in Communication, Women in Film, Women in Management, Women in Business, Women in Health Care Administration, Women in Commercial Real Estate, and many others, have invited me to speak at meetings, and their members have openly shared their experiences with me.

Working Woman asked their readers to respond to my article by sending in written Type E stress self-analyses. The responses provided additional valuable insights into the nature of stress problems in high-achieving women, and formed the basis for a follow-up article in fall 1985.

Other publications—*Cosmopolitan, Self,* and even *The New York Times*—ran pieces on the stress of trying to be everything to everybody, and cited Type E by name. Clearly, stressed women throughout the country were recognizing themselves in the clarion call of the Type E trumpet.

The wealth of information collected from these wonderful sources is interwoven throughout this book in the form of short case studies or vignettes. The cases, of course, have been altered to protect confidentiality.

Sometimes, a character might even be an amalgamation of two or three actual women.

Note that I define the term "high-achieving" as a psychological state rather than as a sociological status. In other words, the term refers to a way of thinking more than to a specific level of achievement per se. Thus "high-achieving" describes any woman with multiple roles who desires to excel in those roles. So the phrase refers to characteristic ways of thinking about achievement, rather than to how high on the career ladder a woman may be, or whether she is married or single, or working at a paid professional job or as an unpaid volunteer in the community. In the psychological sense, achievement motivation is measured by a concern and desire for excellence, not necessarily by objective standards of attainment, success, or status.

Therefore, Type E stress can affect any woman, of any age, in any position in life, who is trying to juggle multiple roles and who strives to *achieve*. The definition also includes women who are thrust into achievement efforts by economic circumstances or life crises, like death or divorce, as well as those who pursue achievement principally for its own sake. The "E" is emphatically *not* reserved for *E*xecutives only, although many executive women suffer from the problem.

While this book is written by a woman, to women, about women, it is also about women in relationships with men. It concerns, specifically, the ways that men and women are different with respect to how they feel about achievement and the stressors that affect their lives. The book also examines how Type E stress affects women's abilities to relate intimately and healthfully with men.

I hope that men, too, will read this book, or at least that women readers will share their new insights and behavioral changes with the important men in their lives—not only husbands or boyfriends, but also men with whom they work.

Ultimately, men must participate in the solutions to women's stress dilemma. Trying to understand what makes the high-achieving women in their lives tick is an important way that men can lessen the burdens that promote Type E stress and endanger women's well-being.

This book is an attempt, then, from my perspective as a high-achieving woman, practicing clinical psychologist, and corporate management consultant, to shed some light on the reasons why it is so stressful today to be a woman who struggles to attain excellence in her life.

My intention is to move beyond merely describing the everything-to-everybody syndrome, and to expose and examine the underlying psychological conflicts, confusion, expectations, fears, and concerns that give rise to the pressure and stress under which so many women literally labor.

Working with women who strive to excel in both their personal and working lives has led me to construct a psychological profile of the overstressed, high-achieving woman who I believe, in an analogous way to the Type A man, is at high risk for stress-related physical and/or emotional illnesses. I hope that many readers will identify with the Type E profile, for with awareness and recognition comes the opportunity for change.

The book does not stop with massaging the dimensions of the problem. It offers concrete advice in the form of behavioral exercises and tactics to reduce Type E stress and build better stress resistance. Chapter 11 is a 21-day program designed to train you in the development of effective coping skills for managing the barrage of demands that threatens to overwhelm Type E women.

There is no way totally to avoid stress, nor would

you want to do so. Stress is an inevitable part of life and, in its positive sense, stress is what we experience and label as challenge, motivation, inspiration, and purpose.

You can, however, learn to reduce negative stress, or dis-stress, that compromises your performance and achievements. You can make stress work for you rather than against you. There are ways to alter your thinking and behavior in order to clear away the psychological barriers, obstacles, or trouble spots that can make life for a high-achieving woman more difficult and stressful than it need be.

As you will see, you *can* learn to alter your stress habits, to contain stress within optimal boundaries, and to enhance your sense of self-control so that you are more at ease with your life and freer to enjoy the fruits of your achievements.

CHAPTER ONE

Wanting It All

WOMEN'S need to achieve is not a fad. It is a fact.

But women who have a need to achieve often wonder whether this ambition is a blessing or a curse. Many have deep concerns and anxieties that their desire to excel in both the work *and* personal realms might somehow backfire and cause them to fail in one or the other, or both.

The woman who strives to excel in both her career and personal life feels caught in a zero-sum game in which someone always loses. If she concentrates her energies on career priorities, she feels as if she is failing her family or cheating herself out of a healthy, fulfilling personal life. Conversely, dedication to the needs of her husband or boyfriend or children may seem to preclude her chances for career advancement.

And there are other strains.

High-achieving women wrestle with the dilemma of how to succeed in a world that rewards stereotypical male values while still maintaining their attractiveness, their sexuality, and their sense of themselves as women. Competitiveness, assertiveness, and independence— traits widely conceded to be what is needed to get ahead in the career world—fly in the face of deeply ingrained cultural beliefs about what it means to be "feminine." When women display such traits, they are labeled pushy, aggressive, and, well, *bitchy*.

While women want to succeed, *need* to succeed, few want to give up their cooperative natures in exchange for male competitiveness. While women yearn to be competent and independent, few would forfeit their parallel need to be loved and nurtured by a man; few women would trade their emotionality and need for intimacy for cold rationality and social withdrawal.

Despite the difficulties and pressures, American women are still marrying in substantial numbers and continuing to bear children. But for the first time in history, more American women work than remain at home.

The nation's distaff labor force is 50.1 million strong, and growing. Women earn $500 billion a year, and take home nearly one-third of the nation's pay. In two-thirds of American families, the women work full- or part-time. There are 19 million working mothers in America. Nearly 50 percent of contemporary "new" mothers work today; estimates are that 75 percent of new mothers will be working women within five years. Amazingly, only 5 percent of U.S. households today fit the stereotype of a working father with a stay-at-home mother and minor children.[1]

Of even more significance are women's attitudes and commitment to their work. Large numbers of women are intent on the pursuit of a successful career—a lifelong involvement in what has heretofore been predominantly a male arena. They are not taking on jobs simply for economic survival.

And women are finally starting to make it.

To proponents, the surge of women into the workplace is a triumph of feminist ideology and the durability of the Women's Movement. But economic realists accept the fact that America cannot successfully compete in the international sphere with half her population *not* striving for excellence.

Detractors, though, decry the trends as evidence of the fall of the American family. Some even blame the sexual revolution for penis envy run amok.

Regardless of the reasons, it is a striking fact of enormous dimension—historically, politically, socially, and psychologically—that there are more high-achieving women in the world today than ever before. Women who are making it, who have made it, or who have high aspirations to succeed are gaining and wielding power, influence, and control in the professional and business worlds.

Although the picture of women's achievements and opportunities is far rosier now than ever before, the picture is far from perfect. American society is still marred by the feminization of poverty. Women earn only 59 cents for every dollar earned by males in comparable positions. Women still comprise the vast majority of pink-collar clerical, teaching, nursing, and support roles in industry. And there still are insidious and pervasive prejudices against women that present all-too-real impediments to their advancements and equitable financial rewards.

Yet, times *are* changing.

Women in their mid-thirties to mid-forties—those daughters of the sixties and liberated women of the seventies—are conspicuous by their number in corporate structures. They have a decade or more of experience under their belts, and are quickly closing the credibility gap. These women represent an awesome wave of talent and energy, the reverberations of which are felt throughout formerly sacrosanct male corridors.

Age prejudices are slowly shifting; being fifty or even sixty doesn't have the over-the-hill connotation it once did. Older women, too, are out there competing in the working world, some admittedly not out of choice but to survive the aftermath of mid-life divorce or widowhood. But many start a new career, return to work, or continue working as a way to maintain meaningful, productive involvement in life.

And young women in their twenties, the first-generation beneficiaries of the feminist awakening, seem to have unbounded expectations and ambition. Colleges and graduate and professional schools are graduating record numbers of women who begin adulthood with the assumption that they *will* have a lifelong career just as educated men have always had.

But, for the most part, American women still want what they have always wanted—a husband and a family, or an enduring love relationship with a man. Yet, they want something more. They want to participate in society in meaningful ways beyond their biological privilege of bearing babies and their cultural responsibility of child rearing and nurturing. They are motivated to achieve goals of their own, beyond the vicarious glow of their husbands' achievements.

Success and achievement have different meanings or connotations for women than they have for men. In general, men confine their achievement criteria to the arena of work, money, and professional or corporate status. Women, on the other hand, apply a literal double standard. To feel "successful" as a contemporary woman means not only attainment by objective standards in the workplace, but achievement in the personal arena of life as well.

In conversations with patients, I have frequently listened to men describe themselves as "successful" or "a success" even though their personal lives are replete with failed or disrupted relationships with women and/or children. This is not to say that such a man's life may not be troubled or unhappy, but he typically leaves his own self-perception as "a success" uncontaminated by any personal "failures."

On the other hand, I have never heard a woman

refer to herself as "a success" if her personal life is unsuccessful by her own criteria, even though she might measure up fully to comparable male standards of success in terms of money or status. She is far more likely than the man with an unhappy personal life to contaminate her entire perception of herself as a successful person if her personal life is wanting. And the woman today whose achievements are confined to the home and family finds herself not only in an ever-shrinking minority, but also feeling "unsuccessful" by society's contemporary widened standards.

Success for achievement-oriented women today is defined as achievement in both realms: career *and* personal. But the success formula is a calculus that often yields enormous frustration and exhaustion. There seems to be only one way for women to play the game and win: be *E*verything to *E*verybody. Many working women adapt to the enigmatic problems of trying to "have it all" by pushing themselves to *do* "it" all themselves, and to excel in all their roles, often at tremendous cost to their physical and emotional health.

Bombarded with daily life stress, working women are swelling the epidemiological ranks of ulcer cases, drug and alcohol abuse, depression, sexual dysfunction, and a score of stress-induced physical ailments, including backache, headache, allergies, and recurrent viral infections and flu.

They suffer in legion numbers in various degrees from what stress specialist Barbara B. Brown calls "states of unwellness"—those in-between states in which one is not sick enough to have a real diagnosis, but where stress incubates and serious stress illnesses, such as heart attacks, strokes, and ulcers, insidiously breed.

Of course, many women seem able to accomplish truly dazzling juggling feats. In spite of heavy work-loads, they manage a host of other commitments to family, personal relationships, community and other organizations—for a while. But behind the dazzle, behind the multifaceted competence and ostensible strength, you can almost hear the stress bombs ticking away.

Too often, the high-achieving woman is the proverbial candle burning at both ends. What's worse, she has unwittingly baited a trap with her own competence: she is the victim of her own success. Paradoxically, the more she demonstrates that she *can* do, the more others demand of her. She indeed proves that she can do it all, and her admiring fans—at home and at work—scream for more. Her driving achievement needs force her to stretch her resources ever thinner until she gets caught in a self-perpetuating *dis*-stress cycle.

At some point, her complicated life may begin to backfire, and everything that she has worked so hard to attain and maintain may appear threatened. The stress takes its toll on her physical health, her moods, her personal relationships, her career—in short, on her life. Recognition of her own limitations may further threaten her self-esteem and heighten feelings of inadequacy. She may fight back by trying to do even more, but it won't work; it can't work.

The solution, however, does not lie in capitulating, sacrificing, or forfeiting a rich and complex life with fulfillment derived from all domains. In fact, research has shown that multiple roles benefit women so that those who have jobs and families have a greater sense of well-being than those who have only one or neither.[2]

The issue is learning to handle the stress that dual achievement goals can involve. Rather than foregoing multiple roles or achievement needs, the key is to redefine the behavioral criteria for successful fulfillment of whatever roles a woman chooses for herself. In this way, she can "have it all" without nearly killing herself by trying to "do it all."

The first step in breaking the dis-stress cycle is the

recognition that coping by trying to be everything to everybody will not work in the long run. Trying to respond continually to the demands of others—or to the insatiable compulsion to prove your prowess in all areas—is the path to neither success nor happiness. Quite the contrary, it is a clear prescription for failure and illness.

The core issue is how much *control* a woman feels she has over the demands of and on her life. But control, as we all know, is difficult to maintain during times of such drastic social and historical change. It is hard to keep your balance when you are riding the wave of what many commentators have called the greatest change in the fabric of American life and social institutions since the Industrial Revolution: the sexual reconfiguration of the labor force.

It has changed child-rearing practices.

It has changed relationships between men and women.

It has changed the structure of the family.

It has changed the definition of sex roles.

It has changed living standards.

It has changed corporate culture and policies.

It has changed educational institutions.

And it has had a profound impact on the psyche of the American woman.

With the explosion of opportunity has come a female revolution of rising expectations—and an avalanche of stress.

Much of the stress arises because women often feel deep conflict between work and love, between competing demands for their time and attention. Unlike men, who can derive satisfaction from being "good providers" to their families *because* of their careers, women often feel compelled to prove that they can be good wives and mothers, or good girlfriends, *in spite* of the fact that they work. Cognizant of their minority position in the upper echelons of corporate and professional power, women still try to prove their competence and worth at work *in spite* of the fact that they may be wives, mothers, or single women with active personal lives.

Gloria Steinem points out that she is routinely asked whether it is possible for a woman to have it all—a career *and* a family. But, she notes, does anyone ever ask the same question about a man? Obviously, it has been possible for men all along. But it *is* a real issue for women. How can they achieve success in multiple domains without succumbing to the ravages of stress or getting caught in a self-perpetuating dis-stress cycle? There's the rub.

But before we get to Type E stress in women, let's consider the implications of the fact that how an individual copes with the stressors of her or his life has an immediate impact on something as fundamental as survival.

CHAPTER TWO

Type A Men
and Type E Women

JUST over a decade ago, two medical researchers brought terror to many hard-driving Americans with the news that becoming the victim of a heart attack was not just the unlucky outcome of a dice throw in some genetic or celestial craps game.

What doctors Meyer T. Friedman and Ray H. Rosenman announced was that so-called cardiac "accidents"—heart attacks—were not accidents at all, but the consequence of certain chronic behavioral responses to stress. To a significant extent, heart disease, they showed, was the predictable culmination of a self-destructive personality and behavior pattern: *Type A,* the human accident waiting to happen.

In their book *Type A Behavior and Your Heart,* Friedman and Rosenman reported the results of a longitudinal study of 3,000 healthy, middle-aged men. All subjects were observed and interviewed with respect to certain behavior patterns; they were also examined for coronary heart disease. Half were identified as Type A; the remaining 50 percent were classified as Type B.

Type A behavior was described as "an action-emotion complex that can be observed in any person who is *aggressively* involved in a chronic, incessant struggle to achieve more and more in less and less time, and, if required to do so, against the opposing efforts of other things or persons."[1]

Stated more simply, Type A behavior is characterized by an extreme sense of urgency, hurry, and impatience; intense competitiveness; free-floating anger, hostility, and irritability; and a preoccupation with quantifiable measures of achievement—how *much* money he is making, how *many* rungs up the corporate ladder he has been promoted, how *many* material possessions he has acquired, et cetera.

Type B behavior was defined simply as the *absence* of Type A characteristics.

The original interviews were conducted in 1961. Eight and one-half years later, the researchers recontacted their sample to examine them for evidence of heart disease. The group labeled Type A, on the basis of observable and reported *behaviors*, were found to have twice the rate of coronary heart disease as those whose behavioral patterns were called Type B.

The findings were simultaneously enlightening and frightening. Although the relationship between Type A behaviors and heart disease was not perfect—there are men who got heart disease who were not Type A, and there were Type A men who did not get heart disease—the odds against the relationship weren't favorable enough to bet your life on.

The good news, the life-saving news, was that if you could recognize the Type A behaviors and personality in yourself, you could do something about preventing a heart attack by *changing* or altering the behaviors.

Friedman and Rosenman included a number of characteristic behaviors in their description of the coronary-prone individual. Type A individuals do everything rapidly—walking, moving, eating, talking. In speech, they tend to emphasize words in rapid, machine-gun fashion, and often speak in a pressured, hurried cadence. Typically, they are impatient with the rate at which things happen, including how fast other people speak. Often, they interrupt others or finish others' sentences.

Type As hurry themselves in almost all activities. They tend to be fast drivers and they suffer intensely when they find themselves held up in a traffic jam. Since they are interested in the *number* of things they can get done, they frequently do more than one thing at a time. They may read mail while talking on the phone, for example, or think about business difficulties while driving to work or playing tennis. They tend to overschedule their time, and find it difficult to relax or do nothing at all. Spending time on relationships or conversations that do not fit in with their own personal achievement needs is experienced as annoying and wasteful.

Type As are extremely competitive and hostile. Constantly keeping "score" and making invidious comparisons, they try to achieve more than do other people. Their goals are defined in quantitative, not qualitative, terms. Success is defined as having *more* of everything— more money, more possessions, more activities—not in terms of subjective, qualitative measures of how well life is actually going in an emotional or interpersonal sense.

Type As attribute their successes (and many Type As are highly successful by objective, material standards) to their ability to get lots of things done faster than others. Frequently, they display behavior illustrative of their constant aggressive, competitive struggle against time and against other people, such as fist clenching, knuckle cracking, teeth grinding, and other symbolically hostile gestures.

The mechanism that links Type A behaviors with heart disease is believed to be the physiological stress response. Under conditions of stress, which chronically exist for Type As due to self-imposed time pressures, the body mobilizes itself for a primitive "fight-or-flight" reaction. The stress hormones (adrenaline and cortisol) are discharged, the heart rate increases, the mind is hypervigilant, the central nervous system is in a state of alert—all body systems are, so to speak, "go." The danger lies in overstimulation of the arousal system, causing abnormally high levels of stress hormones which, in turn, result in dangerous levels of cholesterol and fat in the bloodstream and eventual clotting and blockage of the coronary arteries.

In short, getting too uptight too much of the time can kill you.

The Type A concept has spawned the development of a whole new field called Behavioral Medicine, whose practitioners teach stress management. Patients are taught to interrupt the arousal or stress response through such techniques as biofeedback, deep relaxation or autohypnosis training, and behavior modification. Type As are taught, for example, to drive in the slow lane, to monitor their activities so as not to do two things at once, or to become more patient listeners.

Great strides have been made in the prevention of heart disease and other stress-related ailments as large numbers of hard-driving, ambitious men have come to see themselves in the Type A profile and to heed their doctors' or wives' stern warnings to *slow down*.

The original Type A concept was based on research with entirely male samples. But men certainly aren't the only Americans pushing themselves hard for success in the eighties. While studies in the last decade have documented the presence of Type A behaviors in women as well, the Type A prototype is not a personality profile with which many women easily identify.

The classic embodiment of the Type A personality is the hard-driving, impatient, competitive, aggressive, antacid-chomping executive or professional with a single-minded focus on getting to the top and staying there, and who measures life in quantitative terms. It is hard to conjure up a quick image of a woman in that picture.

This is not to say that there isn't a female counterpart to the overaroused, overstressed, high-risk, Type A personality, or that high-achieving women do not experience intense time pressure. But the nature of women's *stressors,* the reasons behind their stress, and the behavioral coping styles of women are different from those of men.

In our culture, for example, women are explicitly trained *not* to be aggressive, hostile, or competitive no matter whether they are under stress or not. Traditionally, women have been the nurturers and have attended to qualitative issues—like how well or happy everyone is—while men have provided quantitative attainments.

Back in 1974, when Friedman and Rosenman's book came out, I was married, completing my doctorate in social and clinical psychology, and starting a research career at The Rand Corporation, a well-known think tank in California. I could recognize lots of Type A men in the corridors of Rand, and I knew many women, including myself, who were suffering from high levels of stress.

The women I knew wanted to succeed in a "man's world" and have a part in changing that world and its rules. But the research findings troubled me.

It seemed to me that the stress of success—indeed success itself—meant something different to women than it did to men. Although I was a liberated working woman of the 1970s, I had been a traditional little girl in the 1950s, and career was only part of the picture. Success meant way more than just how much I could earn or how high I could be promoted. It meant how well I could do all the things that would make me feel successful not only as a professional psychologist, but also as a *woman,* according to my own standards.

And my standards were killers: I would be a wife, gourmet cook, gracious hostess, skilled homemaker, tasteful decorator—and stay calm, cool, and pleasant at all times. I would be a terrific therapist, researcher, teacher, consultant, and writer—and show no signs of strain. Eventually, I planned to have a family, as well as remaining a devoted daughter, friend, sister, all-around confidante and pillar of strength to everyone who would need me and love me. And while I was at it, I wanted to be thin and beautiful, too.

My achievement needs, and those of my female friends and colleagues, were splayed as broadly as shells from a fired shotgun. We were trying to be everything to everybody, and the resultant stress seemed better labeled Type E than Type A. But if Type A behavior, which is largely geared around achievement in the workplace, could kill men, what could happen to Type E women?

The high-risk personality profile that resulted from that pioneering Type A study seemed to miss the essence of how the women I knew, including myself, characteristically coped with and felt about stress. It was difficult to identify with the incessant struggle against time and other people to get to the top that is central to the concept of Type A stress. Instead, the women I knew that felt highly stressed were struggling with the problem of trying to cover all bases as *women*, vis-à-vis men and children, while simultaneously trying to build viable and successful careers as *people*.

Instead of the single-minded, one-dimensional Type A personality that strives for more and more and more, Type E women feel pulled in multiple, often conflicting directions by a seemingly endless stream of demands from family, work, husbands or boyfriends, and community and/or professional organizations. Since achievement and success mean fulfillment in both career and personal domains, Type E women often assume unrealistic and excessive burdens. They want to keep everyone's approval—that is part of how they know that they're succeeding—and they cope with the demands by trying to do it all, often at a substantial cost to their emotional and physical well-being.

The Type E woman typically evaluates herself against cruelly perfectionistic standards of what she thinks she "should" be able to do or what she imagines others expect of her. Partial successes are judged as failures. It is as if she is trying to prove that she is entitled to "have it all" by making herself indispensable to others.

But she rarely does enough really to satisfy herself.

Most often, she is hassled, not happy, with the life that she has presumably created or chosen. With so many demands impinging on a finite supply of time, her daily schedule is crowded and precariously balanced. Minor inconveniences, such as a late delivery or a broken appliance, may trigger rage or near panic. And sometimes trying to cover so many bases produces a kind of mental fragmentation. When she is at work, she may find herself distracted by household responsibilities or personal relationship problems; at home, work-related pressures and worries may keep her from being truly present and available to her husband/boyfriend or family.

The resentment and frustration produced by continually putting others' needs ahead of one's own—the everything-to-everybody Type E coping style—inevitably creates feelings of hostility. But women, as a rule, do not express anger or aggression as overtly as do men. In work settings, for example, men who lose their tempers and raise their voices may not be well liked, but they are generally listened to; women at work who show their tempers or whose voices crack with rage are dismissed as "hysterical," and their emotionality is frequently used against them to undercut their credibility. More frustration results and additional stress mounts.

In many cases, women who are stressed may not even recognize their feelings as anger. Instead, they may disguise the rage as depression or victimization.

"Everyone expects so much of me," she might say. "I guess I'm not good enough to satisfy them."

And so the anger comes out in other ways—as resentment against perceived oppressors, as coldness or withdrawal, irritability or abruptness, or in moodiness or bouts of emotional volatility.

Because women are culturally the providers of nurturance and caretaking, they far more than men suffer the particular strains of what psychologists call *stress contagion.* Ever ready to listen and be understanding, many women feel their friends', husbands', boyfriends', children's, coworkers', or bosses' stress rub off on them. They frequently worry and feel upset or depressed about other people's troubles, and are frustrated by not being able to make things all better for everyone.

The really dangerous part of the Type E personality is the self-perpetuating and ultimately self-destructive nature of the stress cycle it produces. As she proves how much she can do and how well she can perform, the demands expand.

In response, she pushes herself relentlessly to do more, stretching her resources thinner and thinner, with little capacity to say "No," to draw effective lines of self-preservation, to filter demands into manageable priorities, or just to call "time out" and relax.

Delegating tasks to others, especially on the home front, may make her feel like a cheat or a fraud. Or she may reject help on the grounds that no one will do the job as well or as efficiently as she can anyway.

Eventually—inevitably—she will be tapped out. The recognition of her limitations may further threaten her self-esteem, and she may push herself toward even greater danger. Women caught in a dis-stress cycle may forfeit sleep for additional working hours, smoke cigarettes and drink countless cups of coffee (or use more stylish, expensive drugs) to keep going. Some resort to alcohol or tranquilizers as cost-efficient ways to "unwind" (actual relaxation takes too much time). Pressure can make them snappish, irritable, or belligerent. They may begin to retreat with headaches, excessive sleeping, substance abuse, illness, or depression.

For Type E women, physiological arousal becomes a way of life. They are almost always "on," in one role or another, pushing themselves to do their best and to please others. We know from the Type A research that chronic physiological arousal puts the body under unbearable strain and predisposes the stressed individual to cardiovascular disease as well as a myriad of other emotional and physical afflictions and problems that are caused or exacerbated by stress.

The Type E woman, then, should also be identified and treated as a high-risk personality. In the next chapter, you will have the opportunity to assess your own stress experience in order to determine to what extent you fit the Type E profile.

Like her male Type A counterpart, the Type E woman should be encouraged to practice effective stress management. But what can she do to break out of the self-perpetuating and self-defeating pattern? Merely telling her to smell the flowers, drive in the slow lane, or breathe deeply for ten minutes a day seems woefully inadequate for getting at the kinds of stress that high-achieving women feel.

Indeed, Type E women are caught in much deeper mental quicksand.

Type E stress is a *cognitive-behavioral* syndrome. This means that really to get a grip on her stress problems, the Type E high-achieving woman must first understand the underlying roots of the problem in psychological terms—how she thinks about herself, her achievements, and her relationships with others. This complex of beliefs, attitudes, values, assumptions, and constructs comprises what psychologists broadly refer to as *cognitions* or, metaphorically, "mindsets," "mental programming," or "tapes that play in your head." As we will see, Type E stress is continually fueled by a set of dysfunctional cognitions that serve to exacerbate and perpetuate the dis-stress cycle.

The other part of the syndrome is *behavioral*, indicating that the Type E woman's problem is not all in her head, but also in her actions and behaviors.

To get to the core of her problem, the Type E woman has to do some probing into her own cognitive system in order to give herself the necessary attitude adjustments for interrupting the vicious stress cycle. And, of course, she must change her behavior accordingly.

In subsequent chapters I examine in depth the Type E woman's thorny dilemma in the context of deeper psychological issues that bear on her feelings of competence, value, and self-worth. And, I point the way out of the mental quagmire.

But first let's turn to a Type E stress inventory that gives you a method for doing a candid self-assessment of your own stress profile. And let's see if you are at risk, if you are Type E.

CHAPTER THREE

A Type E
Stress Inventory

THE art of clinical diagnosis lies in the ability to ask the right questions.

The inventory that follows was designed to help you take stock of your ways of thinking about stress, as well as your typical stress habits and patterns.

But the inventory has more than that one purpose. Psychotherapists often ask questions for strategic reasons to help patients gain insight by examining a particular problem from a new or different perspective. In the process of asking yourself the questions, you will not only be assessing your own level of Type E stress, you will also be learning more about the underlying dynamics of the problem, helping to sensitize you to the nature of the cognitive and behavioral factors that contribute to the Type E dis-stress cycle.

The inventory is organized into three sections. Part I essentially asks the question: Are you a Type E woman?

Part II is a survey of attitudes, beliefs, and assumptions that underlie and fuel the Type E stress cycle.

Part III is a checklist of physical and emotional symptoms of stress, or problems in which stress is a strong predisposing or contributing factor. The list is intended as a self-checkup to make you more aware of your current stress-related symptoms. It is also designed to remind you of the potential problems that chronic dis-stress cycles, if left unchecked, might produce in the future.

Complete the entire questionnaire before turning to the scoring instructions that follow.

PART I

For each statement below, circle the number of the answer that best describes how often the statement applies to you.

1. I feel resentful that so many people make demands on my time.
   2. Usually   1. Sometimes   0. Rarely

2. I make the time to do the things that are really important to me.
   0. Usually   1. Sometimes   2. Rarely

3. I feel more comfortable doing a job myself than showing someone else how, or taking the chance that he or she will do it wrong or poorly.
   2. Usually   1. Sometimes   0. Rarely

4. It seems like there's just not enough of me to go around.
   2. Usually   1. Sometimes   0. Rarely

5. It's difficult for me to turn down a request from my husband, boyfriend, close friends, or children, even when there is a real conflict with my work commitments.
   2. Usually   1. Sometimes   0. Rarely

6. I try to spend at least fifteen minutes a day just doing nothing at all.
   0. Usually   1. Sometimes   2. Rarely

7. I wonder why I push myself so hard.
   2. Usually   1. Sometimes   0. Rarely

8. Despite my best attempts to plan a realistic schedule, it seems as if unanticipated things throw it off.
   2. Usually   1. Sometimes   0. Rarely

9. I feel rushed, pressured, or hassled during the day.
   2. Usually   1. Sometimes   0. Rarely

10. I feel like I'm being pulled in lots of different directions by the needs and expectations of others.
    2. Usually   1. Sometimes   0. Rarely

11. I do the things that other people expect me to do before I do something that is pleasurable and relaxing for me.
    2. Usually   1. Sometimes   0. Rarely

12. When I get involved in activities or organizations outside of work, it seems like I end up in charge, or assuming a large burden of extra responsibility.
    2. Usually   1. Sometimes   0. Rarely

13. No matter how hard I try, I feel like I haven't done enough really to feel satisfied with myself.
    2. Usually   1. Sometimes   0. Rarely

14. It is difficult for me to ask for help or to delegate work to others.
    2. Usually   1. Sometimes   0. Rarely

15. When my job and home responsibilities conflict, it's easy to find an acceptable solution.
    0. Usually   1. Sometimes   2. Rarely

16. I feel that I might crumble from all the pressure I'm under.
    2. Usually   1. Sometimes   0. Rarely

17. I try my best to be just about perfect in all the activities my life involves.
    2. Usually   1. Sometimes   0. Rarely

18. I feel satisfied with what I am able to accomplish in a typical day.
   0. Usually   1. Sometimes   2. Rarely

19. I feel too tired, irritable, or pressured to enjoy my life.
   2. Usually   1. Sometimes   0. Rarely

20. No matter how tired I feel, I'm available to other people in order to listen and help them with their problems.
   2. Usually   1. Sometimes   0. Rarely

21. People take advantage of my competence and I wind up doing more than I really should.
   2. Usually   1. Sometimes   0. Rarely

22. Once I get home from work at day's end, I can relax, unwind, and calm down.
   0. Usually   1. Sometimes   2. Rarely

23. I set realistic limits on my time commitments and willingness to say yes to requests from my family, husband/boyfriend, or friends.
   0. Usually   1. Sometimes   2. Rarely

24. I do the things I have to do instead of doing the things I want to do.
   2. Usually   1. Sometimes   0. Rarely

25. It seems like I try to earn others' approval by doing things for them.
   2. Usually   1. Sometimes   0. Rarely

26. I feel frustrated, overwhelmed, and out of control by the demands of my life.
   2. Usually   1. Sometimes   0. Rarely

PART II

For each statement below, decide the extent to which you agree or disagree with the feeling or thought that is expressed. Circle the *number* of the answer that best fits your position.

1. Many men feel threatened by the success and achievement of a woman with whom they're romantically involved.
    4. Strongly agree
    3. Agree somewhat
    2. Disagree somewhat
    1. Strongly disagree

2. I expect the people who are close to me to understand the pressure that I am under and to help me out without being asked.
    4. Strongly agree
    3. Agree somewhat
    2. Disagree somewhat
    1. Strongly disagree

3. I believe that I am achieving as much as I should.
    1. Strongly agree
    2. Agree somewhat
    3. Disagree somewhat
    4. Strongly disagree

4. It's possible for a woman to be too smart and successful for her own good.
    4. Strongly agree
    3. Agree somewhat
    2. Disagree somewhat
    1. Strongly disagree

5. It's a safe assumption that if you do a lot for other people, they will be there for you when you need them.

    4. Strongly agree
    3. Agree somewhat
    2. Disagree somewhat
    1. Strongly disagree

6. It's nearly impossible to have a family *and* a career and not be under constant pressure and stress.
    4. Strongly agree
    3. Agree somewhat
    2. Disagree somewhat
    1. Strongly disagree

7. It seems like other people's approval and liking of me is dependent on the number of things I do for them.
    4. Strongly agree
    3. Agree somewhat
    2. Disagree somewhat
    1. Strongly disagree

8. It's easy for me to judge how well I'm doing in life compared to other women.
    1. Strongly agree
    2. Agree somewhat
    3. Disagree somewhat
    4. Strongly disagree

9. In order to feel successful, I need to achieve my goals in both the personal and career areas of my life.
    4. Strongly agree
    3. Agree somewhat
    2. Disagree somewhat
    1. Strongly disagree

10. My needs to be taken care of or nurtured have been adequately fulfilled as an adult.
    1. Strongly agree
    2. Agree somewhat
    3. Disagree somewhat
    4. Strongly disagree

11. You can count on life turning out to be fair.
    4. Strongly agree
    3. Agree somewhat
    2. Disagree somewhat
    1. Strongly disagree

12. I am often pulled in conflicting directions by the demands of my career and the demands of my personal life.
    4. Strongly agree
    3. Agree somewhat
    2. Disagree somewhat
    1. Strongly disagree

13. I feel comfortable and secure when I am dependent on other people.
    1. Strongly agree
    2. Agree somewhat
    3. Disagree somewhat
    4. Strongly disagree

14. It often seems like I have to prove that I can be a good wife (or girlfriend or mother) *in spite of* the fact that I work.
    4. Strongly agree
    3. Agree somewhat
    2. Disagree somewhat
    1. Strongly disagree

15. When a woman lets herself *need* a man, she's bound to feel anxious and insecure.
    4. Strongly agree
    3. Agree somewhat
    2. Disagree somewhat
    1. Strongly disagree

16. My feelings about myself and my achievements seem to change and vacillate a lot.
    4. Strongly agree
    3. Agree somewhat

   2. Disagree somewhat
   1. Strongly disagree

17 If I could do everything "right," other people would like me more.
   4. Strongly agree
   3. Agree somewhat
   2. Disagree somewhat
   1. Strongly disagree

18. Earning the approval and love of others is not as important to me as being successful in my career.
   1. Strongly agree
   2. Agree somewhat
   3. Disagree somewhat
   4. Strongly disagree

19. It seems like I do the equivalent of two full-time jobs.
   4. Strongly agree
   3. Agree somewhat
   2. Disagree somewhat
   1. Strongly disagree

20. People in my life see me as having unlimited resources for helping them and doing things for them.
   4. Strongly agree
   3. Agree somewhat
   2. Disagree somewhat
   1. Strongly disagree

21. It's often the case that the traits that help a woman get ahead in a career cause difficulties in her relationships with men.
   4. Strongly agree
   3. Agree somewhat
   2. Disagree somewhat
   1. Strongly disagree

22. The way I feel about myself depends largely on the way other people feel about me.

    4. Strongly agree
    3. Agree somewhat
    2. Disagree somewhat
    1. Strongly disagree

23. It seems like other people lean on me more than I lean on them emotionally for help with their problems.
    4. Strongly agree
    3. Agree somewhat
    2. Disagree somewhat
    1. Strongly disagree

24. It makes me feel guilty when time commitments to my work cheat my husband/boyfriend/children out of the time and attention they deserve from me.
    4. Strongly agree
    3. Agree somewhat
    2. Disagree somewhat
    1. Strongly disagree

25. It's easy for me to envision the circumstances in which I would feel like a total success.
    1. Strongly agree
    2. Agree somewhat
    3. Disagree somewhat
    4. Strongly disagree

PART III

Next to each item listed below, indicate how often the experience happens to you: frequently, sometimes, rarely, or never. Put a check (√) under the column that best fits you.

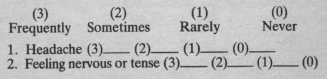

(3) Frequently	(2) Sometimes	(1) Rarely	(0) Never

1. Headache (3)____ (2)____ (1)____ (0)____
2. Feeling nervous or tense (3)____ (2)____ (1)____ (0)

3. Feeling hurried, rushed, or pressured
   (3)____ (2)____ (1)____ (0)____
4. Backache or muscle pain in neck, shoulders, arms
   (3)____ (2)____(1)____ (0)____
5. Fatigue/exhaustion (3)____(2)____ (1)____ (0)____
6. Feeling down, depressed, blue
   (3)____ (2)____ (1)____ (0)____
7. Having too much to drink or overindulging in other substances (3)____ (2)____ (1)____ (0)____
8. Feeling "used up" or "burned out"
   (3)____ (2)____ (1)____ (0)____
9. Feeling "uptight," anxious, overwhelmed
   (3)____ (2)____ (1)____ (0)____
10. Skin rashes (e.g., hives, psoriasis)
    (3)____ (2)____ (1)____ (0)____
11. Sleep difficulties (trouble falling asleep or staying asleep) (3)____ (2)____ (1)____ (0)____
12. Temper outbursts/anger
    (3)____ (2)____ (1)____ 0)____
13. Feeling overworked or overwrought
    (3)____ (2)____ (1)____ (0)____
14. Having a "tight" chest or chest pains
    (3)____ (2)____ (1)____(0)____
15. Having a "nervous" stomach, indigestion, heartburn, pain (3)____ (2)____ (1)____ (0)____
16. Feeling worried or insecure about the future
    (3)____ (2)____ (1)____ (0)____
17. Feeling down on yourself
    (3)____ (2)____ (1)____ (0)____
18. Feeling exploited, hurt, let down by other people
    (3)____ (2)____ (1)____ (0)____
19. Feeling "hyper," irritable, "speedy"
    (3)____ (2)____ (1)____ (0)____
20. Feeling trapped, stuck, paralyzed
    (3)____ (2)____ (1)____ (0)____
21. Eye strain, sore eyes
    (3)____ (2)____ (1)____ (0)____
22. Nausea or dizziness (3)____ (2)____ (1)____(0)____

HOW TO SCORE THE INVENTORY

For Part I, add up the numerical scores of your answers to each question. Your total will range from 0 to 52.

To score Part II, again add the numerical scores of your answers for all 25 questions. This time, your total score will range from 25 to 100.

To score Part III, give yourself a score of 3 for every check mark in the "frequently" column; a 2 for every mark in the "sometimes" column; a 1 for every mark in the "rarely" column; and a 0 for every mark in the "never" column. Now total the scores for the symptom checklist. Your score will range from 0 to 66.

HOW TO INTERPRET YOUR SCORES

Your three summary scores contain important information about your own Type E tendencies.

Part I. On the question of whether you fit the profile of a woman suffering from Type E stress, a score of 20 or more on Part I suggests that you are in the high-risk range. In other words, you are caught in a Type E dis-stress cycle and should begin *now* to reverse the self-defeating direction that this kind of behavior and feeling pattern inevitably take.

A score of 35 or more is a red flag indicator that you are sufficiently overaroused with negative stress to be at high risk for stress-related health problems.

A score below 20 indicates that your Type E tendencies are reasonably well contained, but you should nevertheless continue monitoring your stress levels in order to keep them within tolerable limits.

Now take a few minutes and review the 26 statements in Part I. Think about some instances from your recent experience when you felt the way the statement suggests. Try to become more aware of the ways in which you contribute to your own stress cycle by biting off more than you can reasonably chew, and pushing yourself beyond your physical or emotional endurance limits. The greater your awareness of Type E stress, the more control over your stress levels you can attain.

Part II. Your score on Part II is an indicator of the degree to which you hold typical Type E beliefs, attitudes, assumptions, and values. On this scale, a higher score indicates greater agreement with Type E cognitions; a relatively lower score reflects a lesser tendency to hold or agree with Type E cognitions.

A high score—in the range of 60 to 100—indicates fairly to very strong Type E beliefs and attitudes. This means that your ways of thinking about yourself, your achievements, your dependency needs, your expectations of yourself, and your mode of doing things for others to gain their approval predispose you to Type E stress. These cognitive factors underlie and fuel the dis-stress cycle. In subsequent chapters you will learn how to unravel some of the mental tangles that perpetuate your stress problem.

Part III. Your score on Part III is a relative measure of the frequency of occurrence of stress-related symptoms. Any score greater than 0 indicates the presence of some stress-related symptomatology, although it may be relatively rare.

However, if your scores to Part I and Part II are in the Type E profile range, your symptom checklist probably indicates an elevated frequency of stress-related symptoms. A score of 35 or higher is another serious red flag that your health is already jeopardized by the stress that you are under right now. A score in the moderate range—15–34—indicates the presence of symptomatology that should be monitored and treated so that it lessens, or at least doesn't get worse.

Baseline Measures. Now that you have your scores

you have baseline measures against which you can measure your improvements over time. After reading the rest of this book and implementing the techniques and ideas that are recommended, you should periodically return to the inventory, at, say, three-month intervals, and reassess yourself. You can measure change in terms of reducing Type E stress, altering self-defeating attitudes that perpetuate the stress cycle, and improving your health and psychological well-being by reducing the frequency of stress-related symptoms.

If you're a Type E woman, your immediate stress level may have risen just as a result of taking the inventory. You may be feeling alarmed about the degree of stress that your life entails, and be worried about the consequences.

But that is the purpose of the inventory: not to alarm you unduly, but to raise your awareness level, to identify your Type E stress problems, and to help you realize that your problem is shared by many high-achieving women like yourself who feel trapped by their own behavior patterns and ways of thinking.

Making a candid self-appraisal is the first step toward developing solutions to Type E stress. The next step is getting yourself motivated to change.

Now that you know where you fit in the Type E profile, we can begin to probe, to pull back the layers of this complex syndrome and look at some of the reasons behind Type E stress.

And once we understand the reasons, we can better implement the solutions.

CHAPTER FOUR

The Dilemma

STRESS is in part a social disease. It is an adaptation to social and cultural conditions.

From this perspective, Type A stress can be understood as the male adaptation—albeit self-destructive—to the high-speed, high-tech, high-information, high-competition society of late-twentieth-century America. Type A stress is a symptom of the adaptation to cultural acceleration.

While Type E stress encompasses some of the same high-pressure characteristics of Type A, women's adaptation to their sociocultural circumstances has been different from men's. Women have not only had to adapt to the rate of change, they have been exposed to a vastly different set of social and cultural stressors. While men have obviously been affected by the changes that women have undergone in the last decade or so, the changes, after all, have happened *to* the women.

So Type E stress can be viewed as the female adaptation to the awkward period of social-historical change of late-twentieth-century America. In this sense, Type E stress is the psychological price that contemporary high-achieving women are paying for equal opportunity before society has worked out the details. Ironically, the consequences may be equal rights to ulcers, coronaries, high blood pressure, and a host of other stress-related maladies.

If you scored high on the Type E inventory you're not alone. Type E stress is virtually epidemic today among women who are striving to achieve in roles that are uniquely female—wife, girlfriend, mother, daughter, and the like—as well as in the *full* range of roles in which they now participate as people on an equal footing with men. Many of these women adapt to the crush of demands by Type E coping: pushing themselves to do it all. It is a widespread, high-status social disease among women.

Women have indeed come a long way. They are seriously participating in the career world and making an impressive go of it. But for most high-achieving women, their "other side"—the more particularly female set of roles (whichever set they may choose to play)—is still operating in full gear.

The consensus of social observers studying change in the American family is that, while significant and notable changes have taken place in the amount of sharing or helping behavior by men with respect to traditional woman's work, women continue to bear a far heavier weight of responsibility than men for household management and child-rearing matters.

The dilemma for the high-achieving woman is that by participating in the work world as a *person*, while maintaining her roles as a woman, she is doubly inundated with stress.

"I'm not pressured," one thirty-seven-year-old radio executive, a wife and mother, said to me. "I'm crushed. Pressured would be a vacation!"

The high-achieving woman who strives to "have it all" (whatever that means to her) has, to begin with, the basic set of stressors that have always gone along with the territory of just being a woman. Some of these stressors include her relationships with men (romantic and platonic), with women, and with children (as well as the decision of whether or not to have children).

And women experience the stress of maintaining their physical attractiveness in a society that (Joan Collins notwithstanding) continues to exercise a crippling double standard with respect to how age is worn by men and women. Add to this already considerable set of stressors the fact of having to deal with the tensions that arise as a function of the unique female physiological system. Stressors like premenstrual syndrome, pregnancy, menopause, and the like affect only women.

Just coping with what women have always had to deal with in the first place is stressful enough. Now add to that simmering cauldron the additional stressors to which high-achieving men on the fast-track in their careers have always been exposed and to which contemporary career women are at least equally exposed.

"Type A stress sounds like it would be a relief," quipped one wrung-out female executive. "The stressors on men and women are just different."

In addition to exposure to the *same* stressors that men experience, high-achieving women endure the further stress that comes with the status of being a member of an upwardly striving minority group in a sea of majority male members who, in many instances, have a vested self-interest in maintaining the status quo.

And whereas high-achieving women may have equal rights for advancement in a legal sense, they are competing with a heavily weighted handicap. In effect, the Type E woman has two jobs—or, at best, a job and a half. She not only "moonlights," in the sense that her second job begins when she comes home from work, she "dawnlights" as well. Working women with children to send off to school are often awake and working from the crack of dawn. Few men striving for career achievement are burdened with the same load of caretaking responsibility.

So the contemporary high-achieving woman is faced with the dilemma of going for it all, and enduring the cost of potentially debilitating stress, or foregoing some or all of what she wants to be in her life.

The short answer to this dilemma is that she can—and I fervently hope she will—continue to go for having it all, as long as she comes to her senses about the wisdom, realism, and consequences of doing it all herself.

The Type E woman's dilemma is, in a way, an arithmetic problem. She adds up all the things that she is asked to do, is expected to do, or feels that she should do, in all of her roles. The catch is that it totals more than one mortal, however talented and competent, can safely do.

Instead of using an additive model, women need to start thinking in terms of new role categories that are formed by the combination of roles. By virtue of their combination, these "hyphenated" roles should be qualitatively and quantitatively different from the sum of their parts. In other words, a woman who is a professional–wife–mother should not be expected to do the same things as three separate individuals with singular roles—a professional, *and* a wife, *and* a mother.

It is apparent that the long-range solutions to many of the causes of Type E stress require social change, an alteration in the status, roles, and attitudes of men and women, and adjustments in the home and workplace. But women who are suffering from the crush of their own life stress need some answers today. They need to know what to do until society catches up.

What women, as individuals, can do is make some constructive changes in the way they respond to the stressors in their lives.

Type E women need to learn new and better coping skills to deal with the very real stream of demands that their busy lives entail. They need to learn effective fightback strategies so that they can regain greater control of the rate and intensity of the stressors to which they are exposed, as well as their own responses to those stressors.

As women begin to change as individuals, men will change as well. That much of the social revolutionary process stimulated by the Woman's Movement is already well under way. And when significant numbers of individuals begin to change the ways they think and act, societal change ultimately occurs.

WHY YOU SHOULD BREAK
THE TYPE E STRESS CYCLE

The glimmering promise that she might be a true Superwoman, and thereby earn the love and approval of others, lures the high-achieving woman along the dangerous path of Type E coping. As long as she believes that it is possible to be everything to everybody and remain untaxed or undamaged physically and/or psychologically, she is caught in a self-defeating trap. She will keep coping by trying to rise to each and every occasion, pushing herself beyond safe or reasonable limits, without adequate regeneration and rejuvenation of her resources, until she is thoroughly depleted by her own good intentions.

The necessary condition to breaking the Type E stress cycle is to abandon the Type E coping style. You must stop trying to be everything to everybody. If you don't, what is dazzling for a while will become debilitating over the longer term. And the quality of your life will be diminished in many ways by the chronic low boil of negative stress.

Type E Stress and Your Health. Negative stress, of

whatever type, has deleterious effects on your health. This is essentially accepted by most members of the medical and psychological professions, as well as by most health-conscious laypersons.

Chronic overarousal taxes the body's physiological system, and results in fatigue, debilitation, and depletion of the body's immune defenses. Stress either contributes to, causes, or in some ways aggravates just about any disease or illness you can think of, including cavities (the saliva becomes more acidic under stress).

Your stress symptom checklist in the preceding chapter is your own evidence of how stress is currently affecting your health.

Type E Stress and Emotional Well-Being. Not only does stress play a key role in precipitating just about all forms of mental illness, it affects mood, self-esteem, cognitive acuity, and behavior among otherwise "normal" individuals. Exposure to chronic, unremitting stress can lead to feelings of burnout, depression, emotional "flatness," anxiety, and uncertainty.

In short, Type E stress is not good for your head. And the negative feelings associated with stress can themselves become the source of further stress, concern, and tension.

Type E Stress and Relationships with Men. Love relationships are also negatively affected by stress. And inevitably the relationship problems produce their own stress, contributing to the vicious cycle.

There are many ways in which the stress to which women today are exposed, as they struggle to achieve in both their personal and career lives, affects and is affected by their relationships with men. At the most obvious level, sheer exhaustion resulting from the chronic demand overload is dangerous to your sex life. A recent Masters and Johnson study,[1] in fact, documented the finding that career-oriented women had more trouble getting in the mood for sex than those who are unemployed or in boring jobs. According to researcher Dr. Constance Avery-Clark at the Masters and Johnson Institute in St. Louis, the factor of limited time for intimacy accounts for the differences.

"These couples are often unable to spend much time together because of their demanding schedules, and the career wives frequently report difficulty making an effective mental transition from their professional lives to personal time with their respective husbands," commented Dr. Avery-Clark.[2]

Dual-career couples are challenged and stressed by a whole new set of issues and decisions that traditional couples have managed to avoid, usually by default on the part of the woman. Power balances are changing, expectations are often strained, and couples frequently experience daily hassles in working out agreement on such matters as money, how to spend quality time, respective responsibilities, and so on.

Stress can also interfere with clear thinking and effective communication.

Just as women have worried about the dangerous Type A behavior of their overdriven husbands, men, too, should attend to the problem of Type E stress in women. No one is benefited in the long run by a woman running herself into the ground, least of all her man.

Type E Stress and Children. The quality of relationships with children, too, is compromised by excessive stress. When negative stress depletes you of your vital resources, the children who need your attention and energy are necessarily getting shortchanged. And you are presenting a strung-out mother as a female role model.

Type E women often worry about the effect their behavior or mood has on their children.

"Sometimes I think the only attitude they can read in me is resentment," one career mother told me, "and that's the last thing I want them to think I feel about them. It's just that there's nothing left after a whole day of work. You know, if I don't change for the sake of my own health, I ought to just for the sake of my kids."

Type E stress can also strongly affect a woman's decision regarding whether or not to have a baby. If as a single woman, or as a married woman without children, she is experiencing Type E stress, what, she asks herself, would happen if she added a baby to all of this?

The point is that the current level of Type E stress may be distorting a critical life choice. This is not to say that choosing *not* to have children is bad, wrong, or otherwise undesirable. But the question is best evaluated in the context of a well-managed life. A Type E woman facing this choice (with her biological clock ticking away) might better ask, "If I could learn to reduce my stress level by breaking the compulsion to be everything to everybody, would I like to have children?"

Type E Stress and Work. If the negative effects of Type E stress on your health, emotional well-being, and personal relationships aren't enough to convince you to modify or moderate your behavior, consider the effects on your job or career.

Chronic stress is the single greatest contributor to burnout. This overwork syndrome of emotional, cognitive, and physical exhaustion seriously impairs the motivation required to achieve at work.

Stress rubs off in the atmosphere, too. Work stresses you, and you stress those in your work environment. This stress contagion can be palpably felt in such pressure-cooker environments as advertising agencies, stock brokerages, professional and executive offices, and hospitals. In this sense, stress is a communicable disease.

There are, as I discuss in the chapters ahead, many points at which Type E stress and work-related issues—including achievement, corporate politics, and office romance—overlap. And of course, as mentioned previously, there are all the stressors in the workplace that men have traditionally been exposed to, and, in large numbers, have succumbed to with coronaries or other illnesses. These stressors now lie in wait to prey on women, too.

Gaining control of Type E stress is not a matter of equality; it is a matter of survival.

Other Reasons. If you need even more reasons why you should break out of the Type E stress cycle, try some of these on for size: Stress feels terrible; it saps your potential for achievement in all areas; it ruins your looks. And it is rooted in some dangerous mythology or, perhaps, ingenuous propaganda.

Writing in *Esquire's* June 1984 special collector's issue devoted to women, Adam Smith notes that the mythical images of the Superwoman "are buried deep in the unconscious." But whose unconscious—men's or women's?

He goes on to a delightful dissection of a passage from Proverbs in the Old Testament that describes the "virtuous woman." Quoting from *The Bible Designed To Be Read as Living Literature,* Smith writes:

> She has a family because "her children rise up, and call her blessed." She is a very efficient homemaker:
>
> *She riseth also while it is yet night*
> *And giveth meat to her household,*
> *And their task to her maidens.*
>
> So she is up before dawn, delegating tasks. And while Proverbs says, "Her clothing is fine linen and purple," she is very much at home in the pinstripe power suit. She (this mythical biblical Superwoman) is in real estate—
>
> *She considereth a field, and buyeth it;*
>
> in agriculture—
>
> *With the fruit of her hands she planteth a vineyard.*

in manufacturing and selling—

She perceiveth that her merchandise is profitable:

Her lamp goeth not out by night. . . .

She is not afraid of the snow for her household;
For all her household are clothed with scarlet. . . .

She seeketh wool and flax,
And worketh willingly with her hands. . . .
She maketh linen garments and selleth them;
And delivereth girdles unto the merchant.
Strength and dignity are her clothing;
And, she laugheth at the time to come.

So the virtuous woman is buying fields, negotiating the mortgage, planting the vineyards, determining the state of the textile market, dealing with merchants as to linen garments and girdles—and don't forget, not all the maidens to whom she delegated could be expected to do their tasks perfectly; some of them must have showed up late, or loitered with the local louts. What, you might ask, did the virtuous woman's *husband* do?

Her husband is known in the gates,
When he sitteth among the elders of the land.

That's what he does, he sitteth. And praiseth her, saying:

"Many daughters have done virtuously,
But thou excellest them all."

Well, I would, too. Praiseth, that is. Superwoman! I think the virtuous woman was invented by a man.[3]

As Smith suggests, it does make one wonder. Who did come up with the idea that a woman could—indeed, should—do it all?

But behind your own Type E behavior is the belief that being everything to everybody is both desirable and possible. Maintaining this belief can have damaging effects on self-esteem.

Columnist Ellen Goodman suggests that the mythical ideal Everything-to-Everyone woman rises early each morning with enthusiasm. Breakfast is merrily shared by Mom, Dad, and kids, and the family members all arrive at work or school promptly and eager to begin the new day. Dressed for success, our mythical ideal engages in important work, executing command decisions. When, at the end of the workday, the family reunites, there is a gourmet dinner (prepared, of course, by our heroine). Following a lively political discussion among the entire family, the woman and her husband-lover go to bed, whereupon she enjoys multiple orgasms until midnight.

The truth of the matter is that today's typical high-achieving woman is often deeply exhausted, tense, or otherwise suffering from the negative effects of the stress cycle in which she is caught. Holding this kind of idealized myth in your mind is a dangerous criterion against which to measure your self-esteem. If you believe that you *ought* to be able to function as well as the mythical Superwoman, you believe in a self-defeating ideology.

And the slick Madison Avenue television ads that portray the all-day/all-night Superwoman whose hair never even so much as droops add to the dilemma. Someone someplace expects this to be you. If you buy into that mythology, you're buying into trouble. Or if you know better, but the men in your life are taken in by the seductive image, you're in even bigger trouble. Not because the image isn't desirable, or that it isn't attainable—some of the time. But the subliminal message is that you should be just as perky as that woman all the time, or else something may be wrong with you, and it may be more serious than your hairspray. The mythical ideal is presented as the Everything-to-Everybody woman—powerful and decisive by day; sexual, feminine, and alluring by night—a standard against which American women can or should judge themselves. Needless to say, in the harsh light of reality, the Type E woman who is attempting to be everything to everyone and is running herself ragged in the process fails to measure up. The results: lowered self-esteem and perpetuated stress.

WHAT YOU CAN DO ABOUT TYPE E STRESS

Since Type E stress is a cognitive-behavioral syndrome, the problem exists at the levels of how you *think* and how you *behave* or act. It logically follows that the solution or treatment for the problem lies in changing your thinking and your behavior. You must, in effect, give up trying to be everything to everybody, and start exercising more strategic control of your finite personal time and resources. In moderating everything-to-everybody behavior you will also be moderating stress levels. And you can reasonably expect to learn to transform as much stress as possible from negative to positive, and to keep stress levels contained within optimal ranges of performance and feeling. To do so presumes an awareness of stress-related behavior and feelings. It also presumes insight into the nature of the stress problem itself.

WHAT LIES BEHIND TYPE E STRESS

The phrase "everything to everybody" has an intuitive, bellringing meaning to most women. But what does the term really mean? In the next five chapters, I examine the nature of Type E stress by dissecting it into its component parts or factors: *Excellence Anxiety, Ego Confusion, Excessive Self-Reliance, Erroneous Ex-*

pectations, and Everything-to-Everybody Behavior. From these different perspectives, I attempt to probe and illuminate some of the major psychological issues, conflicts, confusions, strains, and tensions that underlie and fuel the Type E stress cycle.

By combining what you learn on the cognitive side with the behavioral perspective of everything-to-everybody behavior, you should have a pretty good "fix" on the problem of Type E stress in general. And when the nature of your own Type E stress pattern is within your sights, you will be in a position to focus your attack.

You will, of course, need some new cognitive and behavioral skills as your artillery for countering the barrage of demands that assault you every day. The skills for breaking out of the Type E stress cycle are in this book. A training program for learning the skills through rehearsal and practice is systematically laid out for you. I hope you will commit yourself to learning new and more adaptive coping skills and, more important, will implement those new skills in the effective management of your daily life.

But before we turn to the issue of how to change, it is important to look first, in some depth, at each of the five factors that comprise the constellation I call Type E stress.

CHAPTER FIVE

Excellence Anxiety

On a balmy June evening in 1963, I had my first real attack of excellence anxiety.

It happened at the awards ceremony held by the ninth-grade graduating class of Louis Pasteur Junior High School in Los Angeles, where the class president announced the results of the student body poll anointing certain class members with such coveted titles as "Best Looking Girl," "Most Likely to Succeed," and so on. The fates were not kind to me that fair evening. I received the dubious distinction of being named "Smartest Girl in the Ninth Grade."

I remember my reaction as if it happened yesterday. I felt as if someone had punched me right in the stomach. My eyes burned as the anger mounted within me. This was a perverse blow. My social life in high school was ruined in one fell swoop before I even got there. Who would like the smartest girl? What boy in his right mind would want to date the smartest girl?

This, gentle reader, was before woman's liberation.

In 1963, the general cultural instruction to female children with high IQs was to keep their brains under wraps, especially around boys. Social popularity and cerebral prowess—not to mention genuine ambition— simply did not go hand in hand for girls. At least, that's the way life seemed to me on that particular evening.

Later that night, back in the haven of my bedroom, the pent-up dam burst forth in a torrent of tears. I cried hard, heaving sobs on my mother's lap. "They might as well have branded my forehead with a big, red 'S' for 'Smart,' " I wailed.

My dilemma was that I liked being smart, and I had absolutely no intention of foregoing my academic ambitions. But I also wanted to have a normal social life with boyfriends and girlfriends. I wanted both, and I felt deeply conflicted. It all seemed so unfair.

Hearing my cries, my father came into the room. "What's wrong, baby?" he gently asked. "They voted me 'Smartest Girl,' " I gulped between sobs. "And now nobody's gonna ask me out on dates and I won't be *popular*," I explained.

Without missing a beat, my father replied, "Honey, any boy who's not going to like you because you're smart is someone *you* wouldn't really like very much anyway."

Suddenly I stopped crying.

The feeling of anxiety connected with achievement motivation has reared its ugly head on many occasions since 1963, though I comfort myself by recalling my father's wise words. The fact is, lo these many years later in the era of women's liberation and comparable worth, the thought of success still causes many women to experience sensations of internal discomfort ranging from vague feelings of apprehension or arousal to full-blown phobic reactions.

This link between achievement motivation and internal, psychological discomfort in women is what I call excellence anxiety, an albatross of conflict around the Type E woman's neck. High-achieving women are often the victims of their own confusions or fears regarding achievement. As a result, they construct unnecessarily difficult psychological hurdles on their way up the career ladder or in their personal relationships that make the actual pursuit of success more stressful. Sometimes, excellence anxiety gets them off the track, thereby further contributing to the overall stress cycle.

The reasons, as we shall see, for the link between achievement motivation and psychological discomfort in women are complex. But gaining insight into some of the dimensions of the problem is of great value in conquering Type E stress. Once you become aware of the tangle of motives that seem to be pulling you in multiple directions, you can get a handle on straightening yourself out by clarifying your own values about achievement.

Unresolved or maladaptive thoughts and feelings about achievement and its relationship to femininity, acceptability, desirability, and lovability fan the flames of negative Type E stress. Resolving excellence anxiety, and reducing the stress that it produces, lies in understanding more about achievement motivation and how it differs for women and men.

ACHIEVEMENT MOTIVATION: A CONCERN WITH EXCELLENCE

Research on achievement as a motivation or need that differs among individuals was spearheaded by psychologist Dr. David McClelland of Harvard University in the late 1940s and early 1950s. This pioneering research yielded a methodology for studying achievement motivation as well as a rich theoretical basis on which generations of psychologists have built their research.

But only in the last decade or so have psychologists begun to sort out the complex relationship between achievement motivation in women and its relationships to other competing and compelling motivations, including, particularly, the drive to be accepted and approved by others, especially, though not exclusively, by men.[1]

Let's begin by defining some terms. Achievement motivation, technically called need achievement or nAchievement, is defined as a *concern with excellence*. The motive is thought to lie latent within individuals' personalities and to be activated by certain appropriate circumstances. So given the right set of conditions, a person with a high need to achieve, or strong achievement motivation, will strive not only to succeed, but to excel as well.

The original research on achievement motivation used a technique called projective testing to measure the need to achieve. The method entailed showing the research subjects a set of standardized pictures known as the Thematic Apperception Test, or TAT. The TAT, much like the Rorschach, or inkblot test, is used to measure latent or unconscious motivation by analyzing the content of the story that a subject tells in response to an ambiguous picture.

For example, a story that a subject tells in response to a picture of a boy reading a book might include references to the fact that he is a "top student" or that he has an "important test and is studying hard because he wants to do well." These references would be thematically coded as evidence of achievement motivation.

Using this projective technique, researchers sought to discover the "buttons" that would activate or stimulate achievement motivation imagery in the stories of their subjects. But the researchers found that the techniques that increased achievement motivation in men were not the same as those that stimulated achievement in women.

Specifically, when men were told that their performance on the TAT was a *competitive* task, their achievement scores showed the predicted increases, as compared to men who were given the pictures with no additional motivating instructions. But when women's competition "buttons" were pushed, no increases in their achievement themes were found.

However, when the instructions for the TAT emphasized *social acceptance* rather than competition, the women's achievement scores jumped higher than even the men's. In other words, telling women that good performance on the test would mean that they were likable heightened achievement motivation, whereas telling them that good performance would be viewed competitively failed to raise their achievement scores.

Further research has shown that achievement motivation has different cognitive meanings to the two sexes. In women, the need to achieve is virtually fused to the need for what psychologists call *affiliation,* or the need for social approval and acceptance—by both women and, particularly, men. Women who are high scorers on the need for achievement measure are also high on the need for affiliation. In other words, most high-achieving women are also those most concerned with pleasing others and with having status in the eyes of others.

In high-achieving men, however, no such relationship to affiliation exists. In fact, men with high achievement needs are explicitly *unconcerned* with making friends.

The research reflects the deep, culturally ingrained belief in many women that their achievement motivation might put them at risk of social ostracism. Somewhere along the line, women are given the message that they may risk social disapproval for outstanding achievement, especially in the realm of the male, competitive world. So women may experience profound internal conflict between what seem to be competing drives: to achieve, and to be liked, especially by men.

WOMEN AND THE FEAR OF SUCCESS

In 1968, psychologist Matina Horner carried the under-standing of women and achievement forward by ad-vancing a theory that women's achievement motivation was compromised or diminished by a competing motive—fear of success.

Horner's research built on McClelland and others' earlier work, although she used a different and more modern stimulus cue. This time, subjects were given a one-sentence opening line and asked to complete the story any way they wanted.

Female subjects were given the cue line: "After first-term finals, Anne finds herself at the top of the medical school class." Men were given the cue line: "After first-term finals, John finds himself at the top of the medical school class."

Horner devised a scoring system for what she de-scribed as "fear-of-success" imagery. Stories were scored for evidence of fear of success if they contained any of three themes: (1) social rejection—for example, a fear that success would be linked with loss of friends or with being sexually unattractive or unfeminine; (2) more general guilt and anxiety about success—for ex-ample, fear that the person will be unhappy or unfemi-nine or unmasculine; and (3) bizarre or hostile themes, or denial of the cue altogether—for example, stating that Anne was really a code name for a group of students.

The widely reported finding of Horner's study was that 65 percent of women who wrote stories—but only 10 percent of men—displayed at least one fear-of-success image. This vast difference in the prevalence of psychological imagery that reflects underlying con-flict and strain about achievement is key to under-standing excellence anxiety.

Women tended to depict the character, Anne, in

their stories as being unfeminine, miserable, isolated, and/or rejected by men as well as by other women. The *woman* who finishes at the top of her medical school class apparently does so at the price of sacrificing achievement in her personal life, according to women's projective imagery. The *man,* on the other hand, is seen as achieving academic success without foregoing social acceptance or other desirable qualities, according to the men in the study.

Horner was also interested in how women's fear of success expressed itself in competitive tasks. To study this question, women were asked to do a timed task unscrambling anagrams. In one condition, the subjects worked alone, thereby minimizing competition cues. In the other condition, however, women were tested in a group.

Once again, the fear-of-success theory gained confirmation. Women who had written stories with a lot of fear-of-success imagery also tended to show poorer performance in a group than they did when they were tested alone. This decrement in performance was especially pronounced when the group condition included men as well as other women. Since the traditional feminine role proscribes competitive success—except within strictly female domains—women who expressed more fear-of-success imagery in their stories lowered their performance under group conditions in order to be less threatening or undesirable to the others in the group, particularly the males.

EXCELLENCE ANXIETY AND THE STRESS OF SUCCESS

Although research attempting to clarify the nature of achievement motivation in women continues, one thing is clear: The way that the need for achievement operates in women is different from the way it seems to work for men. For women, striving for success can arouse stress because the motive challenges other equally important, or perhaps even more important, needs in women for affiliation, social approval, acceptance, and the maintenance of their valued femininity.

Why is achievement so threatening to women? In the first place, women are trained to associate femininity with such traits as submissiveness, dependency, and passivity. But in order to achieve in the contemporary career world, women need to be assertive, independent, competitive, and ambitious. These two sets of traits—what is required to *achieve,* and what is required to be *acceptable* as a feminine woman in the traditional sense—produce an obvious strain.

At a more primitive, unconscious level, a woman's striving for excellence, achievement, and success in traditionally male domains can arouse deeply buried fears of abandonment, of retaliation from those who are being surpassed, of rejection and disapproval from loved ones, and of loss of femininity and sexual desirability.

These can be psychologically crippling fears.

Kathryn, a thirty-three-year-old woman who recently divorced her professional husband after a two-year separation, unveiled her own excellence anxiety as a contributing factor to her stress-related problems. Despite her good academic record and an early history of achievements, she recounted a "spotty and disappointing" career history over the past seven years.

Over that period, Kathryn had tried a number of varied pursuits. She had started with nursing, moved to computer sales, jumped to career counseling, and finally to certification and a job as a paralegal. When I met her, she was considering a stint in real estate.

Kathryn knew that the key to surviving the disruptive circumstances of her divorce was to become more self-sufficient, autonomous, and independent in her career. Consciously she wanted to succeed, and she held high standards for judging her performance. But she remained mystified by her remarkable and consistent capacity for self-sabotage. Every time she began to do well at a new career, she became frightened, depressed, unhappy and, not surprisingly, unsuccessful. She attributed the cause of her unhappiness to making "another bad career choice," and vowed to start over in something new. She believed the magic solution lay "outside" of her in the proper selection of the "right" career.

During one counseling session, she recalled that her family "didn't help" when it came to bolstering her career decisions. She explained that her father wrote her a series of letters cautioning her against becoming too assertive and successful lest she place herself "out of the market" in terms of desirability to men.

After this recollection, Kathryn was able to see that her family training and traditional feminine self-image caused anxiety whenever she started to succeed and behave in autonomous, assertive ways no matter what job or career she was pursuing. Her fear was that her competence would make her unattractive to men. If she demonstrated that she could actually take care of herself, she erroneously reasoned, no man would ever want to marry her again and help to support her financially.

Moreover, Kathryn's mother, her principal female role model, was a highly traditional wife for whom assertiveness and independence were virtually foreign behaviors. Trained to be a "nice little girl," Kathryn was encouraged to behave like her mother, like a "lady." So when Kathryn behaved as an adult in ways that were more like her professional, successful father, she experienced excellence anxiety associated with a fear of losing her mother's love and approval, and risking her father's outright rejection.

As Kathryn worked through these issues in therapy,

she was able to clarify that she held achievement as a value independent of what her mother or father had taught her. And she recognized that by holding herself back due to her fear that her career success might alienate men, she was hurting only herself. What *she* really wanted was to be self-supporting and financially independent, so that her choice of a man wouldn't be distorted by the need for financial support.

The unlinking of motives—separating achievement motivation from affiliative needs—is a key component to therapy with Type E women. Clarifying your own values about achievement and uncovering your unconscious or perhaps latent fears that achievement might have negative social consequences will help you to address those fears and to develop rational, adaptive responses.

EXCELLENCE ANXIETY AND ACHIEVEMENT UNCERTAINTY IN WOMEN

In addition to competing and conflicting drives, excellence anxiety has other causes. Women experience greater uncertainty about their achievement because they are less able or less likely than men to evaluate their performance against that of others. This is because women's achievement motivation has what psychologists dub a *process orientation,* whereas men's achievement motivation is said to have an *impact orientation.*

Process orientation means that an individual has an autonomous concern with achievement that is not based on competition or rivalry. Instead, achievement is evaluated against a standard that is internal to the woman herself—how well she thinks she *should* be able to do.

The process orientation toward achievement also means that women are concerned with building competence at the task, and will try as hard as is required to attain competence, independent of how well others do, or how hard others try.

Impact orientation means that men approach achievement on a task as a way to impact the environment and, thereby, gain power. Their orientation is competitive: Striving for success is embedded in a standard of comparison with other men.

It is a fundamental psychological principle that uncertainty breeds anxiety. Uncertainty about their achievement breeds excellence anxiety in Type E women.

Another well-documented principle of psychology is that the *social comparison process*—collecting information from relevant others—reduces uncertainty and, therefore, lowers anxiety. This is not to say that finding out how you are doing compared to others is always pleasant or satisfying, though often it may be. What we are looking at is the anxiety associated with conditions of uncertainty. And information from others reduces the uncertainty that causes anxiety.

Consider the following facts in the context of women's and men's respective orientations to achievement.

Women seem to be at a comparable disadvantage because of their autonomous process orientation in which the emphasis in judging achievement is on how well they do compared to an internal standard of how well they believe or think they *should* do. Yet they essentially remain uncertain about how well they are doing compared to others because they simply don't pay attention to others as a way to judge their own achievement. And because women often remain autonomous in evaluating themselves, their expectations and standards can become unrealistic, with consequent feelings of inadequacy and failure.

But men approach achievement as a way to be competitive and to have an impact on other people. So they naturally evaluate themselves according to a competitive or comparative standard of how well they are doing stacked up against other men. Since their impact orientation focuses their achievement assessment on the actual performance of other men, their standards are likely to be more realistic than women's.

This is not to say that women should become more competitive. It is, however, to recommend that when they evaluate their achievement, women attend to input from relevant reference groups of similar women who share similar burdens. In other words, if you rely on how well other women *actually* do, instead of an imagined standard of how well you think you *should* do, you are likely to have more realistic, less burdensome, and less perfectionistic achievement pressures.

HOW WOMEN AND MEN EXPLAIN THEIR SUCCESS

Some of the most interesting findings come from studies that look at the attributions people make for their own behavior and for the behavior of others. These studies have systematically examined how women and men explain the reasons for their success as opposed to their stated reasons for their failures.

The basic experimental design involves having subjects complete a problem-solving task. The experimenter then lets the subject know whether she/he succeeded or failed at the task. But the subjects' successes and failures are actually manipulated by the experimenter, and don't in any way reflect true outcomes.

After the task is completed, the subject is asked some questions about her/his performance. In particular, the researchers are interested in the explanation she/he gives for the outcome of success: Does she/he say it's because of *ability?* Is it because she/he tried hard, because of *effort?* Is it because the task was *easy* (in the case of success) or *difficult* (in the case of failure)? Or is the reason for succeeding or failing seen as a matter of just plain *luck?*

The differences between men's and women's attributions are fascinating.

In the first place, men are likely to attribute "success" to their own *ability,* whereas "failure" is attributed to the inherent *difficulty* of the task. Note that when the outcome is success, men don't claim that the task was easy to explain why they did well; they claim that they are highly able.

Women show a strikingly different pattern. When they are told that they have succeeded on the task, women tend to attribute it to *good luck.* But when the outcome is failure, women tend to attribute it to their own *lack of ability.*

And the different explanations for women's and men's success extend to other people's attributions as well. When observers (of both sexes) were included in the studies, their explanations for the success or failure of the male or female subjects differed according to the sex of the subject.

Male *and* female observers tended to see a male's ability as the reason for his success. By inference, we could say that the subject created the impression of high ability when he was observed succeeding at a task.

But consider what happened when male and female observers saw a woman subject succeed at a task. Their explanation for her success was the *amount of effort* she expended ("She tried harder") or the *ease of the task ("She* succeeded, so it must have been easy"). Or, like the female subjects themselves, the observers said that the success was due to good luck. The observers' impression of the female subject's ability, however, was apparently unaffected by learning about her success.

These differences in how people explain the reasons for male versus female success (or failure) are called *sex-linked attributions*. Sex-linked attributions constitute significant cognitive distortions in the way both women and men understand female achievement. And the implications of these differences, both psychologically and politically, are disconcerting.

Consider, for example, the implication of seeing your own successes as being due to luck rather than to your ability. Obviously, since luck is inherently unstable and unpredictable, basing expectations on this kind of attribution would necessarily attenuate your expectations for success. Attributing success to luck minimizes your degree of control, and creates the perception in your mind that your achievement is an "iffy" affair, dependent on the wholly capricious whims of fate and circumstances. While good fortune is sometimes a factor in furthering achievement for many people, constantly discounting your own ability as the preeminent factor in your successes amounts to self-devaluation and produces lowered expectations for future success. Lowered expectations become self-fulfilling prophecies.

For women attempting to advance through the corporate ranks, consider the fact that others see women's successful performance as being due to hard effort, whereas they see men's successful performance as evidence of high ability.

Psychologically, the relationship between ability and effort is compensatory. This means that all things being equal (like luck and task difficulty), the person with greater ability will not have to try as hard, or exert as much effort, as the person with lesser ability. Conversely, the person who tries harder, we infer, probably does so to compensate for lower ability.

Given this compensatory relationship between effort and ability, we begin to get some psychological insight into the reasons why women do not get promoted as rapidly as men, and are not paid as highly. Obviously, factors such as overt and covert discrimination policies and chauvinistic sexist prejudices contribute significantly to the discrepancies. Since promotions are typically based on attributions of high ability and only secondarily of hard work, sex-linked attributions also operate against female advancement. The focus here is on internal psychological mechanisms that distort the meaning of women's successful performances and, thereby, interfere with women's attempts to influence the impressions of their superiors positively.

Recall, also, that the research findings characterize women as process-oriented, autonomous achievers. In other words, women probably *do* try harder because their orientation is to do as well as they can at the task or project, whereas men do what they need to do to have an impact on others, and judge their performance in competitive terms.

If women are seen as being *intrinsically* motivated—knocking themselves out for the sheer sake of knocking themselves out—then extrinsic rewards like salary increases will not be seen as necessary incentives. After all, some may argue, why pay women more money when they're already working as hard as they can anyway?

ACHIEVEMENT GUILT

Many women experience heightened anxiety and guilt when they learn that they have succeeded at a particular job or project. The psychological discomfort and problematic behaviors that accompany this form of excellence anxiety are often not readily understandable to the women themselves.

Shelley is a case in point. A trial attorney in her late

thirties, she came to consult with me because of a blossoming drinking problem. But Shelley didn't believe that she was drinking because she felt depressed or unhappy—at least it never started that way. Shelley was a binge drinker, not an everyday alcoholic. Every few weeks or so, she would drink excessively, to the point of memory lapses, and eventually passing out.

She awoke the next day with so vicious a hangover that generally she was forced to call in "sick" to the office. Following each drinking episode, she was beset by feelings of guilt, remorse, self-deprecation, and self-revilement.

As we examined her drinking problem in therapy, I asked Shelley to keep a diary of her moods and to keep a record of the events or situations that precipitated mood changes and drinking behavior. And I told her to review mentally the events that had precipitated her last three drinking bouts.

Shelley did her homework and produced the key to her drinking problem, although the connection among events, feelings, and drinking had eluded her in the past. She found that her drinking was triggered by finishing or settling a case, and *winning*. She recalled that her initial reaction was a mixed one—happiness and satisfaction on one hand, but deeper, gnawing feelings of stress, discomfort, and depression on the other.

In further analyzing the nature of the stress response, Shelley was able to see that her successes made her feel anxious and fraudulent. The anxiety came from her uncertainty about her performance in the future (despite what was a stellar record of litigation) and from the perceived pressure from her partners to "keep up the good work." And since she was unsure and insecure about her own ability, she often felt like a fraud or imposter when she won a case. "Maybe," she would say, "it was just a case of lucking out or of trying harder." Despite an impressive professional track record, Shelley still lacked confidence in her talents and abilities as a trial lawyer.

The level of stress that success engendered sent her for a drink, which she handily rationalized as "celebrating her victory." But inevitably she would lose control of the drinking and "create a disaster of myself," which would then validate the perception that she was "really no good."

Many women suffer from feelings of anxiety or guilt over their own excellence—whether they really are as good as their performance would indicate—though relatively few develop as severe a symptom pattern as did Shelley.

DISCOUNTING THE GOOD NEWS

In addition to sex-linked attributions, high-achieving women tend to process feedback from their environment about success and failure with a cognitive "filter" on their mind's lenses. It is as if the filter enhances the intensity of negative information feedback about failure, poor or mediocre performance, or even performance falling short of perfection—while minimizing or discounting the positive feedback or good news.

With this distorted filter on your perceptions, negative feedback from significant other people in your life can spiral into full-scale depression. Your self-esteem is assaulted with the attributional input that failure has occurred, and failure—remember sex-linked attributions—is due to lack of ability. This kind of erroneous thinking quickly escalates into labeling oneself as a failure, and to such denigrating overgeneralizations as "I can't do anything right," "I'm inadequate," and other self-sabotaging attacks.

Positive information is discounted in many ways. As we have seen, successes are attributed to external factors like luck, or the ease of the task in question, and are not used to bolster self-confidence by making the male attribution that success is due to ability. Or the source of the compliment or praise is denigrated or devalued. So the good news about a woman's ability, competence, or talent doesn't get adequately processed so as to nourish her ego.

Francine suffered terribly from this problem on a writing assignment that eventually ended her writing career. She was working on a lengthy technical report document with a team of three others. The group's working style was to circulate chunks of their written output to one another for critical comments and feedback.

Francine was anxious about showing anybody anything she had written until she had done four drafts and it was letter perfect. But she complied with the team's request and circulated a ten-page draft document.

Her three team members returned comments. All of them liked much of the work; all of them had some critical, constructive comments on the work. But Francine had an anxiety attack.

She became so concerned about the past negative feedback that her future writing suffered. No amount of coaxing would convince her that the editors had said positive things, too. The good input was discounted and rationalized ("They were trying to be kind") into having little meaning to Francine about her own ability. Eventually, she left writing altogether and opted for another job.

When it comes to processing success feedback in life, men seem to have it all over women. Men let the good news come into their heads, and they process the data about their accomplishments as evidence of, and flattery to, their able egos. But research shows that women use the *negative* outcomes in life as input into their self-esteem. In other words, successes are discounted with respect to ability, and are laid to other reasons—trying harder, good luck, task ease, or even ulterior motives of male superiors. And failure information (which for Type E perfectionistic women can mean anything short of flawless) is processed as evidence of low ability.

EXCELLENCE ANXIETY AND RELATIONSHIPS WITH MEN

The change in women's career status has altered the basic fabric of many relationships between men and women, not only marriage. Traditionally, women have needed men for, among other things, status and financial support. If your husband was a doctor, lawyer, or business tycoon, you were Mrs. Doctor, Mrs. Lawyer, or Mrs. Tycoon. The vicariously derived status that a woman received by virtue of being married to a successful man gained her entrance into social circles, a sense of identity, and a prescribed function. In simple terms, he went out to earn a living; she took care of everything else.

Enter the successful, high-achieving woman. She doesn't need the status of being Mrs. Doctor or Mrs. Attorney-at-Law. She has her own status. She *is* a doctor, attorney or whatever. And she also has her own money. Ergo, the power balance in the relationship shifts.

The challenge that confronts the partners of successful women is straightforward and powerful: If a woman doesn't need you for status or money, then you have to work at getting her and keeping her with affection, sexuality and, basically, with *yourself*. That is a frightening proposition for men with less than solid self-esteem.

Excellence anxiety is in part rooted in a fear that

has a rational basis. This fear is that becoming a successful, achieving woman will, ultimately, be too threatening to the men in your life and, therefore, will result in abandonment or rejection. And the sad truth is that many men are deeply threatened psychologically by a woman's competence, intelligence, success, and power.

The psychoanalytical explanation for why some men are so threatened by smart, successful women goes back to dear old mother. To a little boy, the theory goes, the mother is a large and powerful figure with control over such valuable resources as food, affection, praise, and acceptance.

Successful and healthy resolution of the mother-son relationship requires that the boy learn to identify with his "more powerful" masculine role model—his father—and to establish his own gender identity as a male.

In turn, the boy is taught, via a virtual implosion of cultural signals, styles, and norms, that men are stronger than women, and that women need a male who is more competent, independent, and powerful to protect and take care of them. For a man with this kind of psychological history, a dependent woman is necessary in a romantic relationship in order for him to feel like a "real man"—the independent, strong provider who goes out to kill the proverbial beast and bring home food to the family.

Enter the liberated woman of the eighties. She is female, attractive, and sexually interesting just like Mommy. But she is also successful. She is smart and capable outside the confines of kitchen and bedroom. So she stirs up deep, primitive feelings in some men that recall how it felt to be intimidated by a big, powerful mother. Today's woman is not even dependent on a man financially. She goes out and slaughters the beast herself. And she cooks it, too.

A man who grew up in a traditional family with a bread-earner father and a submissive, dependent mother, may well feel threatened by a high-achieving woman. Often the reasons are not clear to him. He knows only that somewhere deep inside he does not feel as sexually capable because his masculinity is not defined by her traditionally feminine helplessness and dependency.

Let me emphasize that not all men are threatened by high-achieving women. On the contrary, there is a growing awareness and recognition among men of all ages of the immense value of having an equally competent partner in the person of a lover and/or wife.

Many such men have had maternal role models different from the traditional homemaker. And certainly we can anticipate profound changes in the early learning experiences of male (and female) children today whose mothers are themselves high achievers. Other men have overcome traditional prejudices and now recognize the desirability (and added economic pleasure, too) of a woman who is truly an equal, treasured partner in all respects. These are the liberated men of the eighties.

Nevertheless, despite encouraging changes in men's attitudes toward women, the fact remains that deeply rooted cultural sex-role prescriptions, psychological associations, and sexual wiring are hard and slow to change.

The Catch-22 of being too smart and successful to be desirable to men is a widespread anxiety that plagues more than single women trying to find a mate. Women with longstanding marriages are discovering the subtle, and sometimes not so subtle, changes that occur in their husbands when they return to and/or excel at work.

Ann and Leo had been married twenty-seven years when they came to consult with me about their problems. Having raised three children, all of whom were off in college, Ann decided at age forty-seven to start her own business. Leo was a reasonably successful, mid-level executive for a company where he had worked for the duration of their marriage. Leo was proud of the fact that, unlike his own mother, Ann didn't "have to work" to support the family.

But when Ann's parents died and left her some money, she decided that given the freedom offered her by virtue of her empty nest, she wanted to start a new venture and make it work. She opened a catering business to capitalize on her domestic talents. The business boomed, but the marriage busted.

As Ann's business success increased, Leo became irritable and depressed. Then he developed scrotal pain for which his doctors could find no organic or physiological explanation. Leo turned off completely to any sexual relations with Ann. In response, she became sequentially frustrated, angry, and then depressed. "My business success ruined my husband and my marriage," she sighed, and bemoaned the fact that, "it all seems so unfair."

I worked in therapy with both Leo and Ann, independently and in joint, marital sessions. Leo was able to gain insight into how some basic unresolved issues about his own mother surfaced in the form of sexual problems when the circumstances of his life confronted him once again with a strong and powerful woman like his mother. To Leo, Ann's bold entrepreneurial success represented her power and his own inadequacy. Ann's insight into the psychodynamic nature of Leo's problems helped to reduce her anger, and enabled her to focus on more constructive ways to reduce their joint stress level and rebuild their marriage.

Single women with successful careers frequently feel that they are simultaneously attractive and yet off-putting to men. While many men give lip service to wanting an independent, smart woman, the reality of a relationship with such a woman makes them uncomfortable. These men may end their relationships by giving excuses or explanations that fail to address the real problem, and instead leave wounded women in their wake.

Barbara and Joe had been dating for about four months. Barbara is a twenty-nine-year-old with a master's degree in mathematics and engineering, and a plum job at a large corporation in which she manages more than thirty computer programmers, operators, and systems analysts. The company compensates her with a very handsome salary with which she provides a comfortable life for herself and her child from a previous marriage.

Barbara and Joe had met through a video-dating service. On the dating service's biographical data form, Barbara had listed her occupation as a DP (data processing) Manager. When Joe called, he explained that he had selected her on the basis of her occupation—she was "just the kind of successful, independent woman" he was looking for.

About two months into their relationship, Barbara realized that Joe really didn't understand what she did for a living. Joe spent most of the time talking to her about *his* career goals and ambitions. But, she recalled, he never asked her about what she actually did at work other than, "Did everything go okay at the office today?"

"He thinks I'm a programmer," Barbara mused. "What'll he do if he finds out I'm in charge of a thirty-million-dollar project and make three times as much money as he does?"

She realized that the basis for Joe's lack of understanding was her own reticence about revealing her actual success level for fear that it would scare him away.

"You might as well find out his reaction now rather than later," I advised.

Barbara told Joe the next evening over dinner about her career and also about her aspirations for the future. The following weekend, Joe announced that the relationship wasn't working for him sexually and suggested that they start seeing other people.

Fortunately, Barbara's reaction was not unduly painful. "Actually," she said, "I guess I expected it all along. I just sensed that even though he always talked about wanting an independent, successful woman, he probably wouldn't be able to handle the competition. I'm glad I found out now rather than six months from now. It could obviously never have worked out with Joe in the long run."

Barbara vowed that in the future she would disclose the full picture about what she did for a living within the first few dates. Based on her experience with Joe, she could appreciate the value of the disclosure strategy as a viable screening mechanism for separating men with whom she might have a future from those who could never really be serious relationship candidates.

Another unhealthy pattern in relationships is the "behind-the-doors-switch." The man wishes to be seen with a successful, smart woman in order to impress others with his own intelligence, ostensible strength, and liberalism. But behind closed doors, in the privacy of their personal relationship, he demands to "wear the pants." He may bark orders or criticize the woman mercilessly. He may insist that they have sex when he wants to in the manner and style that he desires. In short, her rights as an equal in the relationship are severely abbreviated. It is as if he needs to test his masculinity by subduing and dominating an "independent" woman.

It is the Taming of the Shrew 1980s style.

Interestingly, there are some women who go along with this kind of arrangement and, while their reasons do not bespeak psychological health, they find the relationship tolerable because it allows them to indulge their feelings of helplessness, passivity, submissiveness.

"At least with him," one bank vice president said of her verbally abusive husband, "I don't have to be in charge all the time. Hell, I'm not in charge of anything with him, not even my own body."

EXCELLENCE ANXIETY AND ACHIEVEMENT SELF-SABOTAGE

The concern that excellence and achievement might be threatening to men affects women's behavior in work relationships as well.

Marsha is a forty-two-year-old advertising executive with a large, national agency. After a successful career in the New York office, Marsha decided to transfer to California, following her divorce.

But after only three months in the new office, her performance was falling far short of her normal standard. She felt barren of creativity and worried that somehow she had lost her knack for writing advertising copy when she crossed the Rocky Mountains.

In therapy, it became clear that when she came to California Marsha was banking her hopes on starting her life over again with a new man. But she feared that the men in her office (who were the only men she knew thus far in the West) would be put off if she excelled the way she had in New York. Marsha was holding herself back in her work, albeit unconsciously, as a way to make men like her. This insight seemed to unblock her creativity and effectiveness. Soon her self-esteem increased and her dating life improved as she began to feel better about herself. And she was well liked and admired in her office.

There are other ways in which high-achieving women sabotage or undermine their achievements. Some, for example, allow their energies to be drained off by frustrating relationships with men. And their achievement potential is thereby diminished.

Sharon, for example, knows that at age thirty-six her "biological clock" is running out of time for her to have the two children she claims she wants. But she first needs to find a husband, since her fantasy is that of a traditional nuclear family—a husband, a son, and a daughter.

The trouble is that Sharon's relationships just don't work out, despite the fact that she anguishes over her men greatly and puts a maximum amount of effort into "making the relationship work."

The real problem is that Sharon has had four consecutive affairs with married men, three of whom stayed married to their wives, and the fourth, while he got divorced, decided that he preferred to remain without any further commitments to anybody, including Sharon.

Sharon suffered almost chronic anxiety throughout all her affairs, so much so that her health was affected and so was her career. With a Ph.D. in a scientific field, Sharon's career success required that she complete research projects and publish her work in academic journals. But her unhappy love affairs, and her anxiety over the years going by with no successful relationship, were compromising her discipline, motivation, and energy.

In therapy, Sharon began to understand that her selection of unattainable men was an unconscious way to deflect attention and concentration from her own career and into obsessive rumination and strategizing over whether or not her man of the moment would be willing to leave his wife for her.

Sharon revealed that she felt anxiety about being an "egghead scientist" and, despite the fact that she was very attractive, feared that making it in her field would mean that a man wouldn't find her desirable as a woman. So by choosing married men and unsatisfying, difficult relationships, she drained off her achievement energy and was failing to accomplish her ostensible professional goals. Because she wanted the men to marry her, she was able to maintain the protective rationalization that *she* was ready for a committed relationship, but that they just weren't up to it. Sharon eventually realized that her own excellence anxiety about achievement had been causing her to sabotage both her career and her personal relationships.

Some women sabotage their achievement by using alcohol, drugs, or food as their focus of addictive behavior in much the same way that Sharon gets hooked on unattainable men. Psychologically, if you blame your drinking problem (or weight problem, or relationship problem) for your not achieving your potential, you avoid the real issue of testing the boundaries of your talent and ability.

Louise, for example, is a smart, potentially attractive but immensely overweight woman of twenty-eight. She already is a junior partner in a large, successful accounting firm. Despite her impressive career, Louise feels like a failure because of a barren personal life.

The managing partner of Louise's firm referred her to me because of some recent "personality problems" she was having at the office. She had become increasingly short-tempered with the associates and some of the partners, especially the men. The fallout from her hostility had already led to a confrontation by her partners demanding that she seek help for her apparent problems.

In therapy, Louise admitted that her irritability arose from her frustration regarding her empty romantic life. She said that she resented, even hated, men because they "hold something as superficial as your weight against you. I want someone who will accept me the way I am. I'm a successful accountant. So what if I'm heavy? Men are so shallow."

Eventually Louise recognized how she was sabotaging her achievement desires to have both a career and a relationship by choosing to remain fat. Throughout the several months of her weight-loss program, Louise experienced anxiety as she approached what felt to her as the "true test" of her value and worth. Without the layers of fat to protect her psychologically from her own potential, her therapeutic task was to develop alternative ways to cope with her stress that did not include using food consumption as a form of sedation.

Another form of self-sabotage that affects many Type E women is the "eleventh-hour power failure."

In this pattern, the woman consciously pursues a goal highly symbolic of her achievement strivings: for example, a graduate degree or certificate, passing the bar exam, getting a part in a play or movie. Consciously, the goal is something she really wants to achieve. The event has enormous psychological significance to her. She has defined the accomplishment to mean the equivalent of a definitive test of her intelligence, worth, talent, and so on.

And right before the big day, the power fails. She gets sick. Or she loses her voice. Or she becomes phenomenally depressed and anxious. Or she becomes "accidentally" pregnant right before launching on an important new career promotion.

This is not to say that there are no such things as just plain accidents. (As even Freud is reputed to have said in response to the insinuation that his ever-present cigar was a phallic symbol, "Sometimes a cigar is just a cigar.") And sometimes, of course, accidents, illnesses, or mishaps do happen on the eve of an important, achievement-laden event. But the point is that *stress* is the great mediator—it is the stress that achievement conflict and pressure create for many women that compromise their resistance to infection, or reduce their coping abilities. The pattern of spotty achievement that results has a disturbing ring of the self-fulfilling prophecy. So another good reason to get your head straightened out about achievement issues is to ensure that you'll be well and functioning when the opportunities for establishing milestones arrive.

Yet another common form of self-sabotage among high-achieving women is the "I wasn't looking for it, honestly" office affair. Often women unwittingly set themselves up for an office romance by denying themselves a fulfilling personal life. They try to simplify their lives by concentrating only on their career, and trying to eliminate the outside interference of personal involvements.

Into this vacuum walks the office lover. He's attractive, she's vulnerable, and the circumstances of proximity breed the entanglement.

The problem is what happens if or when the affair ends. All too often, it is the woman who loses her job, or is passed over for promotion, or is "encouraged" to seek employment elsewhere to avoid the discomfort of the affair's aftermath. It's office policy, you see.

The best protection against being unduly vulnerable to romantic entanglements in a work environment is not to deny yourself a personal life while you build your career, but rather to create good-quality relationships outside of the office with several people—men and women—who are supportive, validating, and emotionally fulfilling.

Excellence anxiety contributes to overall Type E stress not only because of the fear of success in women, but also because of the fear of failure. In fact, women who sabotage their own achievements, both in their careers and in their personal lives, often feel caught between a mental rock and a hard place. They feel the tug of what psychologists call an avoidance-avoidance conflict. The way to avoid failure is to succeed; and the way to avoid success is to fail.

Obviously, working to reduce excellence anxiety by overcoming both fear of success *and* fear of failure will reduce the cognitive strain that unresolved fears and conflicts about achievement can produce.

HOW TO MANAGE
EXCELLENCE ANXIETY

The management and control of excellence anxiety begins with the recognition that this problem is common in highachieving women. From my vantage point, the transitional state of societal and cultural standards and expectations about women's achievements makes it effectively "normal" to have excellence anxiety. There is far more than a grain of truth in the apprehensive feeling many women share that their achievement might isolate them, or make them less desirable to *some* men or women, or backfire in another way.

In the clear light of acceptance that excellence anxiety in high-achieving women is common and probably not damaging *if* contained within manageable limits, the next step is to make a conscious, intentional, deliberate choice about what excellence means to *you*. Examine your feelings about achievement in your work. Define clear, realistic, and measurable goals. Imagine yourself fulfilling those goals; actually try to see yourself behaving as if you had achieved success and excellence from your own personal standpoint.

Decide if you really want to succeed. What does that mean in the context of your work? And what do excellence and achievement mean to you in your personal life? Do you want to be married? Do you want your marriage to be different? Do you want to have children? How would you feel if you didn't?

Ask yourself the hard questions. And listen to the answers. If you decide that you are, in fact, committed to achievement in both realms (whatever the term "achievement" means to you personally), then you have made a choice. The rest of your behavior and cognitions—what you actually do and how you think about your life situation—will follow with some determination and effort on your part.

Given that a certain level of arousal or stress (besides being unavoidable) is actually productive and positive, the important thing to keep in mind is that nobody ever said that becoming successful in either your work or personal life was going to be easy. It hasn't been a rose garden for men, so why should excellence come easily to women?

Accept that stress comes with the territory for a woman who has achievement strivings in both her work and personal life. Your job is to cut down on the excess psychological harassment you cause yourself with unresolved, confused, ambivalent feelings and fears that get in your way like a psychological obstacle course.

Type E women who experience the cognitive pressure of excellence anxiety need to work toward clarifying their personal definitions of success, and need to establish milestones along the way for which they give themselves interim rewards and reinforcements. They also need to work on disentangling the connections between achievement motivation and the need for affiliation. Although both motivations are psychologically healthy and desirable, they need to be kept as separate issues from the perspective of stress management. In other words, work on refining these concepts until the two motivations feel compatible, congruent, and not entangled.

For example, accept the proposition that you want to excel in your career and you want to be accepted in groups of friends, community activities, and by the important man or men in your life. But the truth is that people whose heads stand above the crowd are the targets of jealous potshots. Further, accept that some people may, in fact, not like you because you are smart and successful. It's not fair, rational, or reasonable. But, alas, that is the way it is.

As my father reminded me, you wouldn't want those people to be close to you anyway. After all, does it make sense to want to befriend somebody who would prefer for you not to succeed rather than for you to succeed? Who needs friends like that?

There are some catty, jealous, hurtful people out there who ought to be filtered out of your life. Dr. Hans Selye, the "father" of modern stress theory, identified as one of the most lethal forms of stress that caused by another person to your psyche by way of insidious insult, betrayal, hostility, and the like. As he advised in a piece of enduring wisdom, self-preservation requires that such people be cut out of your life so as to protect you against the debilitating effects of stressful interpersonal relationships.

Obviously, there are some blood relationships that are not voluntary and over which you may not have total control. But all stressful relationships should be identified as dangerous stressors to everybody's health—especially yours—and addressed before the damage is irreversible.

The bottom line about affiliation is that not everybody is going to like you, no matter how many psychological pretzel bends you try to do to demonstrate your flexibility and prove your likability. Nor do you really need to have *everyone* like you. Your affiliation needs can be better met by becoming selective about the number and quality of friends that you do allow close to you.

As a general rule, women who have similar experiences in terms of their work and personal lives are likely to be your most appropriate reference group. Try to be sensitive to the attitudes of those close to you regarding your achievements, those milestones that are important to you. People who genuinely love and support you will support your successes and empathically share your joy. While it is difficult to acknowledge and act on the realization that you have outgrown an old friend, it is important to do so, especially if the relationship has become draining and uncomfortable for you.

Achievement motivation is a drive that needs to be nurtured and protected. This is an especially important and difficult point for many Type E women when it comes to men. It is on this issue that excellence anxiety, laden with the dual fear of success and fear of failure, and the accompanying fears of abandonment and rejection, most frequently occurs. And as we have already seen, the anxiety is not without basis; there are men out there who may be attractive and indeed lovable on the surface who simply are unable to relate in a healthy way to a successful, motivated, high-achieving woman.

Again, the most adaptive approach to handling this disconcerting fact is to use your own achievement motivation as an operative filter for sorting out men. Like the case of Barbara earlier in this chapter, you're far better off knowing early, rather than later in a relationship, if a man is threatened by your achievement motivation or intelligence.

But, you are thinking, it's not always easy to spot. They talk such a good game.

Of course, I acknowledge that the signs that a man is unconsciously threatened by a strong, achieving woman are often not readily apparent in a relationship. But if you can refine your sensors, lots of clues are there. You just have to be willing to look.

Begin by examining your tension level when you are with a man. If you experience anxiety, discomfort, or a vague sense of unease when it comes to discussions of your work or other topics related to your professional achievements, ask yourself some questions. Does this happen with all men, or with only some men? If your answer is the latter, might not your discomfort be something that you're picking up from the man? If you feel that way with every man, the place to look is within yourself.

Examine the pattern of relationships in a man's life. Does he have women friends? Coworkers? Has he had other relationships with working women? What happened with them? Does he show signs of healthy respect and regard for women?

A high-achieving woman needs a partner who is truly and exactly that: a partner. A man who merely tolerates a woman's career motivation or, worse yet, patronizes it as though it were an entertaining diversion but not as serious or important as his own career, belongs in another era, and certainly with another woman.

Being a high-achieving woman entails a certain amount of stress and pressure just by the nature of being a woman in the world of the eighties. The last thing such a woman needs is an enemy to her achievement in her own midst.

Resolution of the issues of how to satisfy your achievement needs while maintaining and satisfying your needs for approval, acceptance, and affection—the need for affiliation—will go a long way to relieving excellence anxiety. By becoming selective and self-protective, in appropriate ways, with respect to the kinds of women and men with whom you choose to have close relationships, the fear that people won't like you if you are successful will abate.

Healthy people, with a secure sense of themselves, will like you and befriend you if you are achieving and likable (i.e., friendly, outgoing, giving). People who are not healthy enough themselves, or not secure enough in their own accomplishments or identity, may begrudge you your achievements. These kinds of friends or lovers can be dangerous to your health.

Another essential cognitive correction for Type E women to make is their own sex-linked attributions. Recall that men attribute success on a task to their own ability, and failure to outside factors. In contrast, women make the damaging and demoralizing attribution that their failure is due to their lack of ability, and that their successes are due to good luck or hard work. This sex-linked distortion in the processing of information about successful performance has significant implications for every woman who wishes to maximize her potential and actualize her achievement strivings.

Excellence anxiety arises, in part, because of these selective distortions in processing positive feedback from the environment. In other words, if you do not accept successful performance as evidence of your ability, it is extremely difficult to build a cognitive track record for yourself on which to build future expectations that are attainable and consistent with your actual ability level.

When you properly integrate information about your own performance, taking care to make the most accurate attribution possible about an event, you will build a base of information about yourself that will serve you well in setting and meeting expectations of yourself in the future and in reaching your full potential. Distorted processing of success that involves discounting, undervaluing, or otherwise disavowing your ability will lead to underestimation of future performances and to chronic underachievement.

Ultimately, the resolution of excellence anxiety as a source of cognitive stress depends on the Type E woman coming to terms with herself as a feminine woman who has a desire to achieve. It is her relationship with herself—her ego and self-concept—that is the subject of the next chapter.

CHAPTER SIX

Ego Confusion

THERE is only one mental concept that each of us has that is at the same time both objective and intensely subjective. This cognitive picture, of course, is the self-concept: How "I" (the subject) thinks about "me" (the object). So by definition, nobody can ever be fully "objective" about herself.

The concern that we all share with our egos is normal and healthy. We all find the subject of the self—*ourselves*—interesting, relevant, and important. In fact, having a clear, stable, and strong sense of self is a criterion of psychological good health. Conversely, going through life with a distorted, inaccurate, or unstable sense of who you are can be highly stressful and unhealthy.

Although we can't be fully objective about our self-concepts, we can strive to achieve the clearest and most accurate picture of ourselves as possible. Like a road map, your self-concept provides you with a point of guidance about where you are moving in life—who you get close to or keep your distance from, what goals you are pursuing, what you think you can and cannot accomplish, and so on.

The input we rely on for constructing our ego picture or self-concept is the collected, assorted reflections that we perceive in the words and actions of others vis-à-vis ourselves. How other people relate to you, in other words, has a significant impact on all facets of your self-concept: its form (how you see yourself), its affect tone (how you feel about or toward yourself), and its value (how you set your own self-worth or self-esteem).

Our self-concepts are also a composite of our entire life's history of the way we have thought of ourselves in the past, and the way people who have been significant to us for one reason or another have thought of us, either by virtue of what they told us or of how they acted toward us.

But sometimes the reflections, especially for high-achieving women, seem more like a bizarre set of fun-house mirrors. Yet feeling confused, unsure, ambivalent, negative, or bemused about yourself is no fun at all.

In fact, ego confusion is a major source of underlying stress in Type E women.

Women who straddle the double-domain life—work and personal—are frequently given mixed messages that can catapult them into states of psychological conflict, confusion about themselves, and resultant stress.

Society is in transition with respect to how, collectively, women are seen, both physically and psychologically. At the individual level of daily interactions with other people, confusion abounds. Some people make you feel that your style and substance are terrific; some people make you feel fraudulent; some downright dislike you for no good reason that you can uncover, other than that you represent or symbolize something that is negative to them. And since our sense of ego—our self-concept—is largely an internalized projection of how other people see us, it is no wonder that many women today feel confused about their self-concepts.

A lot of people of both sexes feel ambivalent, threatened, jealous, intimidated, or otherwise uncomfortable in the presence of a high-achieving woman. Type E women, after all, are striving to be everything as women (vis-à-vis men, children, and other women) and to do everything that men have always done, too. Think about it. The impact of this achievement can be awesome, especially to those who themselves have a shaky ego.

When other people feel ambivalently about you—because of what you represent, not because of who you really are—they act in ways that belie their ambivalence. They may behave erratically, inconsistently, unpredictably, or irrationally. The effect on you can be crazy-making.

Ego confusion results when other people give you mixed messages about who you are. The protection for your own ego integrity lies in sorting out how much of the way other people treat you is a function of you, of them, or of the unique interaction between you.

THE TWO-PART SELF

Ego confusion arises, in part, from a split that exists in the self-concept of many Type E women. The split represents, at minimum, a dichotomous, or two-part, self: the working/professional person and the woman in her personal and home life. The size and location of this split, and the severity of its repercussions, vary from individual to individual, depending on the stage and circumstances of her life.

For some women with achievement needs in both realms, the split in self-concept is a barely visible fissure. They have found a way to integrate the two sides without too much strain. They feel relatively psychologically comfortable in terms of how they see themselves and how others see them. This kind of woman will be more resilient to stress.

But for many more high-achieving women, the pain involved in knowing themselves and in integrating the two or three or more parts that they feel comprise their egos is far greater. The split is not a tiny fissure but a gaping chasm. They feel an enormous strain trying to figure out just which side represents their true, or truer, nature.

There is strain, too, in the constant hat-switching that women's multiple roles demand. By definition, change is stressful, and women change roles several times a day.

A stable and secure ego is the front line of defense against massive bombardments of outside stressors.

THE STRESS OF TRANSITION

The fact that Type E women suffer from ego confusion does not mean that they are crazy or even severely neurotic. Ego confusion is, to a significant extent, the psychological consequence of our changing social order. As attitudes and opportunities have changed, both men and women have been tossed in the throes of transition. Since what it means to be a woman today is not the same as what it meant ten or fifteen years ago, a certain degree of ego confusion seems inevitable for every woman who has been caught up in the wave of historical change.

The renowned psychologist Erik Erikson tells a story about a sign that he saw over a bar in a Western town. It read: "I ain't what I ought to be, and I ain't what I'm going to be. But I ain't what I was!" This sentiment fits many women in the 1980s.

As with excellence anxiety, the reasons, ramifications, and manifestations of ego confusion in Type E women are complex. But as with other cognitive sources of stress, increasing your insight into the causes of ego confusion is an important step toward interrupting the stress cycle.

The hallmark of psychological health and stress resistance is *ego integration.* Feeling that the various parts of your personality and behavior fit into one congruent whole builds ego strength. A strong and integrated ego can withstand the impact of ambivalent or mixed messages from others, who may feel confused about themselves and about high-achieving women as a group.

SELF-ASSESSMENT EXERCISES

A good place to begin is to examine your own self-concept. Number a sheet of paper from one to ten. Then write down ten adjectives, nouns, or phrases that answer the question, "Who am I as a working woman?" Force yourself to come up with ten answers.

Next, number another sheet from one to ten. This time ask yourself, "Who am I as a woman in my personal life?" Again, answer with adjectives, nouns, or phrases.

Now compare the two lists. How much overlap is there? How much discrepancy?

Ask yourself some other questions about this exercise as well. How difficult was it for you to complete each list? Did one list come to you much more easily and fluidly than the other? Perhaps you have a clearer picture of yourself as a working woman, but a far less clear picture of your attributes or defining characteristics in the personal domain. Or vice versa. How much time did it take you to complete the two lists? Which list do you like better? Which one has more positive traits or descriptors? Which has more traits with negative connotations? How much strain do you subjectively feel between the two lists?

I conducted this exercise with a woman who came to see me because of disruptive anxiety bouts associated with dating men. Elaine is in her early thirties and has had a series of relatively long-term relationships with men, though she's never been married. Recently, however, she had decided to take a six-month hiatus from men while she invested all her time and energy in a new entrepreneurial business development plan.

Now that the plan was completed, and the most intense part of the working period was over, Elaine was ready to rejoin the world of dating. But suddenly she felt as though she didn't know how to act around men. For reasons that seemed obscure to her, she now felt uncomfortable, unsure of herself, and greatly constricted in her behavior and emotions around any man whom she found attractive, whereas she recalled no such anxiety prior to the six months of intense work.

I asked Elaine to complete the two "Who Am I?" exercises just described. She completed her first list in less than one minute, rapidly providing a description of the way she saw herself as a businesswoman: assertive, confident, professional, knowledgeable, strong, inflexible, domineering, smart, hard-working, and disciplined.

The second list—how she saw herself with men in personal relationships—took Elaine more than five minutes to complete. She repeatedly asked if she could stop with fewer than ten answers, apparently unable to find enough descriptors to characterize herself in the personal realm. Eventually she produced this list: attractive, scared, inhibited, self-conscious, competitive, not feeling good enough about myself, confused, anxious, unconfident, and nervous.

It was as if Elaine were describing two entirely different people. She reflected that she never felt as confused about her personal self until she began defining a clear business persona that she believes will serve her well in the work arena. But as soon as she began to feel comfortable with her assertive and professional business self, she found that she became vulnerable and confused about what all these attributes would mean to her self-perception as a female. For Elaine, it is incongruous to see herself as assertive, confident, and strong, and at the same time to experience herself as a sexual, feminine woman who could feel sure of herself around a man in a romantic context.

Elaine's problem is typical of Type E women who experience ego confusion.

Another interesting and revealing self-assessment exercise is to represent visually the split between the working and the personal side of yourself.

Draw a circle about two inches in diameter. Now divide the circle (either in pie-shape wedges, or in halves, quadrants, et cetera) into the portions of your self that you envision when you conjure your own self-concept. Think of the circle as representing all of your ego in a psychological sense. Where do you see the divisions, if any? Do you experience yourself as an integrated whole circle? Few Type E women do.

Most find that the circle can visually or spatially represent the proportion of themselves they see as embodying a working self and the proportion that is personal. Some carve the circle into several pie parts, each of which corresponds to a role—wife, mother, professional, student, et cetera.

Now take another piece of paper and redraw the parts of the circle that you divided as representing parts of your ego or self. This time, though, try to arrange the pieces in a way that conveys the "distance" that the pieces seem to have from each other. In other words, do you have narrow fissures between the portions of your self-concept, or does it feel like your working self, for example, is really very removed and discrete with no adjoining borders to your personal self?

Elaine's original circle was divided into two parts, with one part (business) comprising two-thirds, and the personal segment about one-third. On the second drawing, she represented the two circle portions about three inches apart on the page. The distance was a psychological representation of the chasm she feels between two seemingly competing, incompatible, or incongruous sides of her self.

SELF-CONCEPT DEVELOPMENT

How do we develop a sense of ego or self in the first place? How do we form a picture of ourselves that we can scrutinize, have feelings toward, evaluate, be proud of, and so on?

Most theories of self-concept formation agree that the way significant others in a person's life history related to her will strongly impact the self-concept of the adult woman. These perceptions, attitudes, and actions of other people are referred to as "reflected appraisals"—the mirror that is held up to your psyche by those around you.

Research has shown that girls and boys are treated differently by adults, and these differences are likely to be incorporated into self-concept development. For example, consider the pet names that are given to children. In general, girls are given diminutive, soft, gentle names, whereas boys are likely to get feisty, punchy, even slightly naughty nicknames. Many adults still think of themselves by the names with which they were dubbed as kids.

Beyond what's in a name, there are other ways in which girls and boys are differentially treated. Boys are given more latitude than girls to explore and to be active in their environments. Girls, on the other hand, are warned about the dangers around them, are more carefully guarded, and are allowed to roam less freely in the environment. So autonomy and independence are built into the rearing of boys; cautiousness and dependency are built into the rearing of girls.

In addition, studies have shown that girls are spoken to more by adults than are boys, which may account for the differential pattern of verbal skill development that the two sexes show: girls develop verbally faster than do boys.

Many women function on the basis of arrested self-concepts. They may still see themselves—psychologically or internally—in much the same terms as they did when they were children, teenagers, or perhaps as adults prior to the changes brought about by the Women's Movement.

One of my patients, for example, is a tall, voluptuous movie and television comedienne who still thinks of herself as a "gangly, scrawny girl with funny-looking features." This self-concept, which is severely distorted in terms of her actual appearance at age forty-two, interferes with her confidence when auditioning for parts that are appropriate to the adult woman that she is, but with which her internal self-concept is incongruous.

The differential treatment and perception of males and females continues far beyond childhood, and the self-concept continues to reflect the appraisals of others throughout our lives.

GENDER STEREOTYPES

An intriguing line of research that bears on the development of ego confusion concerns the stereotypical ways that females are viewed in our culture. Investigators have been quite successful in isolating lists of adjectives that are seen by most people as applying to women, and a parallel list of traits that are seen as generally applying to men.

What is more interesting is the evaluative connotation of those adjectives. Adjectives that have negative connotations include "weak," "nagging," or "frivolous"; adjectives with positive connotations include "confident," "independent," and "affectionate." In virtually every study, the ratio of positively loaded words assigned to men as compared to women was about two to one; conversely, the ratio of negatively loaded traits assigned to women compared to men is also about two to one.

In one well-known study by psychologist Sandra Bem, twenty characteristics each were found to distinguish between people's perceptions of men and woman, among an initial list of some 400 adjectives. The adjectives and descriptive phrases found to characterize "feminine" and "masculine" gender stereotypes are listed below.[1]

Feminine	Masculine
affectionate	acts as a leader
cheerful	aggressive
childlike	ambitious
compassionate	analytical
does not use harsh language	assertive
eager to soothe hurt feelings	athletic
feminine	competitive
flatterable	defends own beliefs
gentle	dominant
gullible	forceful
loves children	independent
loyal	individualistic
sensitive to others' needs	leadership abilities
shy	makes decisions easily
soft-spoken	masculine

Feminine	Masculine
sympathetic	self-reliant
tender	self-sufficient
understanding	strong personality
warm	willing to take a stand
yielding	willing to take risks

These lists reflect the gender stereotypes that both men and women use to describe the characteristics of themselves and each other. And, despite impressive strides of the Women's Movement, everyone knows that stereotypes die hard.

The Type E woman who suffers from ego confusion strives, in effect, to be a member of both lists. And therein lies the strain.

The working woman's experience as she strives to achieve in both personal and career domains involves several changes of trait expressions during the course of a typical day. In the morning, she may act one way with her husband or children—perhaps affectionately, eager to soothe hurt feelings, or cheerfully. When she goes off to work and confronts the demands of her job, she may act analytically, self-reliantly, and forcefully.

Such a woman would have a hard time deciding whether, on the basis of the Bem Sex Role Inventory, she thought of herself in feminine or in masculine terms. Actually, she would do both, thereby creating a potent source of ego confusion and Type E stress.

Like Elaine mentioned earlier in this chapter, if gender stereotypes appear in your own thinking, it is possible that acting in independent, assertive, and competent ways might be stressful because it threatens your femininity or sense of yourself as a woman.

The cognitive correction to this jumble is to start thinking in terms of desirable qualities for *people,* and to conceptualize yourself in terms of your personhood rather than your womanhood or femaleness. This is not intended to serve a feminist purpose, but rather the psychological purpose of removing some of the unnecessary murkiness that clouds many women's sense of themselves.

There are, in fact, many attributes assigned stereotypically to women that would humanize the business world were they to permeate the political and corporate atmospheres. A little more cheerful, compassionate understanding would help everyone.

Conversely, there are a number of qualities traditionally associated with masculinity that are immensely helpful to women with respect to just getting along better in life—such as self-reliance, assertiveness, and the ability to make decisions easily.

An effective step toward integration of your sense of self and reduction of ego confusion is to expose and rehearse those characteristics about yourself that you most value in one domain of your life in the context of another area of your life. In other words, if you like your capacity for clear and direct communication in a businesslike manner at work, and you value your capabilities as a negotiator, try practicing these same qualities in relationships on the personal front. The ability to communicate clearly is a skill that should be transferred, in this example, from the career/business domain to the personal. Conversely, you may value the humor and warmth that you demonstrate in personal contexts, but you may not exhibit these traits openly at work because of your own dichotomous sense of which self is activated. The qualities of warmth and humor are, however, virtually indispensable assets in any human interaction and will serve to advance your interests in the career domain just as they have served you well in your personal life.

Keeping rigid divisions between the way you act in different roles may have very stressful consequences if carried too far. Obviously, a certain degree of separateness and discontinuity between the career woman persona and that of the wife, mother, or girlfriend is appropriate and necessary to social decorum and order. But when the distinctions reach the point where you begin to feel like one person in a work setting and another person entirely in your personal relationships, something is amiss and the stress level intensifies.

Changing hats so many times a day for Type E women is inherently stressful. But changing not only what you *do* but also who you *are,* including how you think of yourself, is an exhausting, confusing, and overtaxing psychological costume change.

SITUATION-SPECIFIC BEHAVIOR

Few people are comfortable applying stereotypes to themselves, whereas they may be quick to stereotype others. This is true because much of our behavior is situation-specific. That is, we act one way in a certain set of circumstances, and another way under different conditions. Because we know ourselves in a broad array of circumstances, we are less likely to fit ourselves into neat categories or trait descriptions.

Roberta, for example, struggled to sort out her self-concept following about six months on a new job in which she received monthly feedback reports from her sales manager on how she was doing as a part of the sales force. The manager's reports were either neutral or critical; praise was withheld completely. The thrust of the criticism invariably included comments on Roberta's "coldness, impersonal attitude, and distance," which he saw as negative characteristics for anyone in sales.

But Roberta got along well with all of her clients, and her sales performance was above average for her department. Still, Roberta felt discomfited by the fear that some people in the office saw her as cold and distant, when she wanted to be seen as appropriately friendly and personable. Roberta began to wonder if she really was cold, impersonal, and distant.

In therapy, Roberta revealed that she knew about the manager's reputation for coming on to women at the office, and she wanted to steer clear of any trouble. So in fact, with the manager, Roberta did defensively maintain a posture of coolness and distance to discourage any advances.

Having clarified why the manager was motivated to see her as cold, distant, and impersonal, Roberta was still mystified by the fact that she had less clarity about the way she saw herself, in terms of distinct personality traits, than others seemed to have of her. And she saw her lack of clarity about herself—her ego confusion—as a flaw.

But psychological research has revealed an enlightening relationship between the willingness, or lack of it, to attribute traits of any kind to a person being a function of familiarity or intimacy with that person. The people least close to you, in fact, are the ones most willing to ascribe certain traits to your personality, whereas you and those closest to you are less willing to ascribe traits to your personality.

The explanation for this phenomenon is that you observe yourself in many situations and, therefore, you know how much your own personality and behavior vary from one circumstance and social situation to another.

And people who are relatively close to you presumably spend more time with you, and also either observe you or hear about your experiences in many varied situations. So those people will be less likely to ascribe traits to you easily because they, too, know that your personality is largely situation-specific. Conversely, people who see you only in one or a few situations will tend to have a "clearer" view of who you are because you are not such a varied stimulus to them. Roberta's manager, for example, could readily ascribe traits to Roberta because that was what he observed when she was in the office. He didn't observe her with clients, or at home with her boyfriend, or with her dog.

Roberta discovered, for example, that she saw herself as capable of both warmth and coldness. What determined her psychological temperature had mostly to do with social context: with the threatening manager, she was aloof and apparently cold; with friendly clients, she was warmer but still reserved and professional; with her boyfriend, she was warm and giving and highly intimate.

Roberta learned that her reticence about assigning summary personality traits to herself was not a reflection of a weak and inadequate ego, but rather of the fact that she knew herself so well that simple, overgeneralized traits like "nice" or "warm" just seemed not to apply to all situations in which she observed herself. Roberta worked on developing a more refined concept of herself, which integrated her ability to adapt her personality to the situational requirements presented to her. She learned to view herself as a woman capable of great warmth and intimacy with the right people under the right circumstances, and also capable of being cold and distant if the situation and self-protection warranted such behavior. Roberta was further able to integrate her self-concept by seeing herself as flexible and adaptable, characteristics that she valued in herself and that consequently helped to buoy her self-esteem.

THE ACTOR-OBSERVER BIAS

Another psychological explanation for the fact that many Type E women feel misunderstood by others, reporting that other people attach traits or labels to their behavior that feel incongruous with the way they see themselves, is called the *actor-observer bias*. What this means is that there is a systematic difference between the attributions or explanations that an actor—a person in a particular situation or set of circumstances—gives for her or his behavior, and those attributions made by observers—others who see the actor behaving.

Essentially, the actor-observer bias indicates that the actor will attribute the causes for her or his behavior to the situational circumstances. The observer, on the other hand, will tend to attribute the reasons for the behavior to the *personality* traits of the actor.

Consider the example of a couple who gets into a row on the way home from a party because she accuses him of flirting with another woman.

"You're nothing but a low-down hit-artist trying to embarrass me and make me look bad in front of my friends," she might say in a fit of pique, making direct attributions to his characterological deficits and personal motivations.

"But you don't understand," he protests. "Everyone at the party had a little too much to drink, and people were just getting flirtatious. Besides, she came on to me. I was just an innocent victim of circumstances."

The underlying process here reveals the actor-observer bias. He (the actor) sees his behavior as arising out of the situation; she (the observer) sees his behavior arising out of his personality.

The actor-observer bias characterizes many interpersonal battles and office disputes.

But for the Type E woman whose life entails exposure to multiple, sometimes competing, situational requirements, the bias can cause considerable distress. While she (the actress) feels that her behavior reflects reactions to various situational requirements, those around her are more likely to label her behavior with personality traits that may have undesirable connotations.

Carol's problem with her boyfriend, Danny, is a good example of the phenomenon. Carol, a busy corporate lawyer with a large firm, is in line for a partnership position toward which she has been working for seven years.

At the time they first came to consult me, she and Danny had been involved for about nine months. The event that brought them to counseling was a severe argument during wich Danny had told Carol what he "really" thought of her personality.

He said that she was, among other things, "selfish," "egocentric," and "inconsiderate." Carol was deeply wounded and confused by these accusations. These characteristics were at odds with the way she viewed herself. In contrast, she conceived of herself as "giving," "thoughtful," and "overly concerned with his [Danny's] feelings and opinions."

"But Danny knows me very well," Carol mused. "If he thinks I'm selfish and egocentric, maybe I am."

Her stress was not only in reaction to the trouble within the relationship, but also in reaction to what this information meant about the way she saw herself. Hence, ego confusion.

In therapy, the reasons behind Danny's attributions about Carol's character were revealed. Apparently, the fact that Carol often worked very long hours, sometimes staying at the office until 9:00 or 10:00 P.M., was interpreted by Danny to be "evidence" that she was not thinking of him, that she could think only of herself. He elevated the significance of this "evidence" to the level of making inferences that Carol's character was flawed by selfishness, egocentrism, and inconsideration.

Carol, on the other hand, was amazed to learn that Danny took her late hours and hard work personally. From her vantage point, she was behaving strictly in response to her demanding work situation. Her legal career required that she spend the time doing the work. It had nothing to do with Danny.

Both Danny and Carol benefited from learning about the actor-observer bias. The information helped them to see the perceptual source of their problem. And it started a constructive dialogue between them about career and relationship values and about how better to demonstrate "giving" and "thoughtfulness" during the necessarily limited time that they could spend together during the work week.

EGO CONFUSION
AND THE AMBIVALENT LOVER

There are other potent sources from the outside that can assault an achieving woman's psyche, and drill holes in her self-esteem and ego.

Perhaps the most insidious is the experience of being "hung up" with an ambivalent man. There is almost nothing as damaging to one's sense of self-worth and integrity than to be the object of another person's ambivalence. It is the eternal daisy game—"he loves me, he loves me not"—tattooed on the psyche. It can rivet a gap right in the middle of even a strong woman's ego.

Sara, at age thirty-four, is a mid-level executive for a growing corporation. She, too, hears her biological time clock ticking, and expresses the desire to find the "right" man and have a family.

She had been seeing George for a year, and she felt they had a lot going for them. George, at forty-five, had been divorced for eleven years. In many ways they were compatible, and seemingly had many of the same goals. Except for one big difference: Sara was ready to get married, but George was, as he explained, "not ready to make a commitment." But he assured her that he would work toward resolving his ambivalence, and give her an answer about marriage.

Over the course of the next few months, George blew hot and cold. Sometimes he would let down his guard and become more open and intimate. At times like this, he was loving and validating to Sara. But at other times, with no apparent warning, he would become distant, removed, and desirous of his "space." Then he would become more critical of Sara, identifying those things about her personality and behavior that he didn't think bode well for a long-term relationship with her.

The point of the story is not George's ambivalence, which is hardly an interesting story at this point, since to many women it reads like a tired old tune plays. What is important to note is the effect that George's ambivalence had on Sara's self-esteem. She concluded, "If he's so undecided, there must be something wrong with me." George's ambivalence triggered Sara's ego confusion.

But what was really wrong in the picture was George's perpetual ambivalence about women and commitment. George had a long history since his divorce of "uncommitted" relationships with women in which he could never quite make up his mind. Sara's misattribution was that the source of George's ambivalence must be a fatal flaw in her appearance or personality.

In the context of George's history, Sara was able to see that the likelihood indeed was that the problem lay somewhere with George. Her problem was why she continued to be involved with someone who was so inconsistent and periodically withholding toward her.

P.S. Sara gave George a deadline to decide, which he blew. She broke off the affair, and married Mr. Right the following year. George, at last report, is ambivalent about his current woman.

The fact is, as I discussed in the previous chapter,

many men are indeed threatened or ambivalent about high-achieving, high-powered women. But Type E women need to avoid the trap of trying to "prove" their lovability and acceptability with men who are unable to provide unambiguous, unconditional love.

And as a functional line of defense against the ego confusion that such relationships can cause, Type E women would do well to stay out of relationships with men who suffer from the crippling effects of chronic ambivalence about women and relationships.

DERIVED AND NEW IDENTITIES

Another reason for the ego confusion that so many Type E women feel has to do with the differences in the way men and women have traditionally derived their sense of identities. Traditionally, women's identities have derived from their pattern of relational ties. It was, in a sense, identity by derivation—they *were* somebody's wife, somebody's mother, and so on.

Men, on the other hand, have traditionally derived their identities from the roles they play in society. They were defined by themselves and by others according to their role designation—doctor, lawyer, or whatever. Men have not derived their identity from their relational ties, except insofar as they inherited title, position, or power from their ancestors.

The interesting implication of these differences is that to a significant extent they still apply. Even though women do not *need* to define their identity by reference to being Mrs. Doctor or Mrs. Lawyer, women still derive a significant source of their identities from being attached in some way to a man.

But women today have expanded their sense of identity to include their own, independent identity in the career world. It appears that women need *both* a sense of themselves as defined by their career niche or title, and a sense of themselves as defined by their relational attachments to a man and/or a family. Yet many women have not yet learned a comfortable way to integrate the two. And the strain between their derived and newly acquired identities compounds the stress of ego confusion.

LACK OF ROLE MODELS

Ego confusion in Type E women also arises from the dearth of good, clear role models of high-achieving women. How many women do you know personally who have achieved their goals in both personal and career domains, and done so without suffering undue amounts of stress? Not many, I'd wager. There are not many such creatures around, although there are vast numbers of women trying to emulate this ephemeral Superwoman.

Of course, there have always been some extraordinary women who made their mark on history and had interesting if not perfect marriages or relationships with men. There are some true heroines, some true superstars whom we imagine can pull off everything without the kind of stress we ourselves experience.

Trust me: Superwomen have Superstress. Some have just learned to manage the stress better than others.

But the number of all-around, successful, high-achieving women, by anybody's count, is relatively low compared to men. This is the necessary result of an era of oppression—a long, dark era. And until the evolutionary changes come about over a few generations, women face the job of devising *ideal* self-concepts of the way they would like to be, in the absence of many flesh-and-blood women after whom they can model themselves. Without clear role models, some women feel like they're making themselves up as they go along, and they may feel fraudulent, false, and painfully self-aware.

Having worked as a flight attendant for eight years, Joyce was determined to succeed in a career in commercial real estate. After passing her licensing exams, she was hired by a conservative, prestigious firm and placed as a trainee in an office with virtually no other women brokers. She was instructed as to the acceptable office attire for a woman—dark suit, white silk shirt, and tie (scarf)—and was also told by her manager that if *she* made it, that would prove that other women could make it, too. The burden of having to prove herself not only for her own achievement, but for the greater good of all womankind, was onerous.

Joyce felt that the men in her office had a stereotyped idea of what a successful woman looked like and of how she acted. But Joyce didn't feel as if *she* had any appropriate role models. Her mother was a traditional countryclub housewife, and she could think of few women that she knew well or "close up" who gave her any guidance about what acceptable, female corporate behavior would look like.

For other women, the lack of role models is compounded by the pressure of knowing that they are the principal female role models for their own daughters.

Suzanne, for example, worries that her two daughters will come to think that working makes you nasty and irritable because she is often short-tempered after a long day at the office. Her stress is compounded by the fear that her ineffective coping is setting a bad example for her daughters, for whom she has high ambitions and aspirations.

"I don't want them to see me unhappy and aggravated about work, because I don't want them to get turned off and give up. And I feel like they think I'm a bad mom because sometimes I'm tired and grumpy when I get home."

Suzanne was able to reduce her anxiety about being an inspirational role model as she learned to manage her own stress more effectively. She came to understand that the best thing she could model for her daughters was that there are techniques and attitudes for managing stress that can be established to increase a woman's resistance to its damaging effects.

IDEAL VERSUS CURRENT SELF-CONCEPTS

In addition to the current self-concept, or *extant self*, each of us also has a concept of how we would ideally like to see ourselves. This concept, technically called the *ideal self*, is the embodiment of our dreams and desires, of how we would most like to be.

But the ideal self operates in another way as well. The ideal self-concept is the psychological measure against which we evaluate ourselves at any point in time. If we ask how we feel about ourselves, what we do psychologically is to compare the picture that we have of ourselves currently—the *extant* self—with the idealized internalized concept of how we think we *should* be. It is precisely the command "should" that causes all the trouble.

It is in the chasm between the self as we see it now and the self as we think we *should* be that self-esteem lies. If the ideal self and the extant self are relatively close together and congruous, the individual's self-esteem is enhanced. If, on the other hand, the perception of the self as it now exists is far away from or far below that of how you think you should be, the effect is to deflate self-esteem, and the psychological consequence is often depression.

Lacking adequate and sufficiently varied role models of women who have successfully "made it" without in the process succumbing to the ravages of stress, we are each left to our own imaginative devices to conjure up the ideal of how we believe we should be.

The problem is that the ideal selves of many Type E women are so overidealized, so unrealistically without human frailties and imperfections, that virtually no mere mortal could live up to the standard. The consequence can be brutal self-castigation and a lowering of self-esteem. When the self-esteem falls, everything becomes more difficult to handle, and coping abilities for handling stress are diminished.

Stress relief for Type E women often necessitates alteration of the extant and ideal self-concepts. One relatively easy and effective approach is to start thinking about the way you would *like* to be, rather than the way you think you *should* be. Women with extreme, unrealistic, and unattainable ideal self-concepts often suffer from the intense pressure of perfectionism, which they generally acknowledge to be both irrational and dysfunctional. When you ask yourself how you *want* to be, also ask yourself if you really want to be a perfectionist. Most women I know who labor under perfectionistic self-imposed standards promptly acknowledge that they would be happier if they were less perfectionistic and judgmental about themselves.

Designing an ideal self in response to the criterion of what you want to be, rather than what you think you should be, helps to transform the ideal self from a self-evaluation tool that can be damaging to self-esteem levels when it is unrealistic and extreme, to an internal guide or source of motivation toward self-improvement.

The key lies in developing a realistic and attainable ideal self-concept, and in learning accurately and usefully to process information from both internal and external sources about who you are in the world.

SOCIAL COMPARISON, REFERENCE GROUPS, AND EGO CONFUSION

Because of their ego confusion, Type E women are driven to ask themselves, explicitly or implicitly, "How am I doing?" The psychological mechanism involves either an event or experience or an internal feeling that triggers the uncertainty-about-self cycle. The uncertainty gives rise to self-questioning: Who am I *really?* How am I doing in life? Am I living up to my own expectations? What do other people think of me?

Remember that uncertainty creates anxiety, and one way that people seek to reduce uncertainty about themselves is to seek comparative information from relevant others. In order to get relevant information to the questions you have about yourself, the appropriate reference groups have to be available. In other words, to evaluate how you think you're doing as a mother, for example, you're going to try to get comparative information from other mothers. Or when you try to evaluate how you are doing in life as a single woman, you would get your most relevant social comparative information from a group of single women like yourself.

The interesting dilemma for many Type E women is *which* group to use as the relevant reference group. Time and again, in my conversations with high-achieving working women who strive to be "good mothers," I discover that the women evaluate how they are doing as mothers against comparison groups of women who don't work—like, perhaps, their own mothers—or mothers whose work involves very different hours, pressures, demands, and so on.

As women have come to learn the value of appropriate reference groups, the membership rolls of professional women's and other working women's networking organizations have swelled. High-achieving women need to seek out other women who are like themselves, both as supportive friends and as appropriate comparison points. Relational ties and comparative information about others' experiences operate to reduce uncertainty and the accompanying feelings of stress and anxiety.

Because of women's autonomous orientation to achievement that I discussed in the last chapter, women are also at a disadvantage with respect to processing competitive information. Men, you recall, are reared to use *competitive* standards against which to evaluate and judge themselves. Women, in contrast, are trained to use *autonomous* standards—how well they do against how well they think they should be able to do. Moreover, few women are really comfortable with external competitive standards for judging their achievements. They are far more likely to seek standards of excellence that arise from their internalized ideal self-concept.

Because of this difference, men are more experienced and adept at using competitive information about how they are doing *versus* other men as input to their self-esteem. Women, on the other hand, are unsure how to process information about how well they are doing as compared to other women in a competitive sense.

The implication is that women rely less on social comparison processes than they do on internal comparisons using their ideal self-concept as a criterion for evaluation. The lack of adequate role models and of appropriate reference group members, as well as the woman's intrinsic tendency to evaluate herself against her own internalized standards, focuses her on the stressful comparison between her self-concept as it exists today and her ideal self-concept, usually driven by the omnipresent, admonishing "should."

EGO CONFUSION AND
FREQUENT SELF-EVALUATIONS

Because they often feel confused and uncertain about
how they see themselves, Type E women tend to
engage the psychological self-evaluation mechanism too
often. The result is a changing sense of self-esteem
that can create and exacerbate mood swings and
depression.

Repeated self-observations can cause the self-concept
and the related sense of self-esteem to fluctuate wildly
as a result of getting too much input or "noise" into
the system. Getting on the scale every five hours to
see how your diet is doing is likely to confuse and
discourage you with random fluctuations, whereas
weekly weigh-ins give you a truer picture of weight-
reduction trends.

Another hazard of overfrequent self-evaluations is
the tendency to exaggerate the meaning of "down"
periods—when your self-esteem is low and you feel
depressed—to indicate the way things are always going
to be.

When I work with a patient who reports feeling low
and bleak about the future, I ask her to draw a mood
cycle on a piece of paper. Typically, she draws something like this:

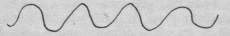

I ask her to plot where she is currently in the cycle.
Generally, her data point representing a low mood is
plotted at the nadir of the cycle (Point A). The problem often lies in her erroneous prediction that the one
data point (A) is indicative of a continuous downward
turn (broken line). Reminding the patient that cycles

involve upturns after down points often helps her to regain her optimism that the more accurate prediction of the future is represented by Point B, on the upswing of her mood cycle.

Keeping the graphic model of the up-and-down cycle in mind can help buffer the negative prediction effects of the low points in your own mood cycles.

For Type E women who suffer from ego confusion, the best method is to collect information about yourself and your impact on the world, and then to use the information for evaluative purposes periodically. Evaluating psychological progress on a monthly basis, for example, will give you more useful and accurate information than evaluating yourself hourly, daily, or even weekly. Too many data points confuse the picture of overall trends.

EGO CLARIFICATION

As I have said, the Type E woman cannot afford to wait until society straightens itself out about how women are perceived, judged, and treated. She must start by straightening herself out about her own ego, and develop as clear and solid a concept of that self as she can.

The key to exactly how the process of self-enlightenment happens is the subject of many a lengthy treatise in clinical psychology. But every great journey begins with the first few steps, and the first step is to spend some time with yourself, thinking about yourself—about the kind of person you see yourself as being and about the kind of person you'd like to be. Try to be specific about the actual *behaviors* that would be involved in every personality trait you use to define yourself and the way you'd like to be.

The next step is to start behaving *as if* you were the kind of person you ideally see yourself as being, how you would most like to be. This is the beginning of change.

Work toward integration of the "selves" that you feel comprise your personality. The more congruous and consistent you can be, while maintaining flexibility and adaptability, the more psychologically healthy you will become and the more stress-resistant your personality will be.

In Type E women, a central link between ego confusion and the dis-stress cycle arises from the need to prove and prove again your value and worth by knocking yourself out to be all things to all people. If, in fact, your sense of yourself is overly weighted by the opinions or transitory reactions of others, you will be likely to respond to their demands and requests in ways that fail to set effective limits and boundaries on your personal resources and coping capabilities.

The cognitive correction to this component of ego confusion is to establish your worth and value as "givens." Then you no longer will have to push yourself to keep proving and reproving your worth in all your roles by acquiescing to every demand or opportunity that presents itself.

It is necessary to unlink the motive to please with the instinct to survive. You cannot be everywhere at once, nor can you do everything for everybody. And the meaning of saying "no" must not put your value or lovability as a woman or as a person into question by yourself or anyone else.

* * *

The effective response to the stress generated by ego confusion is to commit yourself to a process of self-concept clarification. Many Type E women, while burdened with repetitive, recurrent self-doubt and questions about what they really want out of life and where they're really going, generally do not take the time to examine themselves and to create order out of the chaos that they may experience to be their inner self.

Of course, attaining the ancient injunction "Know thyself" is a matter of considerable weight. And there are no shortcut solutions for valid self-knowledge. But an essential ingredient to the process is the *intention* to know yourself, the commitment to the process of trying to understand who you are and what the meaning of your life will be.

The process of ego clarification requires, first and foremost, a candid and committed attitude of self-examination. Go back and review the self-assessment exercises at the beginning of this chapter. How do you see yourself? Try rank-ordering the "Who Am I?" lists in terms of how close you believe each answer is to the core of your true self. Assign a rank of one to the answer that is closest to the core of who you really are, two to the next closest, and so on. This will inform you about the relative importance of these self-descriptors to your sense of self.

Now examine the answers in terms of how you feel about each adjective or noun on your lists. Does it have a positive or negative connotation? Put a plus next to the positive labels, and a minus sign next to those that have negative connotations. What does the balance of positive and negative signs on your lists say about your self-esteem?

Examine your ideal self-concept closely. Is it realistic? Do you know anybody, for example, who meets your criteria for how you would ideally like to be? Is your ideal self a construct invented from how you think you *should* be or from the starting point of how you most *want* to be? The latter is a healthier basis on which to construct a motivating ideal self-concept.

Aside from asking questions of yourself and having the tools to provide answers, you will also need to start observing yourself to gain a better understanding of your "stimulus value" in the social world.

Each of us is a stimulus that elicits responses from other people. As social animals, we interpret what others' reactions mean about our worth and value in life. As I discussed in this chapter, the confusing and ambivalent reactions of others to high-achieving women cause considerable stress in the women themselves. It is the distorted funhouse mirror phenomenon.

Clarifying the meaning and interpretation of input from the social world into your ego concept requires time and concentration. And by time, I mean information gathered over a period of time.

By examining patterns of input from other people about how they experience you, you will begin to identify commonalities. When most of the people you know agree that you are "bright," for example, it is reasonable to accept that appellation as a descriptor of your self: You *are* bright. On the other hand, if only one person sees fit to lay into your ability and intelligence with insult and criticism, a more appropriate interpretation is that the perception is arising from within the speaker rather than being a stimulus property of you.

This fundamental point—sorting out how much of the feedback you get about yourself is really about *you* as the object—is key to stress resistance. Comments and feedback born of jealousy or spite say more about the speaker than about the recipient of the comments. Becoming adept at sorting out the source of social information about yourself requires an attitude of observation—of yourself and of other people. As you develop a clearer picture of yourself, you will develop resistance to the stress caused by unpleasant social interactions.

Developing a clear self-concept requires more than just understanding your stimulus value in the world. But learning how you affect other people can be immensely useful in making you more effective interpersonally. Most Type E women discover, once they adopt an observational attitude toward their experiences, that they have quite a strong effect on other people. This recognition alone helps boost self-esteem, and enhances a sense of self-importance. It helps us all to know that we matter to other people, and that they are affected in some degree by what we do and how we feel. By learning to understand your effect on other people, your life will become more controllable and more understandable to you, and therefore less stressful.

Along with understanding your effect on others, it is necessary to become intimate with yourself. Periodically take the time to be with yourself alone. Take a long walk, or be with yourself in some other way to ponder some heavy questions. Be a philosopher about your life and what it all means to you so far. What are your religious, political, psychological beliefs? How have you been changing in recent years? How have you evolved? In what ways do you want to change or improve? Do you want to stop something you're currently doing?

Knowing how you're doing in life is a matter of overall patterns and trends over periods of months and years, not hours or days or weeks. Many Type E women perpetuate their stress and ego confusion by overexamining their psyches. Paradoxically, their self scrutiny causes confusion rather than clarification, because they are evaluating too much data, too often.

By committing yourself to clarifying your ego concept gradually over time, you will build stress resistance. A clear and positive self-concept functions as a psychological anchor that keeps you protected from the ravaging effects of difficult personal, social, and career stressors.

But do not be surprised if some of yourself remains enigmatic even to you. The fascination with trying to learn about yourself is sufficient to motivate a lifetime's worth of insight development. And, besides, trying to figure out females has stumped some of the greatest psychological minds of all time. Sigmund Freud summed his dilemma up this way: "The great question that has never been answered, and which I have not yet been able to answer despite my thirty years of research into the feminine soul, is: What does a woman want?"

CHAPTER SEVEN

Excessive
Self-Reliance

ONLY a generation ago, women's dependency needs were almost universally acknowledged, indulged, and reinforced. Today, high-achieving women guard against their dependent tendencies as though such needs were the vulnerable Achilles' heel of their psyches.

Dependency is a loaded concept for high-achieving women. It is resonant with echoes of historical traits that women have struggled long and hard to overcome, traits like passivity, powerlessness, helplessness, loss of control, and victimization.

The posture of dependency is seemingly incongruous with the attributes that high-achieving women in the business and professional world are striving to cultivate: assertiveness, independence, autonomy, decisiveness, self-reliance, and personal efficacy.

To many, dependency is an all-too-familiar, seductive lure that might trap them in positions of emotional vulnerability and the pain of rejection or abandonment. To others, dependency might entrap them in cycles of underachievement, loss of self-esteem, and dissolution of identity.

Feeling dependent, in short, can make high-achieving women feel anxious. And for good reason.

Many women have endured deep and painful emotional wounds to their own needs to be cared for, nurtured, and supported as a result of loving and giving too much without adequate reciprocation. And there have been too many casualties as a result of the traditional arrangement in which a woman was dependent on her husband for financial support and, to a large extent, leadership initiative and responsibility. Many women who structured and centered their existence on a foundation of dependency have found themselves, by reason of death or divorce, alone and unprepared for the exigencies of life and self-support.

Understandably, women today are highly suspect of their own needs for dependency, nurturance, and protection. Many view such tendencies as "neurotic," undesirable weak spots in their psyches in need of bolstering and fixing. Because they view dependency needs as inherently weak, dangerous, or neurotic, many high-achieving women are reluctant to express their needs for nurturance or support.

But the desire to have dependency needs satisfied is not necessarily unhealthy or unwise. On the contrary, the inevitable consequence of squelching, denying, or submerging dependency needs is perpetual frustration and eventual resentment and even hostility.

When a psychological need is continually ungratified, the usual result is an exacerbation, rather than an elimination or reduction, of that need. The more a psychological need is denied gratification, the more it clamors for fulfillment. The more, for example, that you deny food to a hungry person, the hungrier and more ravenous she becomes. And so it is with dependency needs.

But it takes courage to be vulnerable. It requires an act of will to trust. Some strong, high-achieving women are finding that they have the same kinds of problems with intimacy that many men have had for a long time. Getting close involves leaning on another for emotional gratification. The dependency feelings that intimacy evokes have long been recognized as a source of anxiety, discomfort, or fear for many men who have been given the traditional cultural training to be strong, self-reliant, and independent.

Today, women are also told by the business/professional/working world to be strong, self-reliant, and independent. So the arousal of dependency needs that intimacy evokes is becoming an increasing psychological stressor.

Many high-achieving women, by their own account, are veritable founts of unmet, ungratified, pent-up, and frustrated dependency needs. This frustration of dependency needs—excessive self-reliance—is key to understanding the dis-stress cycle of Type E women.

One way that Type E women defend or guard against their dependency needs is by placing them on the back burner while compulsively catering to the needs of others. In this sense, the everything-to-everybody core of the Type E style is an effective—albeit ultimately damaging—way to defend against dependency needs.

If you arrange, either consciously or unconsciously, for other people in your life to be more dependent on you than you are on them, and you cultivate and reinforce the expectation that you will anticipate and meet every need and demand of others who depend on you, there obviously will be precious little time even to think about your own needs. And the emphasis on satisfying the needs of others—husbands, children, bosses, et cetera—is a way of shielding yourself from thinking about the pain and frustration of having no one really taking care of your own needs to be nurtured.

So Type E women often submerge their dependency needs by creating asymmetrical relationships, relationships in which the imbalance in dependency is in the direction of others needing them or being more dependent on them than they are permitted to or let themselves be on others.

Saints notwithstanding, it is practically axiomatic that

if you always put someone else's needs ahead of your own, the inevitable price is frustration, resentment, and a sense of exploitation, angry sentiments that fuel the negative stress cycle for Type E women.

In addition to creating asymmetrical relationships and trying to be all things to all people, Type E women deny, suppress, and repress their dependency needs in other ways. They have difficulty asking others for help or requesting adequate support services in a work environment.

The Type E woman is a poor delegator. Delegation of tasks to others, especially on the home front, may make her feel like a cheat or a fraud. Or she may reject help on the grounds that no one will do the job (whether it is laundry, cleaning, meal preparation, or a work project) as well or as efficiently as she can.

Because she does not clearly or comfortably communicate her dependency needs to others, the Type E woman contributes to her frustration cycle by failing to ask for or get what it is she needs. With building resentment, her dependency needs may break through to her awareness and she may find herself asking questions like, "Why doesn't anyone ever take care of me? Why is it always me who has to take care of everyone else? Why can't they understand that *I* have needs, for a change?"

To cope with her frustrated dependency needs, the Type E woman tries, over time, to shut down or minimize those needs and to replace them, instead, with excessive self-reliance.

Traditionally, women have acted out their historical fears of independence and autonomy by exaggerating their "feminine" dependency, often elevating that dependency to the high art of what can only be characterized as "learned helplessness."

But among high-achieving women today, independence and autonomy are prized; dependency is feared. So Type E women often respond to their *fear of dependency* by adopting a posture of excessive self-reliance.

In psychoanalytic parlance, excessive self-reliance can be thought of as a *reaction formation*. Essentially, this means that a particular impulse or need is represented symbolically in a symptom that embodies its opposite. For example, the proverbial "Napoleon Complex," in which a short man who feels inferior and inadequate responds by acting domineering, superior, and with extreme bravado, is a reaction formation. In an analogous way, the Type E woman who consciously or unconsciously fears dependency responds with a kind of reaction formation in which her behavioral style reflects an exaggeration of her autonomy.

Balancing dependency needs in healthy, *interdependent* relationships, learning to delegate, identifying and asking for what you need, such as nurturance, support, affection, et cetera, and accepting normal dependency needs as valid and healthy psychological motives are the cognitive corrections for excessive self-reliance.

Before turning to the cognitive corrections, though, it is useful to explore the concepts of dependency, autonomy, and interdependence, and to define some terms.

DEPENDENCY AS A PART OF LOVE

While dependency as an issue creates psychological havoc for high-achieving women, there is nothing inherently unhealthy or wrong about dependency needs, *providing* they are not excessively intense, not regressive or inordinately immature, and not severely lopsided or imbalanced with respect to the reciprocal needs of the other person.

Of course, when dependency needs *are* extremely intense, or when a person denies or avoids competence in areas that most adults master, or when the dependency is not at all reciprocal, the relationship patterns become disturbed.

But broadly construed, and without negative connotations, dependency needs can be understood as the desire to lean on another person, to rely on another for support, to be relieved of isolation, and to experience that desire consciously as a subjective "need" for another person. Stated in this way, dependency needs are part of the motor that drives love relationships.

In this sense, it is neither incongruous nor impossible to be a self-reliant, autonomous, assertive, high-achieving woman and still need to have an intimate relationship at the core of your life from which you derive nurturance and on which you rely for emotional support. The capability to be vulnerable, to experience need for another person on an intimate basis, and to desire closeness and sharing are virtually prerequisites for a healthy love relationship.

Dependency and need play different roles in healthy versus unhealthy relationships, specifically in this sense: In healthy relationships, the individual feels, "I need you because I love you." But in unhealthy, or what can be termed addictive, relationships, the basis is, "I love you because I need you."

You will note from contemplating these two definitional phrases that dependency in the sense of need for the other is part of any good, healthy relationship. The critical issue is whether the individuals in the relationship *need each other* and are responsive to each other's needs—whether the relationship is *interdependent*. Interdependent relationships permit the expression and gratification of healthy dependency needs, with the rewards of love, security, safety, and trust.

When dependency is one-sided and the interdependence is severely imbalanced, domination, exploitation, and manipulation may result. And when dependency needs are ungratified and frustrated, resentment, depression, stress, and hostility can result.

The point is that a certain measure of dependency needs is normal, healthy, and adaptive to forming intimate love relationships. As with so many other psychological traits, it is the degree, intensity, appropriateness, and interpersonal balance that determine whether the expression of a need is healthy or not.

Close love relationships that provide nurturance and emotional support are among the very best stress resistance resources available.

EXCESSIVE SELF-RELIANCE AND BURNOUT

Just as dependency must be understood in the context of the appropriateness and balance of the needs, so, too, should self-reliance be assessed. Self-reliance is a desirable and healthy trait for both women and men within boundaries; *excessive* reliance on yourself to the exclusion of expressing and gratifying your needs appropriately to rely on, trust, or otherwise derive nurturance from others is not adaptive or healthy. Rather, excessive self-reliance contributes in an insidious way to the chronic stress cycle of Type E women.

Marta's case is a classic illustration of excessive self-reliance and the damaging burnout stress it can produce. At age forty-three, Marta had been married nineteen years to a professional man whose career success had been greatly diminished by a chronic drug and alcohol problem for the last eight years of their marriage.

Although Marta saw her husband as a weak and vulnerable man, she maintained a good deal of compassion and empathy for his problems. Recently, he had begun the recovery process. He had been sober for seven months, and he regularly reminded Marta of his emotional fragility and of his dependence on her. She was asked to tolerate his volatile outbursts; he expected her to subordinate her needs to his. And she bought it.

Marta suppressed expressing any negative feelings toward her husband, however warranted, such as anger, disappointment, criticism, or dissatisfaction, for fear that she might trigger a drinking binge. Marta could not recall a time when she asked her husband to take care of her needs in any way, for fear that the "pressure" of her "demands" would be too great and would somehow be damaging to him.

In addition to her dependent husband, Marta had two teenage children, a boy and a girl. She was a truly devoted mother, participating actively in their sports activities and school projects, and ever-responsive to their emotional needs. Marta felt an extra burden to compensate for her husband's withdrawals and absences from the children's lives due to his drinking/drug problem by "doing even more for them than just a mother would do."

Marta assumed the bulk of both financial and household responsibilities for the family. She worked at a highly demanding technical job that provided a steady, adequate income for the family and provided the necessary stability to compensate for her husband's erratic job performance.

At home, the children were required to do a minimum of chores, since Marta believed their "other activities are more important." Marta shopped, cooked, cleaned lightly (a weekly housekeeper did the heavy cleaning), handled all the family finances, washed the dishes, and fed, bathed, and tended to the family dog.

Marta came to see me on the referral of her physician following a hospitalization for a bleeding ulcer. "I guess I had to get sick to realize how much stress I'm under. I know I do a lot, but I've been doing it for years. There's no one else that can do anything anyway . . . or at least I can't ask them to."

As therapy proceeded, Marta was able to analyze the assumptions she was making that created her excessive self-reliance. She felt exhausted, at "the end of my rope," burned out, and bitterly resentful.

The real thing that was eating away at Marta and interfering with her ulcer recovery was her family's reaction to her illness.

"This was the first time in nineteen years that I've ever even needed anyone to take care of me. And you know what they did? They got hostile! They were mad that I was too sick to take care of all of them. It was unbelievable!"

As we discussed her Type E pattern and stress cycle, Marta began to understand how her cognitive assumptions about relying on herself for everything without acknowledging and expressing her own needs for nurturance had, in effect, created the monster.

"It took getting sick to see that there is no one there for *me*. I always thought—just *assumed*—that after all I've been to them and done for them, they'd be there when I needed them. Oh, they did what they *had* to, but they sure weren't nice about it. They didn't give me the love I really needed."

And as Marta gained insight into her problem of excessive self-reliance, she realized that the problem really started long before her husband's drinking and drug problems even began.

"You know, I set it up from the beginning," she said. "I picked a very dependent kind of guy. I always knew he needed me more than I needed him."

We discussed how the imbalance in dependency needs gave her a false sense of control (her husband's dependency needs really controlled her behavior, more than vice versa), and how, even at a young age, she believed that the safest posture in a relationship was to "count on herself" and to not show "signs of weakness or dependency."

Marta discovered, as her mounting resentment and debilitating stress levels revealed, that she, too, had certain dependency needs. She needed to rely on someone else, and to "let go and have someone else take care of me once in a while." She had always had these needs, she realized, but had submerged them in her compulsive drive to satisfy her family's needs to the exclusion of her own.

In Marta's therapy, we worked on developing several skills. Marta learned to identify and express her needs and, in family sessions, her husband and kids learned to recognize the importance of reciprocating need gratification. Marta learned to delegate tasks at home and at work; she lightened her load and preserved blocks of time in her schedule to do things she wanted and needed to do. She developed the ability to ask for help, and to say "no" to requests that exceeded her resources or desires or abilities.

These changes took time, effort, and commitment from everyone involved, but they turned out to have salutary effects all around. Marta's ulcer healed, and her stress level diminished considerably. Her subjective happiness level also increased considerably.

As the relationship with her husband restabilized into a new kind of balance—less asymmetrical and more interdependent—her husband expressed feeling "good that Marta needs me. She always acted like she could do it all without anybody's help. I didn't feel needed at all. Actually, I always felt scared that she would leave me."

It was, in fact, the dynamic of Marta's suppression of her own dependency that plugged into his drinking/drug problem. By being "helpless" or impaired via intoxication, he unconsciously tried to hold onto Marta by relying on her need to take care of him.

"I don't know why I'm so surprised," Marta remarked. "I trained them all to be that way. I never admitted that I had any needs other than to take care of them. That's what I was raised to think that a wife and mother does. I never asked anyone to do anything for me. I've been bottling up resentment and rage all these years."

Marta's case is quite characteristic of many women's dilemmas, although most situations are not as extreme or clearcut as hers. Nevertheless, Type E women, in general, are reticent to admit to their own dependency needs, and therefore are not skilled at identifying and expressing those needs in a way that leads to their rewarding gratification.

DEPENDENCY NEEDS AND RELATIONSHIPS WITH MEN

There are many reasons why Type E women have difficulty expressing and gratifying their dependency needs, particularly with men. First, of course, is the association that the concept of dependency (in its negative or pathological connotation) has for many high-achieving women who pride themselves on independence and autonomy. But as I have discussed, there are reasonable, normal, healthy dependency needs that form the bonds of interdependent relationships. So why is it so difficult to ask for and say what you need?

For one thing, the nature of the things that women need from men has changed in many respects. As I pointed out earlier, high-achieving women realize that they no longer necessarily *need* a man for financial support or for the derived status of being a professional or businessman's wife. In addition, women's awakening has meant that in many homes and relationships the authority of the male to make unilateral decisions, to initiate leadership, and to have his needs catered to has been challenged. Increasingly, women assert their equal rights to participate in the control of the relationship's destiny, financial resources, and so on.

Moreover, in traditional relationship structures, the trade-off between the husband providing total financial support to the family, and the wife providing, in turn, the nurturance, homemaking, and submissive role to complement her mate's was workable and even equitable. But in the contemporary relationship, husband and wife are often financially interdependent; the family or the relationship is often balanced on the ledger of two contributing incomes.

Furthermore, the change in the typical woman's working status means that her time allocations have drastically shifted. No longer can a woman typically expect to have the day to herself after she's packed the children off to school and sent her husband off to work with a good-bye kiss. Now she, too, spends her day at a job, and comes home tired and drained.

What's more, for most Type E women, work doesn't stop when they come home at night. They merely shift roles again and, relying on themselves, assume responsibility for meal preparation or, at least, seeing to it that the people who depend on them for such things are fed well and on time.

While the high-achieving woman may not *need* a man for financial support or status or leadership, she still has deeper dependency needs for emotional support, empathy, affection, nurturance, protective warmth, and reassurance from her partner. These needs have not been eradicated by women's coming of age. Indeed, successful, competent men, who are healthy enough to achieve intimate love relationships, have strong needs to be listened to, supported, cared for, and nurtured. Why shouldn't high-achieving women have similar needs?

In fact, the woman today who is out competing in the working world may well be more needy of support and comfort after a hellish day at the office than the traditional homemaker ever was.

In a real sense, contemporary relationships are strained by the fact that instead of having complementary needs and roles—he works; she takes care of the home and family—they now have many of the same needs. She is just as tired at the workday's end as he is; he can no longer claim the prerogative of being waited on because he's had a long day at the office. Many Type E women have expressed to me the sentiment that it would be great to have a wife.

In a group therapy setting recently I raised the question of how the women (all Type Es) handled their dependency needs.

"I know I *shouldn't* be like this," one woman admitted, "but I feel that I would like to just let go and allow someone else to just wait on me or shower me with attention or affection sometimes." She went on to explain that because she views her own needs as a weakness and an undesirable characteristic that "other kinds of woman have"—presumably less competent, less successful, or less independent women—she does not express her needs, and they are consequently ungratified. "At this point, my husband doesn't even think I really need any taking care of at all. It makes me angry. I feel cheated. Do I have to act like a dependent, incompetent little girl to get treated with tenderness and care?"

Several of the other women echoed the sentiment that they wished the men in their lives understood that, at times, they have needs to be indulged a bit and, perhaps, even pampered—just as more "helpless," traditionally dependent women do. It seems like a bitter pill to swallow that the price of cultivating competence and autonomy is to give up the human needs to be nurtured, supported, and comforted.

Perhaps, to answer Freud's question posed at the end of the last chapter, what today's woman wants is for men to understand what it is she really needs.

In many circumstances, men inadvertently contribute to the problem of Type E women's excessive self-reliance. For example, many high-achieving women are reinforced for their seeming lack of neediness. The men in their lives may tell them how "refreshing" it is to find a woman who can really take care of herself. Or he may confide what a relief it is not to be involved with another *dependent* woman who drains him of his resources.

In such cases, the woman may feel that expression of *any* needs remotely smacking of dependency will result in painful rejection or reproach. Furthermore, since she has been praised for her lack of overt dependency, she may feel conflicted over expressing or showing any signs of dependency (needing to see him, to hear from him, et cetera), fearing that such expression will cancel out the attraction.

The problem is compounded by the distorted perception of many men that high-achieving, competent women do not, in fact, really *need* men very much at all. But while it is true that many of the bases for needs and dependency have changed, most high-achieving women still want and need emotional closeness and support, sexual love and attention, affection, and the reassurance that comes from knowing that there is someone at the core of your life to whom you can turn for the gratification of such needs.

Men who understand the more subtle, psychological nature of the kinds of things contemporary women need from their relationships with men can be wonderful and rewarding partners. But men who believe that competent women are devoid of any dependency needs whatsoever, for the most part sadly misread their subjects.

Because high-achieving women are often treated as though they don't have dependency needs, they begin to internalize the misperception and to think of themselves as not having the needs, or as flawed for feeling states of need that therefore are left unexpressed.

Some women keep such a tight lid on their inner dependent tendencies that the needs fulminate and erupt in highly emotional, usually ill-timed outbursts that can have damaging effects on relationships.

Sheila's experience with the man she had been dating for nine months, Frank, is a case in point. Sheila is a successful attorney, known and respected by her colleagues for her toughness and skill in negotiations. But when it comes to negotiating what she needs in her relationship with Frank, or any other man, for that matter, her skills as a communicator seem to vanish. While in many ways she felt attached and drawn to Frank, she felt he was too cold and withholding when it came to giving her the kind of tender affection, nurturance, and "cuddling" she craved.

But Sheila never dared even to hint to Frank that she needed or wanted this kind of treatment. She waited, hoping he would come around to realizing that she was "still a woman like any other" and begin treating her in a more loving, nurturant way. The problem was he didn't change either his behavior or understanding of Sheila, and her frustration and resentment deepened.

There were many reasons why Sheila resisted talking to Frank about her dependency needs. She believed that he might "turn off" to her if she admitted that behind her tough negotiator exterior was a soft and gentle woman who yearned for some tenderness in return. "Frank treats me, instead, like a good pal that he sleeps with. . . . I'm like one of the guys to him, except, conveniently, I'm female." Frank, she believed, liked her because of her toughness and independence.

Moreover, Sheila, by age thirty-nine, had practiced a style of excessive self-reliance and submerged dependency needs for so long that the intensity and depth of her frustrated needs frightened even her. She experienced her unmet dependency needs as a kind of psychological Pandora's box, and she feared the consequences of taking off the lid. But her frustrated needs, which continued to bubble toward the surface, demanded expression.

The expression came all right—at about 6 A.M. one morning, when some minor incident blew off the lid. Sheila, much to her own shock and later chagrin, flew off the handle and railed against Frank for not understanding her needs "as a woman" and for "never being there" emotionally for her.

Later, she admitted that the extent of her reaction was exacerbated by nine months with Frank (and a lifetime before that) of suppressing her dependency needs.

For his part, Frank expressed shock, not only at the intensity of her reaction, but at the content as well. He claimed to be totally unaware of Sheila's carefully camouflaged dependency needs, and surprised that she felt hurt. In fact, he had come to believe that Sheila required the "space" to be completely self-reliant, and felt that even such mundane gestures as opening a door for her, or proferring tender or affectionate comforting in the face of a problem in Sheila's life might be construed by her as an insulting, patronizing act.

Sheila's excessive self-reliance reinforced Frank's perceptions. And failing to provide him with corrective information by expressing her needs, Sheila contributed to perpetuating a relationship that frustrated and exacerbated her Type E stress level rather than serving as a haven against stress.

Sheila's story demonstrates the importance of coming to terms with your own dependency needs, and of accepting that such needs can and do exist within the same individual who is capable of acting independently, assertively, and autonomously.

Expecting a man to understand spontaneously what it is that you keep under wraps is an unfair game. A good partner may have some intuitive understanding of your needs, and that is very much to his credit. But *you* are the best source of information about your needs and desires. Expressing your needs in a way that is designed to improve the relationship and heighten everyone's happiness level should not be confused with a demand. Good relationships require mutual instruction in what each one wants to give to and get from the relationship.

Accurately identifying your needs, accepting them as valid and worthy of gratification, and finding ways to get them met are critical steps to take in breaking the no-win cycle of meeting everyone else's needs while denying your own.

DEPENDENCY NEEDS AND FEAR OF ABANDONMENT

For some high-achieving women, the very experience of falling in love can elicit panic reactions rooted in conflicted dependency needs. If you allow yourself to experience or feel need for another person, the possibility exists for emotional pain. Of course, the other possibility also exists: the need will be met and deep emotional gratification will result. In this case, nothing needed, nothing gratified.

Nonetheless, for excessively self-reliant women, the feeling of need for another person, which typically accompanies the experience of romantic love, may trigger high levels of anxiety over the threat of rejection or abandonment.

Rachel's pattern of preemptive breakups exemplifies the self-perpetuating nature of excessive self-reliance.

Rachel is a thirty-year-old physician beginning a career in private practice. She is associated with a prestigious medical group, and enjoys a handsome income and a bright career future. She already, as a single woman, owns a condominium and drives a nice car.

Rachel pushes herself hard to maintain close family relationships and social ties. Even after a long day at her medical office, she manages to invite a few friends over for a fashionably "light" dinner and to be "available" to her friends or family to listen and be supportive.

Rachel also maintains an active dating life. She is "looking" for a relationship that will work as a marriage, though she is unsure, as yet, about having children. An attractive woman, Rachel watches her diet and includes trips to the gym in her busy schedule. She has had many romantic experiences, although, so far, nothing has quite "worked out as a long-term commitment."

Rachel does not, however, feel happy or fulfilled. And she does not, therefore, feel genuinely successful by her own standards. What is missing, she says, "is a man in my life. Someone who would help share the load, and someone who might even take care of me for a change."

Typical of Type E women, Rachel takes care of others—including patients, family, friends, boyfriends, and so on—but no one is really available to reciprocate her needs for nurturance and support. Moreover, Rachel feels that she may not really be entitled to have such needs gratified since, obviously, she is more capable than many women of taking care of herself. Rachel wants a truly intimate love relationship, and a "strong man" on whom she can rely. She says, "I want to need someone in my life and trust that they will be there for me."

So far, so good. The problem is that Rachel never

allows a relationship to last long enough to turn into a long-term commitment or marriage.

Her typical pattern is, first, falling quickly and passionately "in love." She rapidly labels the experience as love and, in most cases, the men have reciprocated the romance in the earliest phases of the relationship. Sometimes, even after as few as one or two intense, romantic weeks, there is even talk of marriage or living together.

Rachel is the queen of the roller coaster affair. As the relationship hits its first romantic peak, a sudden downturn occurs. Suddenly, Rachel is beset by an unspeakable panic. She experiences acute anxiety bouts, and her overall subjective stress index skyrockets.

The content of her upset invariably centers around one theme: What if he leaves me? She begins erecting psychological defenses, seeking to find fault, to criticize, to pick fights, to withdraw and "turn off" sexually as ways to distance herself from the man. The mechanisms operate to protect from "needing" the man too much. If she devalues the man for whom she is starting to feel needy—an emotional and motivational state that Rachel gives lip service to wanting—she can diminish the need and the accompanying dependency panic.

Rachel doesn't trust that any man will really stay with her. She fears that her achievement drive and ambition will ultimately drive a man away from her because the threat will be too great. This excellence anxiety is, of course, typical of Type E women.

And she fears that any man with whom she becomes intimate will expect her to change by becoming more compliant and subservient than it is natural or adaptive for her to be. Like other women who experience role strain and ego confusion, Rachel feels torn between the self that functions as a self-reliant, assertive professional, and a "married self" that she imagines would "have to be more feminine" (i.e., unassertive, submissive, and compliant). Her fears are not founded on anything that the men explicitly say, but merely on the basis that she "feels it to be true" that men really want a different kind of woman for a wife.

Her anxieties are based on her own perceptions of herself in relationship to men, on her belief that every man, eventually, will abandon her. These realizations did not, however, become conscious and clear to her until together, in therapy, we explored the basis for her panic.

Rachel came to see a kind of chain reaction that she set off when she began to feel the dependency that romantic love relationships stimulated in her. The arousal of dependency needs created high levels of anxiety and anticipatory fears of rejection and abandonment. As a defense against becoming too dependent on a man whom she believed would eventually leave her, she became critical and rejecting, thereby generating discord. When the fighting and unpleasantness reached a certain threshold (often within six weeks of the relationship's start), Rachel would break off the relationship herself on the grounds that he wasn't right for her. In effect, and in fact, she made a preemptive strike. Before he left her, as she believed he would *because* she was such a self-reliant and independent woman, she left him.

And so it went, one unsuccessful relationship after the other. And her stress cycled from levels of arousal due to loneliness and dissatisfaction, to panic reactions associated with dependency and "falling in love," to the stressful aftermath of breaking up a relationship and finding herself holding the bag again for all her life's responsibility.

Rachel is a classic illustration of a woman whose self-reliance has exceeded the point at which it is adaptive for managing stress and for building stress resistance. She needs to learn to maintain her balance when she meets a man with whom a relationship is likely or possible. Her own intensity, especially when it is reciprocated, accelerates the rate of intimacy development, and Rachel gets catapulted into a precarious psychological position to which she is unaccustomed and with which she is uncomfortable. That position is one of potential interdependence—needing a man who needs her back. The breakdown occurs when Rachel's cognitive chain reaction gets triggered and she begins unconsciously acting on the belief that she needs him, but he will not need her and will, ultimately, leave her. The unhappy bottom line is that Rachel's stress cycle is self-perpetuated, fueled by self-fulfilling prophecy and unconsciously provocative interpersonal behavior.

DENIAL OF DEPENDENCY NEEDS

Rachel's preemptive strike style is characteristic of many high-achieving single women's patterns of relationship difficulties. But there are other ways in which excessive self-reliance and its corollary of unmet dependency needs contribute to relationship frustrations and problems.

A classic example is yet another version of the self-fulfilling prophecy. In this pattern, the high-achieving woman wears protective psychological armor designed to guard against even her own awareness of dependency needs.

"I don't need anybody in my life," one woman flatly stated to me. "It's been a gradual process of shutting down on the pain. When I was younger, I still thought I wanted to get married, and I let myself feel or imagine what it would be like to be at least partially shielded from so much personal exposure . . . what it would be like to actually let myself need another person, a man, and have that be all right with him, with me, with everybody. But it never quite worked out, and I taught myself to kill the need. And I guess men can tell. . . . I haven't had a date in six months."

In group psychotherapy with other women like herself, this woman began to realize that she indeed felt deep needs for intimacy and interdependence but that she had given up hope that such a relationship was possible. For women who have had long histories, often including failed marriages, of frustration and disappointment of their own dependency needs, the arousal of such needs can be frightening and uncomfortable. As a protective device, this woman, and many others like her, erect psychological barriers to intimacy as a way to insulate themselves from needing too much and therefore risking the possibility of further pain. The price they pay for complete denial of dependency needs is loneliness, alienation, and frustration. These feelings can be far more debilitating and stressful in the long run than confronting and managing the anxiety associated with feeling needful of a man. A healthy, balanced, interdependent love relationship that includes *mutual* nurturance, affection, sexual loving, and emotional support is one of the best prescriptions for building stress resistance.

AUTONOMY AND TESTING THE LIMITS

There are other ways in which the stress of excessive self-reliance plays itself out in symptomatic relationship problems between high-achieving women and the men in their lives. Sometimes, the woman who treasures her independence and autonomy fears that her partner might somehow infringe on those boundaries and compromise her valued attributes. As a response, she may "test" the relationship or "test the limits" of her partner's perceptions of where the control of each begins and ends.

The case of Jane and her husband, Les, is an interesting example of this kind of relationship testing. They came to consult me because of communication problems and sexual difficulties in their four-year-old marriage. The strain in their marriage was, in turn, compounding the Type E stress Jane was experiencing as a working mother of two small children.

As the therapy progressed, Jane and Les revealed an underlying dynamic in their relationship in which Jane used overeating, underexercising, and weight gain as unconscious ways to exhibit her independence and autonomy. The key to understanding this dynamic is that Les was highly disciplined about his eating and exercise habits, and wanted his wife to be the same way.

Jane responded, "I'm an adult woman. I'm responsible for controlling my own food intake, and it drives me nuts when he tells me what to do. It's like he thinks I'm some kind of child that needs direction all the time."

As it turned out, eating was only one area in their relationship that was strained by power struggles and battles to test control. In the bedroom, the frequency and quality of their sexual relationship was a direct function of Jane's weight. When she was thin and in good shape, Les desired her frequently and was a satisfying and attentive lover—so much so that Jane found herself "needing him sexually," a feeling that generated some unconscious resentment in her. By gaining weight (Jane's weight would fluctuate by thirty to forty pounds in a few months' time), Jane could unconsciously "control" her husband by turning him off sexually.

Food was also related to the issue of entertaining for Les's clients. Jane was an outstanding gourmet cook who knocked herself out preparing lavish, impressive meals for Les's business acquaintances and contacts. Jane, herself, did not have a job that entailed business entertainment. So though she thoroughly enjoyed cooking and entertaining, she was careful to remind Les at every opportunity that the "reason" for cooking and *eating* the food she prepared was for him and the advancement of his success.

The problem, of course, was that as Les's business boomed, Jane ballooned. She responded to any degree of criticism or encouragement to diet from Les defensively and angrily. She was, in her words, "knocking myself out for you [Les], and all you can do in return is criticize. It's my business what I eat and don't eat and, besides, I would be a rude hostess if I didn't eat the same food as my guests."

In her less indignant moments, Jane admitted feeling angry and disappointed with herself for "blimping out." In therapy, she also began to recognize the relationship between issues regarding autonomy, self-reliance, independence, and control in her marriage and the ever-present, ever-threatening issue of her weight. Together, in joint session, Les and Jane developed and refined their skills at communication and expression of their feelings and needs. As the various testing grounds for autonomy and control became identified (such as Jane's throwing her weight around), and as the underlying themes of interdependence and control balance were brought to awareness, Les and Jane's marriage took a turn for the positive. Jane lost her surplus thirty pounds, and their sex life resumed its earlier frequency and satisfaction level. And by examining and coming to terms with her own dependency needs in certain areas of their relationship, Jane was less threatened by the interdependence inherent in mutual sexual attraction and gratification.

ROLE-REVERSAL RELATIONSHIPS

Another variation on the theme of dependency needs and how inadequate coping with such needs contributes to the Type E stress cycle is represented by the classic role-reversal marriage or relationship.

In this structure, the high-achieving woman does more than participate in the financial support of the couple unit; she takes full or major responsibility for providing the couple's income. The man in this arrangement typically works at home at free-lance or creative kinds of endeavors, or simply stays at home and tends to household matters, either out of necessity (due to layoff) or choice. The reversal is the stuff of which movies like *Mr. Mom* and television sitcoms are made.

There is nothing inherently wrong or undesirable about this arrangement, provided that: (1) both parties are amenable to the new rules—the wife will earn the family income and the husband will tend to hearth and home; and (2) the nurturance and emotional needs of *both* parties are being recognized and satisfied.

But when these conditions don't apply, stress—for both parties, but particularly the woman—can result.

Heather and Larry, for example, agreed to reversing role responsibilities as a viable way for Heather to pursue a lucrative sales career in the computer field, and for Larry to pursue his desire to be a television writer.

Heather earned a six-figure income and endured a lot of work-related pressure and stress. Her field was highly competitive and she worked on a salary-plus-commission basis. In addition to earning the couple's living, Heather also handled the financial affairs for both of them.

Larry had not yet sold a property, though his work was good and the chances were that he might be successful in the future. In the meantime, Larry puttered around the house and produced a new screenplay about every six months or so. A housekeeper came twice a week to do the heavy cleaning; Larry took clothes to the cleaner, went to the grocery store, and cooked dinner two to three times a week.

They referred to themselves as a "role-reversal couple." For a while, they were proud of the arrangement. Then Heather started developing acute stress reactions. She developed a host of skin rashes that her doctor attributed to "stress at work," and she began to lose her hair. Panicked, Heather came to consult me.

As we explored the dynamic of her marital relationship, Heather explained that, "even though Larry does more domestic things than I do, I still carry the emotional load for the marriage." Since Heather agreed to the role-reversal arrangement—in fact, it was her idea to support them in order to give Larry an opportunity to do creative work—she felt she had "no right to appear weak and needy." She believed that it was necessary for her to maintain a strong "front" so that Larry wouldn't feel guilty for not working in the traditional way like other men.

As Heather's story unfolded, it became clear that her "deal" with Larry included, in her mind, suspending or quashing her own needs to be taken care of in an emotional sense. Heather felt that Larry was keeping up his end of the deal by occasionally cooking, purchasing food, and dealing with most minor household hassles. This, she believed, was "asking enough," since it was "ten times more than most husbands I know of." But while Heather made it a point to be available to listen to and nurture Larry's problems and needs, she was virtually silent when it came to expressing her own.

When they went to bed at night, Heather held Larry in her arms and stroked his head as he fell asleep. Heather cried to me one day as she admitted how much she wanted him to hold her once in a while in exchange.

The punchline of the story is that, after two years of the role-reversal trial (and only one screenplay sold for development for a small amount of money), Larry decided to pack up and leave the marriage. He later explained to Heather that among other reasons, he left because he didn't feel really "needed emotionally" by her, and his manhood seemed somehow to be at stake. He had to leave, he said, because he wanted to see if he could stand on his own two feet as a man and because he needed a woman who *needed* him.

Heather was devastated. "I feel like I'm being punished for my achievements. What's worse is that I thought he needed me so much he'd never leave me. I think that's why I spent all that time denying my own needs and catering to his."

BALANCED INTERDEPENDENCE

Dependency in either party that is imbalanced, immature or regressive in nature, or too extreme or intense can and often does result in the destabilization of the relationship and its eventual termination. Women who have been in a position like Heather's, or women whose assumptions regarding dependency needs also reveal conflicts about how much to need, how much to show that need, and how dependent to make others on you, often learn the hard way that such beliefs are erroneous and ill-founded. The next two chapters examine further how cognitive assumptions underlie erroneous expectations that fuel the Type E stress cycle, and how everything-to-everybody behavior is the result of a belief system that advises you to cater to others' needs at the cost of denying or frustrating your own.

I am not advocating that women abdicate all responsibility for the needs of others who are close to them, nor am I raising a banner of selfishness for all women to salute. What I am advocating as a necessary condition for adequate stress resistance is that women strive to establish balanced, symmetrical relationships (between adults) that mutually gratify needs for dependency, nurturance, intimacy, affection, and so on. Obviously, relationships between minor children and adults are asymmetrical by their very nature and definition. But children, too, can be made more sensitive to and aware of their mothers' limitations of time, emotional resources, patience, and just plain physical endurance.

Excessive self-reliance is a cognitive stance that results from a perpetual cycle of ungratified, frustrated dependency needs. Remember, though, that the Type E trap is baited with the woman's own exceptional competence. She so clearly demonstrates her ability and willingness to respond to the needs of others, and she so often subordinates her own needs for many different reasons as I have discussed above, that there results a kind of collusion between the Type E woman and the people in her life who are dependent on her.

What do I mean by collusion? I use the word to indicate the woman's own participation in creating the cycle of continuous frustration that fuels and perpetuates her negative and destructive dis-stress. Obviously, the men with whom Type E women are involved in love relationships bear responsibility for the problem; for their own set of reasons, the men may choose to deny that their mates have dependency needs, simply as a way of relieving the pressure on them to be nurturant, affectionate, or protective. Or they may misread the signals that, after all, are designed to deceive: The woman who acts as if she is too strong to need support may well be hiding deep and unmet dependency needs. The man who takes such signals as messages to back off from displaying or providing nurturance or tender support is, in a sense, innocently misled into contributing to the woman's own self-fulfilling prophecy.

The collusion lies in the implicit accommodation all parties seem to make to the setup. The husband, lover, employer, or friend whose needs are gratified by the Type E woman is satisfied and, generally, doesn't feel inclined to rock the boat. The Type E woman colludes by failing to identify, accept, and express her needs to stop taking care of others (for periods of time) and to indulge her needs to rest, attend to herself, and to have others provide her with emotional nurturance and caretaking.

Many high-achieving women have described "patterns" in their failed relationships, which they have identified as "picking the same kind of exploitative/manipulative/demanding/controlling man" over and over again.

Becoming aware of the collusion factor is a psychological insight that often alters the perception of such patterns. Type E women who understand how their own suppression of dependency needs or inadequate ways of coping with such needs contribute to their relationship problems also come to see that the real "pattern" is not in the common personality traits of the men with whom they become involved, but in how the women themselves behave and what they do and do not say about their own needs and limitations to those men. The woman's behavior, in short, shapes the man's response. And while it is true that some men may have a predisposition to demand or control, it is the woman's response that reinforces the man's behavior and expectations.

EXCESSIVE SELF-RELIANCE AND WORK

The Type E woman's reticence about expressing dependency needs extends well beyond the perimeters of her relationships with family, friends, and love partners, and contributes to the stress cycle induced by work demands.

Excessive self-reliance can actually sabotage a woman's effectiveness and success at her career by interfering with her ability to ask for and receive adequate support staff for her projects, or her ability to delegate work to others appropriately.

Cynthia's story is a classic illustration of the problem. Cynthia works as a manager in the operations division of a major corporation. She is thirty-three, a divorced mother of two, and is involved in a steady, two-year relationship with a twenty-seven-year-old businessman.

Routinely, Cynthia works a ten- to twelve-hour day, picks up her children, prepares dinner for the kids and her boyfriend, and manages the household with minimal domestic help.

When Cynthia came to consult me, she was feeling upset and stressed about problems at work. After she received a negative performance evaluation from her boss due to a pattern of delays in delivering milestones in the large project on which the company was working, Cynthia realized the severity of her problem.

She accounted for her failure to meet deadlines by citing the number of other competing, personal demands in her life, and wished that her supervisor would simply be more understanding.

As we discussed her work environment and conditions, Cynthia revealed what I found to be an astonishing (but characteristic of Type E women) lack of support services and staff available to her, given her level of responsibility in the company.

While she personally supervised more than twenty-five employees, and coordinated multiple inputs from four functional departments under her direction, Cynthia didn't have a personal secretary. She had to answer her own telephone and take messages for others, type her own memos and duplicate them for distribution, *and* perform her named job responsibilities as manager for the portion of the project that she controlled.

As we talked, Cynthia came to see that an apparent reason for blowing deadlines was that she was doing the work of at least two, possibly three, persons and was, thereby, sabotaging her own effectiveness as a manager. In true Type E fashion, Cynthia had wowed the division heads when she first took the promotion to managerial status by the amount of work her division produced with so low a support-staff budget. Since she never asked for secretarial support or telephone backup, her supervisors assumed that Cynthia didn't need any help and that such valuable support resources should be allocated elsewhere.

To compound the problem, Cynthia operated under the cognitive assumption that she *should* be able to handle the workload by herself and that asking for help or support would be an admission of inadequacy. Although she had never been conscious and explicit about these beliefs, Cynthia was quick to recognize that the underlying assumption that she *should* do it all herself was clearly behind her reluctance to request additional staff. Cynthia could readily see how her style of excessive self-reliance was backfiring—exacerbating her stress level, causing her to fall even farther behind the deadlines, and thereby fulfilling her worst fears that she would be viewed as inadequate and not up to the job.

Cynthia left the therapy session in which she had gained these insights promising to put in a request memo for support staff as an appropriate solution to her problem. She was given a departmental reception-ist and a personal secretary within two days of her request. Her supervisor complimented her on recogniz-ing her management shortcomings ("not delegating to others and trying to do everything yourself") and en-couraged Cynthia to "ask sooner" for whatever she needed in order to turn out a good job *on time*.

Cynthia's story is a clear illustration of a style that characterizes most Type E women, though the mani-festations may be more subtle than in Cynthia's case. Many women experience immense anxiety over the need to ask help of a coworker, supervisor, or even subordinate. They express the fear that they will ap-pear fraudulent, inadequate, or incompetent, believ-ing instead that they should be totally self-reliant.

But self-reliance, in an adaptive sense, includes knowing the limitations of your knowledge and re-sources so that when assistance is required, you cope appropriately by seeking and receiving support. Exces-sive self-reliance in a professional setting can result in unnecessary and costly mistakes, undue anxiety and discomfort, a reputation of not being a "team player," or other backfire effects.

And among women who work in key support posi-tions in organizations, excessive self-reliance is an enor-mous underlying factor in stress disorders.

Helen, for example, was the administrative assistant/ executive secretary to a top corporate CEO. At age fifty-three, she had been with the company twenty-eight years and was proud of her achievements and ad-vances from her entering level as a file clerk/receptionist.

Helen's boss couldn't say enough good things about her. Indeed, he did not hesitate to remind people that "without Helen I wouldn't know how to run my own company." Moreover, Helen's boss was "from the old school." He liked the fact that Helen took shorthand, typed on a "regular, old-fashioned typewriter" (i.e., not a memory writer or word processor), and that "her middle name was efficiency."

Helen had worked for the same boss for the last twenty years, and she was devoted to him. "I have two husbands, in a way," she would laugh. "At least in the sense of two men that I have to take care of. They're really a lot alike—they both need me a lot and I guess I love that. The problem is that they need too much, and I'm falling apart."

Helen's problems started during the last five years or so, when her company converted to new computerized office technology. Helen remained the only "holdout," relying on herself and her efficiency to survive the onslaught of the new Age of Information. But at first slowly, then as a deluge, she became inundated with an avalanche of paper and computer-generated reports to which to respond, and the turnaround time for documents processed by her office was far slower than those in other offices that utilized time-saving technologies.

There were several reasons behind Helen's reluctance to accept the new technologies. She feared the machines, anxious that she would be incompetent at mastering them. Worse still was the fear that the machines would outshine her efficiency, thereby disappointing her boss and rendering her services unnecessary.

In addition to these fears, Helen was also pushing herself to prove that she could do it all herself—classically Type E. Helen also refused to ask her boss for an assistant or secretary. She, like Cynthia, felt that asking for help was some kind of admission of inadequacy or incompetence. Nor would Helen delegate jobs to other secretaries in the office. Delegation meant, to her mind, that "you were too unorganized to be able to fit in all your assignments."

Eventually, of course, Helen's excessive self-reliance caught up with her, and she was deeply mired in a dis-stress cycle that was taking its toll on her health and on her performance at work.

Helen needed to work on accepting that she had long ago earned her value in her boss's mind and that her assumptions about excessive self-reliance were self-defeating. She didn't need to prove she could do it all herself.

Of course, the relationship between a corporate executive and his or her secretary is inherently asymmetrical in terms of who tells whom what to do. But in an important sense, it is a highly interdependent relationship in which both parties rely on the other for achieving positive results or outcomes. The balance, in Helen's case, had to be reestablished by recognizing her own limitations and asserting her rights to have support and assistance for herself.

THE IMPORTANCE OF RENEWING RESOURCES

This chapter has examined a number of ways in which women get caught in Type E stress cycles as a consequence of imbalances, conflicts, or inadequate coping with their own dependency needs. The subjective psychological experience associated with such problems in high-achieving women is often the sense that "everyone wants/needs a piece of me" or "I take care of everyone but there's no one to take care of me but me, and I don't have time for myself."

The asymmetry in nurturance and dependency is felt particularly acutely by working women who have a husband and/or family. For the great majority of these women, the main role of nurturer in the relationship is provided by them. Although such women often work as many or even longer hours than their husbands or boyfriends, when the "day is done," their caretaking and nurturance jobs may just be beginning or, more accurately, picked up where they were left off that morning.

To be sure, significant, notable changes have occurred in the gender role-blending of many couples. Men, reaping the positive side benefits of the Women's Movement, are increasingly discovering that the vulnerable, tender, nurturant, and sensitive side of their nature has salutary effects on their own emotional and mental health as well as on the quality and tone of their relationships with women.

Notwithstanding these shifts in men's willingness to share more in the nurturing process of children and to reveal more of their gentler qualities, women, as a group, have not foregone their need to nurture or their beliefs, values, and assumptions about a woman's role responsibilities vis-à-vis her husband/boyfriend and family.

The trap for the high-achieving woman who suffers from the stress of excessive self-reliance is that her reserves and coping resources are far more depleted by the stressors of work and achievement pressures than were those of her generational forerunners. But her defined role as principal nurturer and attender to the emotional needs of *others* has remained virtually unchanged. The Type E woman is caught in a cycle wherein she puts out more psychological, emotional, and physical energy than she takes back in. There is insufficient renewal of her finite energy. And the omnipresent stressor of trying to achieve in both career and personal realms compounds the problem by acting as a constant drain on the woman's coping resources.

Everyone needs emotional replenishment. The tired body needs rest and relaxation. The tired mind needs respite from worry, agitation, and discipline. And the tired woman, fatigued from trying so hard to give to others, needs to have some giving, nurturance, and dependency gratification reciprocated in order to recharge her emotional reserves.

And she must learn to attend to her own needs as well, to nurture herself as effectively as she does others.

To believe that the need for intimacy, love, and support is a sign of weakness or incompetence is to buy into a dangerous mythology. Nobody benefits from a woman's denial of healthy dependency needs: both the woman and man get the short end of the stick, and their relationship too often becomes a source of additional stress rather than the haven and source of stress *resistance* that it could and should be.

Good, close relationships with both men and women, as well as with children, are among the best buffers against the vicissitudes and stressors of daily life. (I deliberately modified the phrase "close relationships" with the adjective "good," because there certainly are close relationships between intimates that are not healthy, mutually supportive, nurturant, or satisfying; these "not good" close relationships can themselves exacerbate and cause stress.) Other people with whom we share our problems, burdens, confusions, or conflicts, as well as our triumphs, joys, insights, and companionship are the wellsprings from which to replenish our own reservoirs of coping resources.

But in order to draw *mutual* sustenance from a relationship, each party must give to the relationship (in order to feed its reservoir) *and* each party must get from the relationship that which she or he needs.

Balanced, mutually satisfying, nurturing, interdependent relationships are created by both members. Relationships with the "right man" or "right woman" are not found, they are formed. The Type E woman must, in this important sense, rely on herself to identify her needs and to communicate them to others in a way that those needs become gratified.

Accepting that your needs for nurturance, dependency (within healthy, appropriate bounds), and support can and do coexist with parallel needs to be autonomous, self-reliant, and independent is a critical step in the process of reducing the stress of excessive self-reliance. Learning to create and utilize relationships as resistance resources rather than as perpetual energy drains will reduce overall Type E stress levels.

Type E women can learn to be especially effective resistance resources for one another. Too often, women use their friends' ears as a way to ventilate frustration and to emote about their stressful experiences. The listener frequently compounds the stress by underlining the problem ("That's terrible! I can't believe he/she did that to you! Listen to what happened to me . . ."), thereby raising the overall stress level and tone of the conversation. Type E women would be better sources of support to one another if the listener focused on calming the speaker instead of reinforcing the upset, and helped to move the conversation to problem solving rather than mere emotional catharsis.

Being able to identify and express what you want to give to and get from a relationship will likely require altering some of your cognitive assumptions or beliefs about dependency, vulnerability, subjective neediness, and other issues that are problematic for Type E women.

Learning to delegate jobs and responsibilities, a skill I cover in greater detail in a later chapter, is another key step to lowering the stress of excessive self-reliance. Suffice it to say here that delegation requires an acknowledgment of interdependency with others, a willingness to draw limitations around what you expect to be able to do by yourself and an ability to see the act of delegation as an expression of wise self-management and self-preservation rather than as a sign of inadequacy, excessive dependency on others, or other undesirable traits.

The solution to excessive self-reliance is essentially a paradox. You need to be strong and self-reliant enough to let yourself be vulnerable and needful of others. You need to rely on yourself to be the best source of information to others in your life about what you will choose to do, about where your limitations and self-preservation boundaries exist, and about what you need from them in return. And you need to be self-reliant so that you can approach dependency on another—to need, trust, and love—out of choice, not out of desperation and helplessness.

Being capable, competent, and willing to take responsibility for your own life and achievements as a woman will best prepare you for an intimate relationship in which you feel "I need you because I love you," not "I love you because I need you."

CHAPTER EIGHT

Erroneous
Expectations

IMAGINE that you are driving to work, listening to the morning news, and thinking about the day ahead of you. As you approach an intersection where you clearly have the right-of-way, your peripheral vision catches sight of a fast-moving car approaching at a right angle to you.

You jam on the brakes, screech to a halt, and miss the other car by a hair. The other driver waves, shrugs his shoulders as if to apologize, and continues en route without so much as breaking speed.

Moments later, after you have instinctively warded off a disastrous collision by virtue of your quick reaction time, you feel a surge of adrenaline coursing through your veins. Your heart is beating quickly and your palms are sweaty. Your stomach is tight with fear. You are furious.

"You dumb idiot!" you roar. "You damn near killed me! Where did you learn to drive—at Disneyland?" Of course, you are screaming only to yourself, since the culpable driver has long since left the scene, apparently unscathed and unshaken by his reckless act.

Meanwhile, you have to get to work. You're now ten minutes late, and you start to feel one of those terrific tension headaches coming on, as if a rubber band had been affixed to the perimeter of your scalp. "It's going to be one of those days," you mutter.

You are having a classic stress reaction—the primordial fight-or-flight response. But the physiological stress reaction is actually only one part of a complex chain of perceptual, cognitive, motivational, and behavioral responses.

You perceived the approach of the other car, and you interpreted that perception as a threat to your safety and physical integrity. Based on that split-second perception and interpretation, you were motivated to act. You jammed on your brakes, veered to the left, and avoided an accident. But your mind told your body all about how close a call the incident was, and your body responded by getting "worked up," geared for a confrontation, pumped up to fight, or to flee the scene of danger.

The other driver, though, did not appear to be upset. He "interpreted" his perception of the event as a little mistake on his part; perhaps he misjudged your speed and distance. Or his mind was on other things. In any event, to the other driver, a miss is as good as a mile, and there was no cause for distress.

The example demonstrates that stress is more than a response to a difficult or unpleasant event; rather, it is your internal, cognitive reaction to that event: how you think about it.

If you perceive an event to be threatening—in either a physical or psychological sense—the response will be arousal—stress. If, on the other hand, you do not process a particular event to mean that your physical safety or psychological security is threatened, you are unlikely to respond with an aroused stress reaction.

We respond to *our interpretation* of the events in our lives, not only to the events themselves.

The example of a near miss while driving is a concrete instance of the cognitive chain reaction that links perception, attribution of meaning, expectation, and behavior to the stress response.

In a sense, each of us "drives" through life every day, vigilant to threats not just to our physical safety, but to the more subtle clues that our psychological safety—our sense of security, our self-esteem, our belief and value systems, and so on—is somehow endangered. And when we are threatened, we may jam on our "psychological brakes" and stop short, asking ourselves a set of questions such as, "What does this mean?" "What should I do?" "Why did this happen to me?"

The activation of these kinds of cognitions—that something may be amiss and that a problem may exist to be acted on—is the beginning of the chain of mental or cognitive reactions that leads to stress. In day-to-day life, much of the stress we experience is embedded in a complex network of beliefs, values, assumptions, perceptions, and expectations that make up our cognitive-perceptual system. We take the raw data of our experience, what happens to us, and we "process" the data in our internal cognitive computers. The "software" or "programs" that we use to interpret the meaning of our experiences include our values, beliefs, assumptions, and expectations about life.

The way we feel about, or react to, a particular event or set of circumstances is the result of how we process the information. If our cognitive analysis tells us that an event is positive or benign, we may be happy, relaxed, satisfied, or neutral. If the output of our cognitive processing is that an event is negative or that our psychological security is threatened in some way, then our interpretation may cause us to be anxious, upset, depressed, or stressed.

Stress occurs when we cognitively recognize or anticipate a problem that threatens to damage our self-esteem, happiness, and well-being.

But unlike the very real and accurate perception of

a threat in the example of the near-miss collision, many of our perceptions of psychological threats are *not* accurate, real, or even adaptive to our emotional well-being and health. They are the result of distorted ways of thinking, "old tapes" that play in our heads representing self-defeating assumptions, beliefs, and expectations about ourselves that can make us feel inadequate, insecure, and subjectively stressed.

So how we feel about ourselves and/or about events depends on the underlying set of cognitions that we use to process, interpret, understand, and assign meaning to the events. It follows, logically, that one way to modify the stress response is to modify the underlying ways of thinking that may predispose a person to respond to events in characteristically stressful ways.

Psychiatrist Dr. Aaron Beck has pioneered a new approach to psychotherapy, Cognitive Therapy, which is based on identifying and correcting the patient's self-defeating assumptions and cognitions in order to alleviate symptoms of depression, anxiety states, and stress. (A forerunner of Cognitive Therapy is Dr. Albert Ellis's Rational-Emotive Therapy.) Cognitive Therapy has impressed both practicing clinicians and their patients with the rapid and significant improvements in mood that result from correcting underlying cognitive errors in reasoning.

Cognitive Therapy begins with the therapist asking about the patient's feelings and behavior. The therapist then elicits the patient's "automatic thoughts" in relation to those feelings and behaviors. Using deductive reasoning, the therapist moves beyond the level of automatic thoughts to the underlying assumptions, beliefs, and expectations from which the thoughts derive.

The key point in Cognitive Therapy is the discovery of logical errors in the reasoning process that lead from flawed assumptions to the conscious experience of negative, distressful feelings and/or behavior.

Usually the cognitive assumption underlying the patient's symptom is framed in extreme, all-or-nothing terms. Often it is regressive or childish in nature—frequently the assumption, in fact, stems from childhood instruction and internalization of parental values. The flawed assumptions are generally rigid "truisms" to which the patient is attached in some conscious or unconscious way, and to which the patient seldom or never applies rational, logical scrutiny. When the assumptions are examined by the therapist and patient together, the latter soon recognizes their essentially erroneous and irrational nature. Some common examples of flawed assumptions include "Life is fair," "If you're nice, nothing bad will happen to you," and "I have to be loved to feel like a valuable person."

Clues to the flawed assumptions that underlie symptomatic feelings and behavior are liberally provided by the patient's stream of conversation. The alert and adept therapist can literally hear the patient committing cognitive errors in the way she/he thinks and talks about her/his experience. Examples of common cognitive errors include *overgeneralizing* (from one negative experience seeing a pattern of defeat and negativity); *catastrophizing* (seeing events as having negative significance that is exaggerated and inappropriate); *personalization* (seeing yourself as causally involved in negative events and feelings of others when the situation does not rationally warrant personalizing the cause); and *negative mental filtering* (seeing only the significance of negative events while discounting that of positive events).

For example, a woman might describe the events of a particularly stressful week this way:

This has been the worst week of my life. I feel like a complete failure. I just can't do anything right. I know I should be able to do more, but every time I try, I just wind up being a loser. I just know these problems will never end. I feel so guilty that my kids and husband see me this way. I know it makes them feel bad and ruins their week, too. I'm helpless in this situation.

This sample monologue is riddled with examples of cognitive errors that are producing this woman's depression and stress. She is catastrophizing ("This has been the worst week of my life"), assigning exaggerated and extreme labels to herself ("loser," "failure," "helpless"), overgeneralizing ("I just can't do anything right"), and personalizing the reactions of her family, feeling guilty and responsible for the quality of their week as well, and making erroneous negative predictions ("I just know these problems will never end").

In Cognitive Therapy, the patient learns to identify cognitive errors like these and to replace them with more rational, less extreme, and less rigid statements that reduce, rather than enhance, her negative feelings. By applying these logical methods, patients develop better control over their "self-talk" and, therefore, better management of their negative moods and feelings.

For example, a Cognitive Therapist might help the woman above to develop a more rational response to the events of her stressful week this way.:

This week has been more stressful than most. And it is also four days before my menstrual period, so I know I may be likely to be oversensitive to stressful events. I've also been "down" on myself this week—calling myself bad names—so I've kept my "depression and stress filters" on and exaggerated the importance of any bad or partially negative thing that's happened. My family is, of course, affected by my stressed mood. But I'm a person, too, and they love me enough to understand. I'm lucky I have them for support.

ERRONEOUS EXPECTATIONS: TYPE E COGNITIVE ERRORS

Because Type E women are typically intelligent, verbal, and analytical, they are excellent candidates for Cognitive Therapy. In working clinically with high-achieving women who suffer from Type E stress, I have identified a set of self-defeating, stress-producing assumptions that characterize their underlying thought processes. As a summary term, I call the flawed assumptions that underlie Type E stress *erroneous expectations*.

Here are the ten most common erroneous expectations of Type E women that form the cognitive bases of their stressful feelings and behaviors:

1. I have to do things perfectly.
2. I should be able to accomplish more in a day.
3. I should be able to do everything without feeling stressed or tired.
4. I have to please others by doing what they ask me to do.
5. I have to prove myself to everyone.
6. "Having it all" should make me happy.
7. I can't be happy until I "have it all."
8. I can't relax until I finish what I have to do.
9. If I make people need me because of everything I do for them, they'll value me.
10. I should be everything to everybody.

The list could go on for pages. In fact, each of the major areas of concern to Type E women that I have discussed thus far is rampant with implicit or explicit erroneous expectations. Some of the stress of excellence anxiety, for example, emanates from the underlying expectation that "If I achieve, men/women/other people won't like me." Excessive self-reliance, as we have seen, is replete with examples of self-defeating expectations, such as "I can't ask for help" and "I have to put others' needs ahead of my own."

But the ten erroneous expectations above are most closely related to the Type E behavioral stress cycle itself. And my experience in treating Type E stress problems has demonstrated the effectiveness of the cognitive approach: If you can alter the underlying assumptions—the erroneous expectations—behind the stress pattern, you can reduce the level and intensity of subjective stress.

If you are like most Type E women, you will have found yourself agreeing with many of the ten statements. Although, like most, you are probably immediately able to see that the statements as *written down* appear to be somewhat irrational or unrealistic.

In fact, all the statements are cognitively flawed—they are extreme, incorrect, unrealistic, arbitrary, childish, and empirically false. As we explore each of the expectations in greater detail, you will see how self-defeating and stress-producing the cognitions are.

Recall that stress results not from events themselves, but from your interpretation of those events. And your interpretation—the meaning you assign to the event or experience—will be largely influenced by the set of expectations you hold in your head about what "should" and "should not" happen. You can see, therefore, that operating on the basis of erroneous expectations is a significant factor contributing to negative interpretations of events and, in turn, producing the stress response.

The erroneous expectations of Type E women are particularly stress-producing because they are so closely wired to the woman's self-esteem. In this sense, the expectations constitute a list of cognitive "setups" used to bait the Type E stress trap. They are "setups" because they are either unattainable or inaccurate; the expectations are *set up* to create a sense of inadequacy, failure, and the perpetuation of stress. While this cognitive setup is generally not conscious, it is nevertheless damaging.

To conquer the Type E stress cycle and regain control, Type E women must give themselves an attitude adjustment. It's that simple. Erroneous expectations breed and reinforce stress. In their place, more realistic, adaptive, and attainable guidelines for self-management and evaluation are required.

Let's examine the erroneous expectations one at a time, and explore the cognition-feeling-behavior feedback system.

Expectation 1:
"I have to do things perfectly."

Perfectionism is epidemic among Type E women. It is a particularly pernicious standard of evaluation for behavior since, by definition, it is unattainable. Invariably, a great double standard of evaluation characterizes Type E's expectations of perfection: They judge themselves far more harshly than they ever would judge others.

The erroneous expectation that things have to be done perfectly lies behind a variety of stress-related behavioral problems, including procrastination (putting off doing anything so as to avoid making mistakes), tardiness or chronic lateness (due to excessive expenditure of time and effort on endless attempts to "perfect" your appearance, performance, project), and uncomfortable levels of evaluation anxiety (upset and fear about the judgments of others, particularly judgments that will be critical in any way).

As an erroneous expectation, perfectionism also affects your feelings about yourself in negative, undesirable ways. Mistakes, critical feedback, and even very minor errors and flaws are inflated in importance and distorted in significance. A mistake is seen as evidence that you are a "failure." Any criticism, however mild or benign, is experienced as a total negation of self-worth. And the perfectionist fails to experience fully the rewards of her performance, since her harshly critical and deprecating mindset seldom permits her to feel satisfied with how well she has done.

The ancient Greeks believed that only the gods could be perfect. All human beings and the products of their creative impulses and talents were, by definition, imperfect. To symbolize and ensure their belief, artisans and craftsmen intentionally left an error in their work—a chip in a marble sculpture or a weaving flaw in a tapestry—in order to remind themselves and their patrons that they were not so vain as to strive for the perfection of the gods.

Type E women can make important inroads on improving their stress problem by chipping away at the erroneous cognition pushing them toward standards of perfection. Striving toward a performance criterion of doing as well as you can do, instead of trying to be perfect, is far more adaptive, realistic, attainable, and conducive to emotional and physical health.

High achievers need strive only for high achievement, not perfection. Recognizing that perfection is both maladaptive and self-defeating is a necessary step in breaking the Type E stress cycle.

Expectation 2:
"I should be able to accomplish more in a day."

Many Type E women are victims of their own unrealistic, Herculean "To Do" lists.

"I'm very well organized," one of my patients told me. "I make a long list every morning of every single thing I have to do that day. But every night I realize how little I got done, and I feel even more stressed. The next day, my 'To Do' list grows longer, and my stress level gets higher and higher. I should be able to do more in a day."

There are only a finite number of hours in a day during which any individual can accomplish anything other than sleep. Within the sixteen to eighteen or so waking hours each of us typically has, only so many things can be accomplished either physically or mentally. How many things on a list can be done will vary, of course, as a function of what the tasks are and the capabilities, resources, and personality of the list-maker.

But Type E women, on the basis of their faulty expectations, drive themselves to do more and more and more. Rarely if ever do they feel satisfied with the amount that they do manage to accomplish.

Lists are excellent methods for getting organized and setting priorities. But lists are supposed to work for you, to assist you in maintaining control of your stressors. Instead, too many Type E women use their lists as a cognitive whip, goading themselves beyond their limits of endurance by expecting to accomplish unrealistic numbers of tasks, or to complete given tasks in unrealistically short periods of time.

Overly long "To Do" lists also limit your perception of how much you actually did accomplish in a given day, thereby contributing to your sense of disappointment with how much got done. This is because you reinforce yourself for doing only things that are "on my list" by checking off each item as it is completed. But what about all the things you routinely do in a day that take up time and mental effort but do not earn a place on the list because you take them for granted?

Many Type E women do so much every day that they often cannot clearly reconstruct everything they accomplished. They are, however, particularly astute at picking out all the things they intended to do but never got around to completing.

This kind of thinking represents a typical cognitive error in which the weight or value of what did get accomplished gets diminished or undervalued, and what did not get accomplished becomes emphasized and weighted too heavily in the cognitive equation. This kind of distorted evaluation perpetuates the Type E stress cycle fueled by the erroneous expectation that "I should be able to accomplish more."

One way to correct this expectation error is to start collecting the data on how much you *do* accomplish in a typical week. I instruct patients to keep records of what they actually did, instead of what they think they should have done. When they review their records, they are often surprised and relieved.

"I didn't realize how much I actually accomplish," one woman said after keeping a week's records of things she had done. "When I looked over my diaries for a week, I was impressed. I guess I thought I should be doing more because I had the wrong idea about what I was doing with my time. I feel like I can get off my own back now."

Another way to correct this erroneous expectation is to turn your focus away from the *quantitive* dimension of your activities, and start attending instead to *qualitative* aspects of your accomplishments and tasks. In other words, train yourself to think in terms of how important, necessary, or worthwhile a task is, rather than strictly in terms of how *many* things you can get done.

Stress can be reduced and your sense of accomplishment increased by keeping the items on your "To Do" lists down to a reasonable, attainable number. If you chronically overschedule yourself, you will chronically feel inadequate to the task you have unrealistically set for yourself. Short, manageable lists can be accomplished, and the positive self-esteem that accomplishment engenders operates to moderate stress levels. Be realistic about the time you allocate to each task, and take into careful account your own mental and physical limitations of energy, concentration, or endurance.

Getting stuck on a broken-record expectation of doing more and more in less and less time is the essence of classic Type A behavior, the lethal and otherwise damaging effects of which on physical health and stress levels have already been discussed.

Focus your energies on being productive during those times that you allocate to work. Remember, however, that it is "productive"—toward the goal of stress management—to be "unproductive," to allocate time for rest, relaxation, and just doing nothing.

Keep in mind that "To Do" lists are like cleaning house: No matter how much you accomplish today, there will be more to do tomorrow.

Expectation 3:
"I should be able to do everything without feeling stressed or tired."

This expectation is not necessarily consciously verbalized, but the underlying erroneous thinking is belied by the surprise, amazement, disappointment, or upset with which many Type E women describe their stress symptoms.

"I just can't believe how tired and worn out I feel at the end of the day. I know I should have more to give to my kids and husband, but there's just nothing left." This description was given by a woman who worked twelve-hour days as a real estate developer and then managed to fit in a strenuous workout at the gym, followed by a daily regimen of "running all family errands." And she wonders why she's tired?

This erroneous expectation also underlies the commonly displayed attitude among Type E women and other stress sufferers that their bodies are somehow betraying them. When a tension headache caps off a day that has been punctuated by hassles, deadlines, crises, and demands, the Type E woman is apt to characterize the headache as a manifestation of her *own* inability or inadequacy "to deal with things better."

Linda was referred to me by her internist when her medical history began to read like the Ten Plagues of Egypt. Linda suffered from a host of stress-related problems: skin rashes, headaches, hair loss, muscle spasm, asthma, irritable bowel syndrome, an incipient ulcer, and a prolapsed coronary valve. Linda felt convinced that she was doomed. The more she read about the relationship between stress and illness, the more panicked (and symptomatic) she became.

Since Linda and her husband had split up four years earlier, she constantly replayed disaster movies in her mind about what would happen after her spousal support period ended. She saw herself turning into a homeless "bag lady." She had been fully (and happily) supported by her husband during the nine years of their marriage, and had raised two children.

As a result of the divorce, Linda had had to face the prospect of entering the workforce with little more experience than a college degree and nine years as a wife and mother.

But once she began working as a secretary for a large corporation, Linda discovered that she had a taste for achievement and success. In fact, she began pushing herself very hard, working long hours to learn the company's business in order to pave the way for her advancement.

And, indeed, she advanced up through the ranks from secretary to a management position in less than three years. But the management position turned out to be a burdensome, demanding job, and Linda began to experience her work as highly stressful. Her boss was ill-tempered, unpredictable, and prone to angry outbursts at subordinates. He openly voiced his disapproval of promotions from "below" into management positions, particularly when the subject of the advancement was a woman. In short, Linda's advancement soon became an onerous experience.

As a consequence, she began to develop stress-related health problems. At first, her symptoms were mainly severe tension headaches. But Linda responded to her headaches by berating and denigrating herself. She saw the pain as proof positive of what she had long expected: She was not "strong enough" to have a career. She *should* be able to handle this job like other women would, she erroneously reasoned, without experiencing the symptoms of stress. Her interpretation created further anxiety and pressure since, consciously, Linda wanted to be a high-achieving woman.

Whenever a headache would start, Linda felt acutely agitated and worried. She "processed" the somatic stress cue as a sign of her inadequacy. She made irrational negative predictions that her health problems would develop into full-scale debilitating illnesses that would cause her to lose her job. And she feared that her health problems would validate her boss's attitudes that women aren't "tough enough" to be managers.

The agitation that resulted from these cognitive "tapes" in turn created greater arousal, and she began to wheeze with anxiety as she imagined life as an invalid, broken by the "pressures that other women could handle."

Linda erroneously saw herself as the sole *cause* of her stress symptoms. But the reality was that Linda was in a bad environmental situation. Instead of seeing her tension headaches and other stress symptoms as signals that her psychological well-being was being threatened by a poorly managed, capricious work environment, Linda saw the problem in herself. Based on the erroneous expectation that "I should be able to do everything without feeling stressed or tired," Linda saw her stress reactions as flaws, and she pushed herself harder and harder to please her unpleasable boss, and to maintain her responsibilities as homemaker for her children as well.

The first day I saw Linda, I told her about a fascinating experiment in the psychology of learning. The study is the classic demonstration of experimentally induced neurosis.

An otherwise normal, "well-adjusted" laboratory white rat is placed in an experimental cage that is wired with shock grids on the floor. On a random, capricious basis, the rat is delivered painful electric shocks. Within minutes, the rat begins shaking, defecating, urinating, and doing the full range of behaviors evidenced by "neurotic" or anxiety-ridden rats.

The point I was making is that anxiety and stress reactions can be conditioned by the delivery of a painful stimulus (her boss's temper outbursts) on a *random,* unpredictable basis. Her boss was universally acknowledged as having no greater rhyme or reason for his foul moods than getting up on the wrong side of bed. This set of conditions—random painful stimuli delivered on an uncontrollable and unpredictable basis—is sufficient to make *anyone* have stress reactions. Linda's error was in personalizing her reactions and expecting herself to adapt to her stressful situation without evidencing symptoms of stress.

Linda learned that she could exercise a great deal of control over the manifestation of many of her stress symptoms by correcting the underlying erroneous expectation that she "shouldn't" be responding by feeling agitated and stressed. She came to see that her responses were actually appropriate and predictable, given her oppressive work environment. Eventually

Linda decided to leave her job, and she found another position elsewhere. She is not only happier in her "saner" environment, but has discovered that her stress symptoms (headaches, muscle spasm) can be interpreted as "messages" to examine what's going on, either around her or in her own mind, that is likely to set off the stress chain reaction. She has taught herself to take "quieting breaks" at the first signs of impending pain or other stress-related symptoms.

Linda has also learned to accept that stress comes with the territory when you strive to achieve as a woman in the working and personal worlds. Now she realizes that, like other mortals, she might experience the unpleasant physical or psychological consequences of stress from time to time. Linda knows now that instead of betraying her with weaknesses and flaws, her body is an ally, warning her with physical signals that the stress level is getting too high.

Many Type E women deny or ignore their body's signals, failing to heed the warning signs. Whereas Linda created a cascade of stress chain reactions by overreacting to her response to a legitimately stressful situation, other women overlook and push beyond the pain or discomfort on the grounds that such symptoms are simply unacceptable in them. Their irrational underlying belief is that they should be able to do everything without signs of stress or fatigue. Therefore, when they do feel exhausted or discomforted by some tension-induced malaise or other, they push themselves farther, as if to prove that they are strong enough to overcome their body's limitations.

In this pattern, the Type E woman will typically work excessively long hours (at work and/or home) and fail to take enough breaks, naps, vacations, or respites from the continuous energy expenditure. The unhappy—and predictable—result is often a compromise of immune resistance, vulnerability to infection and illness, and exacerbation of the physical stress signals that the woman erroneously overlooked.

Expectation 4:
"I have to please others by doing what they ask me to do."

This erroneous expectation is rooted in the traditional acculturation of female children: Nice girls are compliant, ingratiating, and mindful of the needs and desires of others, especially adults.

This early inculcation of the belief that one should strive to please results in women getting "hooked" on the approval of others as a potent source of social reinforcement. In fact, many women take this erroneous expectation so literally that they genuinely do not see any alternatives; they believe that they *have* to please others and do what is asked of them in order to feel valued and worthy.

Let's be clear that an attitude of selfishness, self-centeredness, and withholding is emphatically not what I am advocating. Type E women need to examine the rational basis for their belief that they *have* to please others by doing everything that is asked or expected of them at whatever cost to their own emotional and physical health. It is fine and, indeed, desirable to do things for other people, especially when love is the motive. But it is neither necessary nor desirable to put your own needs aside, and to compulsively seek to attain *everyone's* approval, recognition, or obligation by virtue of all the things you do for them.

Type E women who are trying to be everything to everybody not only pay too high a price for the approval they seek—in terms of the stress to which they subject themselves—but the formula doesn't even work when actually put to the test. Trying to please everyone by doing whatever they ask often accomplishes just the opposite. Everyone, including the woman herself, suffers from her fragmentation, and the approval that the Type E woman craves—as a parched person craves water to quench a thirst—eludes her.

Many Type E women fear that love or approval will be lost to them if they deny a request or set limitations on their time and resources. But, in fact, people who genuinely have your best interests at heart will respect your self-protective obligation to yourself to exercise restraint over the compulsion to do everything for everyone.

Expectation 5:
"I have to prove myself to everyone."

This belief derives from an underlying sense of insecurity that propels the Type E woman into an almost desperate striving to prove that she is worthwhile, important, lovable, and competent. For many of the reasons discussed in earlier chapters, many high-achieving women feel plagued by doubts concerning their ultimate value and acceptability.

The debilitating nature of holding this expectation lies in the lack of criteria for defining proof. If you always have to prove your value each time a new demand or opportunity arises, then, in fact, you have not *proven* your value at all. Proof, by definition, is a concept that embodies certitude and validation. Once proof is established, the process of proving again and again is unnecessary.

But Type E women continually set themselves up to prove their value at work *in spite* of their personal commitments, roles, and responsibilities; and they strive to prove themselves in their personal lives *in spite* of the responsibilities inherent in their careers.

For many Type E women, the crux of the matter

lies in the concept of "having it all." It is as if they feel somehow compelled to prove that they are entitled to have it all, because they *do* it all themselves.

One of my patients, for example, insisted that she "had" to buy fresh groceries and cook an elegant meal for her husband every night as a way to "prove" that her career ambitions weren't going to compromise her performance (and worth) as a wife. The problem was that she collapsed from exhaustion every night right after dinner, and her husband felt deprived of her time, attention, and sexual affection. This woman came to understand in therapy that after ten years of a successful marriage, she was still trying to prove herself and earn her value. She was eventually persuaded that proof of her abilities and willingness to do "wifely" chores was not necessary and that her relationship would be better served if *she* served "take-out" dinners once in a while and preserved her energy for the more pleasurable perquisites of having a loving husband.

The bottom line here is that your own sense of value and worth should be granted to yourself unconditionally. Once your sense of self-worth is established and solid, the compulsion to prove your prowess and competence at every turn abates, as does the stress cycle it produces.

Expectation 6:
" 'Having it all' should make me happy."

This expectation can be particularly insidious. On its face, the statement may seem reasonable—indeed, didn't Helen Gurley Brown tell us as much?

So what's the problem with this expectation if it seems to be the driving force behind many women's motivation? The problem is that the expectation is stated in language that is too extreme. Happiness is not a black-and-white state of affairs. Happiness, instead, is a continuum of mood states; it is not a stable, continuous, uninterrupted state of mind or being. One is *relatively* happier in nuances and degrees, not in overpolarized, happy-sad, up-down terms.

The implication of a more realistic, adaptable view of happiness (or of the state of being happy) is that there will be some cloudy "down" times periodically punctuating the sunshine. While this may seem obvious, the fact is that erroneous expectations, by definition, are not representative of mature, aware thinking; that is, after all, what makes them erroneous. But maintaining the erroneous way of thinking—that having it all should make you happy—creates poor tolerance for the inevitable "down" times, and can trigger the stress cycle and depression.

Eleanor's adjustment reaction to her first year of married life is a good illustration of how this underlying erroneous expectation serves to exacerbate and compound stress problems.

Eleanor had married Jerry, her second husband, after ten years of single life between marriages, and the development of a successful career in retailing. While Eleanor was single, she sought the brass ring: She wanted to have her successful, lucrative career *and* she wanted to try again to have a successful marriage. Typical of high-achieving women, Eleanor evaluated her "success as a person" as conditional on achieving her personal goals—in this case, marriage—*and* her career goals.

Eventually, after many years of dating and trying to find a man she could marry, Eleanor and Jerry tied the proverbial knot. They honeymooned in Hawaii, and returned to "real life" two weeks later.

But within a few months, Eleanor was worried that "something must be wrong" with her.

"I really thought that 'having it all' would make me happy. It *should* make me happy, I know, and I am happy a lot of the time. But, you know, it's like there are some parts of me that just haven't changed. Sometimes I get blue and bummed out. Sometimes I'm really irritable with Jerry, especially after a day at work during a sale or inventory crunch. And during those times, I worry because having it all should make me happy. It feels like there's something wrong with me. Now it's like I feel pressured to be happy all the time when I'm too tired or grouchy to feel good."

Eleanor's concerns arise from the erroneous expectation that is framed in absolutistic, black-and-white (and therefore erroneous) terms: You either are happy or you're not.

But that's not the way life works. In fact, you may be happier, or you may have more good, pleasant times than blue or sad times, or you feel a deeper, more stable sense of contentment. But being happy is a *state*, not a trait; it is, by definition, transitory and inconsistent. Eleanor's error was in overinterpreting the meaning or significance of her normal "down" or stressed behavior. Since she viewed her transitory states of depression, sadness, or stress as evidence that she must not be "happy," she believed there must be something wrong with her, since now she "had it all." She created cognitive stress via an erroneous expectation.

Expectation 7:
"I can't be happy until I 'have it all.'"

This one, in a sense, is the obverse of Expectation 6: " 'Having it all' should make me happy." The cognition typifies the thinking of many Type E women who are single and, most frequently, those who have never been married.

Here's how it works: The belief reflects an underlying assumption that (a) "having it all" (career plus marriage/long-term love relationship) is a necessary condition for happiness; and (b) as before, "happy" is cast in black-and-white terms.

It is, of course, a perfectly rational and logically acceptable position to believe that "having it all" might make the quality of your life, on balance, *happier*, more satisfying, and perhaps even less stressful. But to assert to yourself that you *can't* be happy until you have it all is to set yourself up for a psychological bellyflop.

In the first place, women who have this erroneous expectation, either at the forefront or buried within their minds, actually depress their own capacity for experiencing genuine states of happiness. One single woman I know describes a kind of "dark cloud" whenever she finds herself having fun and enjoying any activity that doesn't involve a man.

"It's like something stops me," she explained. "I think I must believe that any time away from looking for a husband is a waste. I can't even enjoy being by myself—I always get this vague sense of anxiety, and the cloud comes down. I wish I could just find a man to marry so I could let myself be happy."

This Type E woman's thinking reflects the underlying erroneous expectation that she *can't* be happy unless she has it all. So she defeats herself. Indeed, her experience tells her that she is capable of having periods of enjoyment, satisfaction, or even happiness with women friends or just being by herself. But she sabotages herself with her erroneous belief and her sudden self-consciousness at the realization that she is feeling happy in spite of the fact that, at that particular moment in time, she does not, by her definition, "have it all."

Not only does this expectation prevent many women who are not in relationships *or* who have not yet found their career niches from fully enjoying and maximizing the quality of their lives on a daily basis, it has other stressful ramifications as well.

Because the single woman who believes that she can be happy only if she "has it all" keeps herself down, her orientation toward men may take on a kind of desperate, overeager quality or a depressive aura that can wind up driving the men away. She may even become a chronically "unhappy" person, because of her inability to let herself experience her "up" times. So the expectation can set up a chain reaction whereby the woman indeed has a series of unsuccessful relationships with men, which reconfirms her belief that she can't be happy until she relieves herself of the burden of being single.

A variation on this theme can cause strains and conflicts in relationships with men. The erroneous expectation that "I can't be happy until I 'have it all' " sometimes lies behind the premature pressure politics that are played out in relationships between women who find themselves in the onerous position of trying to elicit a "commitment" from the men with whom they are involved. Unable to tolerate the natural ambiguity that surrounds the early stages of almost all relationships, these women can develop debilitating anxiety and stress trying to cope with the uncertainty of the "Is-this-it? Is-he-the-one? Will-he-make-a-commitment?" stage.

Vicki is illustrative of the problem. A twenty-six-year-old engineer for an aerospace company, Vicki works in a male-dominated environment. Because she is both attractive and friendly, Vicki enjoys the opportunity to date many men. The problem is that few of her relationships last longer than one or two months.

The reason for the difficulty is Vicki's low tolerance for ambiguity (a personality trait that is particularly common among people with engineering training) and her erroneous expectation.

"I reach a point—usually after about a month—when

I can't stand it anymore unless I know where the relationship is headed. So I always seem to do the same thing. As soon as the guy seems interested, I pop off, get emotional, and demand to know whether he's in this for keeps or not," Vicki admitted.

Not only does the inappropriate, premature pressure drive away the interested man, but Vicki's own thinking prevents her from really being happy with her new love affairs. Instead of feeling good, Vicki's underlying erroneous expectation sets off a cognitive chain of stress and anxiety.

"As soon as I start thinking that this man might be *the one,* I get nuts," she described. "I immediately start worrying about whether he is or he isn't, whether he will or he won't commit to me . . . bottom line things like that. And I worry so much about losing him, before I even have him, that I don't even let myself feel happy or feel much of anything other than upset."

Another way in which Type E women set themselves up is by substituting Expectation 6 for 7 when they have a change of status: They get married or they land the career position they have wanted, and then get caught in the cognitive web of Expectation 6, like the case of Eleanor discussed earlier.

In a sense, the term "having it all" is an unfortunate one. It implies that the whole issue is quantitative rather than qualitative. "Having it all," as the term is generally used, refers to having a marriage plus a career. But the term doesn't speak to the issue of quality—*how well* the relationship works, *how satisfying* it is to both members of the pair, *how gratifying* the career position is, and so on.

Erroneous expectations are corrected by substituting mature, realistic thinking for faulty, absolutistic cognitions. Happiness is a continuum; relationships are processes, not merely entities; and careers are created and evolved over a lifespan. These moderating inputs to the erroneous cognitions will help to break the cognitive stress cycle.

Expectation 8:
"I can't relax until I finish what I have to do."

This expectation is so unrealistic as to amount to a life sentence on a stress treadmill. Women who lead demanding, complicated, multiple-role lives invariably have something more to do, no matter what kind of Herculean feats they have accomplished. Children represent a continuous stream of demands; every new job assignment can fill a "To Do" list with details and responsibilities.

To make relaxation conditional on "finishing" *everything* you have to do is, again, irrational and self-defeating. Contrary to the underlying beliefs of Type E women, relaxation is *not* a luxury; it is a necessity to good physical and emotional health. Nor is relaxation of secondary importance as is implied by the cognition that relaxation will be put off until everything is finished—which it never is.

To Type E women, the thought of building in "time off" in the form of fifteen minutes of doing nothing is either so ludicrous as to elicit laughter, or viewed as so wasteful or slothful as to be dismissed out of hand. The fact is that relaxation breaks can interrupt stress cycles and reduce arousal levels, thereby keeping stress within optimal performance parameters and allowing you to "recharge" your physical and mental batteries. You can, in fact, relax, right in the middle of a mess of things to do, if you choose to do so. And the choice might well be the most efficient decision you make.

One of the ironic ways in which this expectation operates is to turn activities that may have begun as forms of unwinding or relaxing into sources of stress. Specifically, I am speaking of the compulsive attitude many women have developed concerning exercise and fitness.

I am wholeheartedly in favor of exercise as a form of stress reduction. My frequent observation has been, however, that Type E women are prone to making their exercise activities part of their obligatory "To Do" lists, and the relaxation properties of the exercise get lost in the shuffle.

"I just can't relax unless I get my workout done. It's gotten so that I get really uptight if I miss even one day. And there are obviously some days in my schedule when I can't fit it in," one woman explained. "But then I feel my stress level building. I sometimes wonder whether the exercise itself unwinds me or just the fact that I got it done is what gives me permission to relax. I really wish I weren't so compulsive about it."

The best correction to this erroneous expectation is to put yourself on a relaxation (or exercise) schedule that is independent of how many things you have accomplished. For example, try (within reasonable circumstances) to give yourself a five-minute "quieting break" every four hours. Just sit or lie down and try to close out the world. Don't focus on any thoughts that come into your head, just let your mind wander at will. After five minutes, return to the task at hand. Repeat the exercise again in four hours.

What you will learn from this exercise is that you *can* relax, even if "everything" isn't finished. And you'll probably also learn that your overall stress level will diminish while your productivity will probably increase.

Expectation 9: "If I make people need me because of everything I do for them, they'll value me."

The cognitive correction for this erroneous expectation may seem like a bitter pill to many women because, in fact, just the reverse is likely to be true. I do not know one Type E woman who does not, at some point, feel that she is being taken for granted or exploited.

The fact that females are trained in our culture to be nurturant means that they are taught how to anticipate others' needs and to act in ways that fulfill those needs. Girls and women are rewarded for being helpful, altruistic, generous with their time, and understanding. But only up to a point.

If you give away your time, others will fail to respect its value. If you fail to set reasonable limitations on your energy expenditures, those limits are likely to be violated and exceeded. If you are the one who stays late in the office taking on the departmental work overload, you are likely to be the one who is expected to do so again and again.

Again, I am not advocating an attitude of selfishness or withholding. Nor is stubborn or arbitrary resistance or refusal to every demand of others advised. But the underlying assumption that people will value you more if you let them take advantage of you is erroneous and self-destructive.

Time and again, I remind Type E women that if they don't respect the value of their own time and talents, no one else can be expected to do so either. Your value in others' eyes is earned more by qualitative than quantitative aspects of your behavior. It is not how *many* things you do, or how *many* ways you can make yourself "indispensable" (another erroneous cognition) that are likely to determine your value except as an adept juggler. Rather, your value is influenced by *what* you decide to do for others and by the *quality* of the job or behavior that you choose to do.

Expectation 10: "I should be everything to everybody."

This erroneous expectation of course forms the crux of Type E behavior. It is, after all, the underlying belief that it is *possible* to be all things to all people that drives Type E women to attempt to cope with the myriad of life demands by trying to be exactly that.

The expectation of yourself to be continuously responsive to, and even anticipatory of, every demand of other people is erroneous on its face. The very term "everything to everybody" implies its impossible nature. As I discuss more fully in the next chapter, Type E coping will exact its toll on your emotional and physical health over the long term, no matter what the short-term gratifications may be from being perceived (or perceiving yourself) as a dazzling Superwoman.

It is faulty thinking to believe that you can expose yourself to chronic, unremitting stress by pushing your resources to the breaking point without suffering debilitating long-term consequences. Busting the erroneous expectation that you "should" try to meet an unattainable criterion is essential to regaining balance and to building effective stress resistance.

Women certainly should not give up trying to achieve their full potential in whatever roles they choose for themselves. While you emphatically cannot survive the frustration, fatigue, and burnout of trying to be everything to everyone, you can be lots of good things to lots of people. You can maintain your achievement goals and learn to modify your behavior getting to those goals so as to reduce the level of negative stress.

Once you alter the expectation that you should be everything to everybody, you will be in a better position to cope effectively with the stream of external demands by learning such behavioral skills as setting priorities, maintaining limitations, exercising control on your energy expenditure and arousal levels, delegating, and being able to say "no" to requests that exceed your resources and/or preferences—all without feeling guilty. These coping skills, and others, are explained in detail in Chapter 10.

Recall that the *two* requirements for building stress resistance for Type E women are changing thinking *and* changing behavior. In this sense, breaking out of the destructive Type E stress cycle requires that the erroneous expectation that underlies and supports the self-defeating behavior pattern be exposed and replaced by more adaptive, self-protective, stress-resistant thinking.

Cognitively, the required change depends on "unhooking" your need for approval from others via what you do for them from your self-esteem and sense of self-worth. When you can give yourself positive self-regard unconditionally, without compulsively testing or demonstrating your value by what you do for others, you will be in a position to regulate more adaptively the inflow of demands and outflow of expended energy fulfilling those demands.

CLEANING YOUR COGNITIVE TAPES

In the beginning of this chapter, I ran through a scenario that is probably a familiar experience to most people who drive, at least in urban areas. The purpose of the example was to highlight the link between external experience—in this case an oncoming vehicle—

and the perceptual, interpretive, cognitive processes that mediate the physiological stress reaction. In the example, the stress reaction followed from the cognition of a threat to physical safety. But we also know that threats, or perceived threats, to *psychological* safety produce stress reactions, too.

You can learn to monitor your own stream of internal "self-talk" in order to identify and systematically cull out and correct "stressogenic" thinking, patterns of language or cognitive errors of logic that precipitate, exacerbate, and perpetuate negative arousal and stress.

Let's return to the earlier example and consider how the internal cognitive monologue operates to fuel the dis-stress cycle.

We left our heroine with the beginnings of a tension headache, late for work, muttering, "It's going to be one of those days."

Let's imagine that we can tune into the frequency band of her self-talk, the internal "tapes" that play in her head. Here's what we might hear over the span of the next hour as our heroine arrives at her office ten minutes late and discovers that she has missed the beginning of an emergency staff meeting called that morning. As she hurriedly assembles her papers for the meeting, her headache rages. Her stream of self-talk might sound like this:

> I can't believe this. First that idiot practically kills or seriously maims me with his car, and then I'm late for work. I'm always late! I can't do anything right. I'm going to look like such a fool waltzing into that meeting late. My boss is probably going to kill me! I can't take this job much longer. It's driving me crazy.

Admittedly I'm caricaturing a bit for dramatic purposes, but not much. In fact, this monologue is very much the way many women's cognitive "tapes" play in their heads when stressors impinge on them. The unfortunate result is *more* stress, *greater* arousal, and perpetuation of a vicious cycle.

The language of our hypothetical sample of internal cognitive self-talk is riddled with exaggeration, extreme statements, overgeneralization, negative self-labeling, unfounded expectations, predictions, and hyperbole.

Is our heroine really "going crazy"? Is the boss going "to kill" her? Is it really accurate to say, "I *can't* take this job much longer" or "I *can't* believe this"? Is she really *always* late? Perhaps she is late more frequently than she would like, and it is a problem that she may want to work on improving. But creating even greater stress by overgeneralizing from "sometimes" to "always," or by irrationally predicting dire, apocalyptic consequences for falling short of perfection only serves to exacerbate stress problems.

These characteristics are the hallmarks of cognitive errors. When your cognitive tapes are replete with stressogenic errors and language, the emotional consequence is negativity: You feel more stressed, depressed, anxious, and uncomfortable.

Ask yourself what you say internally when stress strikes. Do you make cataclysmic predictions if you are unable, for example, to make it to your child's soccer game or school event or to some other obligation? Do you tell yourself that your child will think that you're a bad mother? Or do you call yourself inadequate or a failure?

Examine your own stream of self-talk the next time you start to feel stressed. The best way to clean your cognitive tapes is to write them down, uncensored, and then subject them to careful scrutiny.

To tap into your automatic thoughts regarding Type E stress, try doing the following exercise. Answer all ten open-ended sentences listed below, and write down your answers. Try to be as uncensored in your thoughts as possible. The point is to tune into your *automatic*, uncensored thinking.

1. I have to do things perfectly, *or else* . . .
2. I should be able to accomplish more in a day, *or else* . . .
3. I should be able to do everything without feeling stressed or tired, *or else* . . .
4. I have to please others by doing what they ask me to do, *or else* . . .
5. I have to prove myself to everyone, *or else* . . .
6. "Having it all" should make me happy, *or else* . . .
7. I can't be happy until I "have it all," *or else* . . .
8. I can't relax until I finish what I have to do, *or else* . . .
9. I have to make people need me because of everything I do for them, *or else* . . .
10. I should be everything to everybody, *or else* . . .

Now review your answers. Look for examples of illogical or exaggerated thinking. How about hyperbole or catastrophizing? Do you overgeneralize? See things in black-and-white, overpolarized terms? Label yourself negatively?

When you have carefully scrutinized your automatic answers for cognitive errors, engage in a corrective dialogue with your own self-talk. Replace the cognitive errors with more rational, tempered, adaptive thinking that serves to reduce stress rather than to exacerbate it.

Monitoring your self-talk and replacing erroneous thinking with adaptive, rational statements is a proven technique for reducing stress and altering other negative mood states. If "stressogenic tapes" induce and amplify stress levels, then "talking yourself down" will serve to lower and moderate arousal. And, indeed, modifying your arousal-producing self-talk by replacing it with a monologue designed to calm yourself down and focus you on reality-oriented solutions to the stressors you face is a highly potent form of stress management.

STRESS CONTAGION

Stressogenic talk is not confined to the tapes that play in your own head. It frequently occurs in the conversations women have with their friends.

It has been commonly noted that women have more intimate, sharing, emotionally expressive platonic relationships with one another than men do with other men. And, in general, women's capacities to form emotionally supportive bonds with other women (and/or men) is an invaluable stress resistance resource. Empathic, accepting, mutually reinforcing, and helpful relationships between friends are clearly to be cherished and nurtured.

Notwithstanding the value of emotionally supportive relationships, listen sometime to the way you and/or your friends talk about things that are stressing you. If you're like a lot of Type E women, your conversations might well include such exaggerated and stressogenic lines as, "You won't believe what happened now!" "I'm coming unglued!" "You'll die when you hear this!" The point is not to remove the enthusiasm of the speaker, but rather to comment on the dramatized tone of the language and its stressogenic properties.

When you talk to a friend, you're not the *only* victim of erroneous expectations and cognitive errors. When two friends empathize with each other's problems, a certain degree of *stress contagion* occurs. Women, because of their traditional roles as nurturers and emotional supporters, are particularly subject to worry and upset over other people's—friends or family—problems, and are stressed over their inabilities to make everything better and to soothe the discomfort.

But women could learn to be even better supports and sources of stress resistance for one another if they modified their interpersonal conversations about stress as well as their own internal self-talk monologues. Instead of bouncing off of and amplifying each other's stress levels, women can learn to "talk each other down" by focusing on problem-solving rather than on replaying the stressful event. For example, instead of responding with, "Oh, my God, I just can't believe that! You must be going crazy!" an empathic friend could respond with something like, "I know this is really upsetting you right now, but I think if we just talk it out and think about some solutions, you'll feel better."

In the latter response, the speaker insulates herself a bit from the stress contagion of her friend's upset, while at the same time accurately empathizing but not throwing fuel on the flaming stress.

Other important steps can be taken to reduce or minimize stress contagion, including setting limitations on your own time and energy for dealing with the acute crises or chronic problems of even your best friends. In the arena of friendship, boundaries must still apply, as must self-preservation. Type E women typically are drained by their own openness, availability, and emotional strength. Because they are emotionally open, as well as strong and available, other people plug into them like an energy source. And unless you regulate the outward flow of your own finite resources, it is unlikely that anyone else will spontaneously moderate her or his level of need or demand. The fact that self-preservation and stress resistance require establishing and implementing limitations does not lessen the value of your friendship. Friendship is measured by quality of behavior and treatment as well as intentionality and emotional concern. Quantitative measures, like the *number* of hours you are available to talk on the telephone, or the *amount* of altruistic deeds and actions you demonstrate, are not necessarily accurate indicators of friendship. The key lies in learning to give quality time and attention to friends with the exercise of self-protective limitations against high levels of stress contagion.

The worry and upset over other people's problems that characterizes Type E women (and women in general) is reflective of another kind of cognitive distortion: an assumption of excessive responsibility for the behavior of others. Because of the emotional strength and depth of personal resources that many high-achieving women possess, they often find themselves in the positions of confidant, counselor, adviser, and overall pillar of support to many other people around them—coworkers, bosses, secretaries, husbands/lovers, friends, children, parents, and siblings.

It is, of course, flattering that so many people need you and value your sound counsel about their problems. But you must establish your own enlightened set of criteria about what constitutes *your* realm of responsibility, and what is theirs. All too easily, other people can seduce the Type E woman into carrying too much of the responsibility and burden for their needs, to the point where the woman's own emotional and physical resistance resources are severely compromised and impaired. It is appropriate, for example, to "mother" your children; it is not, however, your responsibility to instruct or "bring up" other adults. You may certainly help them to see their alternatives and offer to support whatever choices they make, but it is not your job to shoulder the burdens of all others who seek your assistance. To do so will figuratively and literally break you and burn you out.

ERRONEOUS EXPECTATIONS
OF OTHERS

It is important to note at the close of this chapter that Type E women are stressed not only by the cognitive errors in their own heads, but also by the erroneous expectations of others.

Type E women often describe feeling guilty if they let down someone else's expectations of them, however unrealistic or stressful those expectations might be.

"I know my husband thinks that 'a wife' *should* cook dinner every night during the week," one woman executive explained. "So even though I often get home later than he does, I make dinner because I'd feel guilty—like I'd be letting him down—if I didn't. You know, his mother always cooked for the family and that's what he expects. And our kids have to eat, . . . so I always cook."

Because this woman never questioned the rationality of trying to live up to the strict code of her husband's unrealistic expectations (his mother didn't work), she never thought to negotiate an alternative solution, such as sharing responsibility for buying and preparing food, bringing home take-out food, or otherwise providing for the family dinner. Instead, she let his erroneous expectation become a source of resentment and stress that festered and intensified in their relationship.

There are many other, far more insidious ways in which the erroneous expectations of others fuel the stress cycle of Type E women. Or, more accurately, how the erroneous expectations of others fuel the woman's own set of cognitive errors and stressogenic assumptions and expectations of herself. It is precisely this interaction between her and others' expectations that constitutes the self-perpetuating nature of the problem. The more the Type E woman proves that she can do, the more others expect of her and demand that she do. As she pushes her resources to their limit, the stress mounts, and so does the intensity and frequency of demands from others.

Breaking the cycle requires, in part, correcting the erroneous expectations of others. Again, this correction must come from altering your own erroneous thinking and behavior. Understanding the complex relationship between the way your everything-to-everybody behavior pattern fits into the need systems and expectations of others who both elicit and reinforce your Type E stress cycle is the subject of the next chapter.

CHAPTER NINE

Everything-to-Everybody Behavior

TYPE E stress, like Type A, is a bad habit.

It is not a psychiatric label, nor is it a symptom or form of mental illness. It is, however, a pattern of behavior that creates chronic *overarousal,* and thereby courts serious trouble in the form of physical and emotional burnout and illness. But bad habits can be broken or modified.

As we have seen in the preceding chapters, the Type E syndrome is comprised of a complex and intricate web of cognitive factors that underlie and intensify the stress of high-achieving women. But the problem is not all "in your head." The bottom line is that Type E women have a real and legitimate behavioral problem.

In behavioral terms, Type E women overextend their time and resources in order to accommodate and acquiesce to the virtually endless stream of demands from personal relationships, work, family, home, community, charitable or religious organizations, and other social sources. They underdelegate, placing excessive burdens on their own performance and sense of responsibility. They are not assertive in saying "no" or in denying requests, needs, or demands from others, nor do they set adequate and appropriate limitations on their own resource or energy allocations. Type E women often recoil from asking for assistance or, if they do ask, they often fail to achieve effective support or help.

They evaluate themselves harshly and frequently. They overdefine the level of effort or number of tasks that are required to fulfill their multiple roles. Consequently, they have difficulty setting priorities and filtering demands or maintaining a sense of order and control over their lives.

Type E women recognize themselves in this profile. But the enigma of Type E coping is like that of other self-destructive behavioral problems or bad habits: You know that what you're doing isn't good for you, but you don't seem to be able to stop or to change, or you want to change but just don't know *how*.

The key is to avoid getting stuck on the question, "*Why* do I do this?" If you have any bad habits that you want to alter—such as smoking, excessive drinking, overeating, underexercising, or Type E coping—the important thing is to *change your behavior*.

When alcoholics or drug abusers sober or straighten up, they often gain many insights into why they got themselves into such self-destructive patterns in the first place. They have to change the behavior *first;* the insights come later. Just gaining insight into the reasons why you do something without actually altering the behavior is worth little in measurable, meaningful terms.

So it is with Type E stress. Altering old, self-defeating ways of thinking or looking at the world that serve to feed the stress cycle is an important part of the change process. But the cognitive component of Type E stress is only one part of the problem; unless the behaviors that constitute the Type E stress syndrome themselves are altered, the change process will be incomplete and unstable.

Changing behavior is a matter of *identifying* the problematic responses to stress, *unlearning* the bad responses, and, finally, *replacing* Type E behaviors with a more adaptive set of coping skills designed to maximize achievement potential, while building stress resistance and protecting against the ravages of the chronic dis-stress cycle.

The next two chapters present a strategic regimen of exercises and a stress-resistance mental workout program to help train you in the acquisition of better coping skills. But first let's examine some of the "whys" behind everything-to-everybody behavior, the ways in which high-achieving women are developmentally, environmentally, and interpersonally conditioned into doing the constellation of behaviors I label Type E.

In this chapter I apply some fundamental scientific principles from the psychology of learning to gain awareness of how Type E women get "hooked" on their own stress patterns, and how mutual cycles of positive and negative reinforcement between Type E women and other people in their lives shape and control behavior. Then I will move forward to behavior change strategies.

HISTORICAL DETERMINANTS OF TYPE E BEHAVIOR

Where does this push to try to be everything to everybody come from? What was the learning process entailed in developing the compulsive behavior of scrambling to meet everyone's needs before your own? Type E behaviors feel deeply ingrained to the women who are so well practiced in their juggling feats. And, in fact, the historical roots of Type E behavior are deep.

Psychologist Carol Gilligan, in her book *In A Different Voice*,[1] describes the development of a moral orientation in females that she calls "care-focused morality." According to Dr. Gilligan's research, this female phenomenon is firmly rooted by early adolescence, and sharply contrasts with male-oriented morality, which is "justice-focused."

To illustrate her point, Dr. Gilligan presented Aesop's fable, "The Porcupine and the Moles," to a study group of eleven- to fifteen-year-old boys and girls and asked them for their solutions to the moles' dilemma.

The story goes that a porcupine approaches a family of moles and asks to share a desirable cave as a shelter from the winter's cold. The moles cooperatively agree and let the porcupine move in. But, to their dismay, they soon find that whenever the quilled porcupine moves about the small cave, they are incessantly scratched and irritated. Finally, the moles ask the porcupine to leave. But the porcupine refuses, saying, "If you moles are not satisfied, I suggest that *you* leave." The moral of the story: "It is well to know one's guest before offering him hospitality."

The boys and girls in the study group responded differently to the dilemma of the moles and porcupine. The boys tended to provide solutions that opted for justice, such as, "It's the moles' house. It's a deal. The porcupine leaves." But the girls looked for conciliatory solutions that would keep all parties content and comfortable, such as, "Cover the porcupine with a blanket."

Girls are conditioned early in life to adapt their behavior according to their care-focused morality. As a consequence, women are predisposed toward behavior that meets the needs of others. And as Gilligan's study illustrates, the "wiring" that makes us feel that taking care of others' needs is the *right* thing to do goes back to early childhood and adolescent conditioning.

There are many other ways, cited throughout this book, in which society culturally conditions girls and boys to be different. Girls, more than boys, are conditioned to be "nice," "sweet," and consequently approval-seeking. They are selectively reinforced for cooperative behavior and for compliance. As the childhood chant decrees, "Sugar and spice and everything nice . . . that's what little girls are made of," whereas little boys are toughened up with images of "rags and snails and puppy dog tails." In this way, Type E women are developmentally conditioned to say "yes" to the requests and demands of others. They are predisposed to being agreeable and pleasing or, at least, intending to be so.

The seeds are sown young for the response to the onslaught of demands high-achieving women experience that results in everything-to-everybody behavior. Women are raised to take care of other people and to seek their approval and love by doing so.

But the roots of Type E behavior extend beyond conditioning to an even more basic or primitive form of learning: the emulation of role models. In other words, much of behavior is learned by way of copying, re-creating, incorporating, or just plain aping the actions of other people with whom we identified.

Where, however, is the role model for the everything-to-everybody woman, this Superwoman, whom Type E women seem to be "emulating"?

The point is that there generally is not a simple, unitary role model for high-achieving women to internalize. As I discussed in the chapter on ego confusion, the behavior of today's high-achieving Type E woman reflects an *amalgamation of role models*. Her behavior is largely modeled on a *combination* of significant figures, generally some traditional women (perhaps her mother), some "heroines" of history or contemporary times, *and* people who have achieved success according to career-specific criteria. Those people include some women but, generally, more men.

Now the difficulty with having an amalgamation of role models is certainly not the richness and complexity of character and style that such a mix creates. Indeed, these results of amalgamation are part of what makes high-achieving women so attractive and interesting to many people. The problem is that when *one* person incorporates an internalized standard that says she "should" be like two or three or even four whole other people, combined, the one woman's resources are inevitably greatly and unrealistically overextended.

Fran, a classic example of Type E stress arising from amalgamated role models, is a forty-one-year-old divorced mother of two children, and a practicing corporate lawyer. She makes an excellent income as a partner in her father's highly prestigious law firm.

When I met her, Fran had been divorced for four years from a man who was also an attorney, though in a different specialty. Since divorcing, Fran hasn't dated a lot or really had much fun at all. She felt bitter about how difficult it seemed to find a "decent man," but despite her romantic and sexual deprivation, Fran insisted that there is "no time anyway between my work and my kids for a man, so what's the point?" And commenting on her stress level, she opined, "I'm so exhausted and pressured that I'd be no fun to be with. If I were a man, I wouldn't want to date me either."

Fran's negative attitude keeps her trapped in a Type E cycle. Part of Fran's stress arises from pushing herself for long hours at work to "do all the things my father did."

"I don't want anyone to ever get the idea that I'm in this position [partner] because I'm my father's daughter. The fact is I'm just as good as he is. But I never stop feeling the need to prove it every day that I'm at work."

And when Fran leaves work, another whole set of behaviors gets activated, based on the figure of her mother as a role model.

Despite the fact that Fran can afford a full-time housekeeper and cook, she insists on cleaning, cooking, and doing the laundry herself so that she feels that

she is doing "everything my mother did for me." Fran
has weekly housekeeping help for heavy chores, but
then, so did her mother.

Fran literally drives herself relentlessly until 1:00 or
2:00 every morning. She goes into the office on weekends "like my father always did," and suffers remorse
from the guilt of "not being home with my kids like
my mother would have been." So to make up for the
time that she works, Fran believes she should stay
home on weekend evenings in order to be with her
kids.

In therapy, Fran realized that she was trying to do
all the behaviors of two completely separate and different people: her mother *and* her father. As her story
unfolded, it became clear that Fran and her ex-husband
also had a highly competitive relationship in which she
"tried to be as good as he was, and then some." To
Fran's way of thinking, entrapped as she was by her
Type E stress, there was no room for a social life or
for having any outlets for herself. But she also realized
how maladaptive and unrealistic her expectations of
herself were, and of how much distress her behavior
was ultimately causing her. She was too exhausted and
strung-out even to enjoy her children or her career—
not to mention the fact of her barren romantic and
social life.

The first thing that I asked Fran to do was to make
a list of all the *behaviors* that she believed were required in order to fulfill her roles as "attorney" and
"mother." Then I instructed her to rank order each list
in terms of how much she personally valued the actions. In other words, I asked Fran to identify the
"best things" about her own mother (since her behavior was modeled after her mother) and the "best things"
about her father as a lawyer (and therefore about
herself).

Together we developed a realistic behavioral schedule for Fran that could encompass the things she val-

ued most about her respective roles, and that she therefore wanted to do, but would delegate to others (her ex-husband, her junior associates, her children, her secretary, her housekeeper) those behaviors that she valued least and were therefore least central to her self-esteem.

Using this approach, Fran realized that the best things about her mother were her warmth, emotional supportiveness, and availability. Since Fran recalled many long, intimate, reassuring "growing-up talks" with her mother while her mother puttered around the house, Fran had come to associate doing housework with being a "good mother." The behavioral analysis helped her to separate the behaviors of conversation and emotional support from the actual activities of housework. In fact, Fran realized that in her case, delegating the bulk of the housework to a full-time housekeeper would free up more of her time really to be like her mother in terms of the things Fran loved best in her memories.

Similarly, Fran worked on modifying and eliminating some of the unnecessary, compulsive ways in which she exerted extra effort to prove herself continually at work. She delegated more work to associates and paralegal assistants, and created more time to spend going out with friends. She also restarted a social life.

Fran's case was a clearcut example of how amalgamated role models—behaviors that are incorporated into our own self-concepts from childhood—contribute to a self-defeating behavioral pattern in which too many demands are loaded onto the limited resources of one individual.

CURRENT REINFORCEMENTS: POSITIVE AND NEGATIVE

Just because Type E behaviors are deeply ingrained does not mean that they are etched in psychological stone. Many bad habits, poor coping patterns, and self-destructive behaviors go back to early historical roots, but nevertheless can be changed for the better.

From the standpoint of developing a strategy for change, the important question is: "What are the reinforcements in my life *today* for my Type E behaviors?"

The most obvious form of behavioral reinforcement is what psychologists call positive reinforcement or reward. When a behavior is followed by a reward, the likelihood that the behavior will occur again is increased. Positive reinforcement is a basic form of *operant conditioning,* learning that is contingent on schedules of rewards and punishments.

In order to develop a better grasp on your own stress-related behavioral patterns, ask yourself what the "hooks" are for conditioning your behavior. Are you looking for positive reinforcement in the form of signs of love or affection? Are you seeking praise, compliments, or other verbal rewards like words of appreciation or indebtedness? Perhaps your main rewards are monetary, or perhaps they lie in the exercise of status and power.

Everyone has her own set of chimes—those things that make you feel good, that you experience as "rewarding." The sources of reward may be external, deriving from the corresponding behavior of other people, or they may be internal in the sense that the woman praises or rewards herself for her own behavior.

One potent reinforcer is the actual chemical "rush" that many Type E women report feeling from their own arousal level. Under conditions of arousal, the hormone adrenaline is released into the system. High levels of adrenaline are correlated with high levels of stress, but adrenaline release is also experienced as "exciting," "stimulating," and "a turn-on."

Adrenaline is even more potent than most artificial stimulants, and many Type E women—and Type A men—virtually get addicted to their high adrenaline levels.

Carol is a successful high-tech salesperson in a fiercely competitive field. She came to consult with me because she was concerned about how hard she drove herself not only to keep up with the rest of the hard-driving, dog-eat-dog salesforce in her company, but also to be "a good wife and buddy" to her husband. The latter, by her definition, meant keeping up her high energy level for conversation, athletics, sex, or dancing in the evenings with her classically Type A husband.

Carol sensed that she couldn't "come down" off her own high energy levels or, perhaps, that she was afraid of a paralyzing "crash." She would get herself pumped up (literally with adrenaline) for her job and keep herself pumped up late into the night with her husband. But she began developing symptoms of sleep deprivation and fatigue, such as irritability and inability to concentrate.

Carol loved the "rush" that she experienced during motivational sales meetings, and she tried to keep herself pumped up on her own adrenaline as much as possible. When we examined her Type E stress from a behavioral perspective, Carol saw that she reinforced her Type E behaviors—driving herself too hard without respite—with her adrenaline rushes. Carol's difficulty was that she attributed her achievements as a successful salesperson to her "high energy level and contagious enthusiasm," and she was afraid that if she "slowed down" or took rest periods when she got home before "revving up" to go out for the evening, she might lose her drive. With inadequate sleep or regenerative rest, Carol was running on fumes.

In therapy, Carol worked on changing her erroneous assumption that relaxing would wind up causing behavioral paralysis. She revised her thinking to accept the necessity of breaks as ways of recharging her high physical and mental energy levels. Carol also committed herself to learning and regularly practicing the relaxation, mental minivacation, and desensitization techniques described in the next chapter.

Many women (and men) voice this same fear of turning down their internal arousal levels. There are some powerful intrinsic motivators and reinforcers involved in achievement behavior, and it is relatively easy and very seductive to get hooked on your own high adrenaline levels. The important point to bear in mind is that periods of arousal spelled by appropriate periods of relaxation or "letting down" are fine. The danger lies in overexposure to chronic arousal levels. Every system, including specifically the human mind and body, needs some "down time" in order to recharge, rejuvenate, and revitalize.

In addition to being reinforced by their adrenaline levels, Type E women receive reinforcement for their behavior from many social or external sources. Women who keep the juggling act aloft are frequently, or at least periodically, the objects of praise, adulation, or regard by admirers impressed by the feat. "This is a woman who can do anything . . . and does!," "You're a Superwoman," or "When you want a job done right, give it to _(your name)_" are the kinds of common verbal praises that positively reinforce Type E stress.

There are also internal sources of reward or gratification for Type E behavior. If you are indeed trying to be a Superwoman, you are likely to pat yourself on the back psychologically for demonstrating Type E behavior. If, in your mind, Type E coping is a formula for success, you will internally reinforce the ultimately self-destructive pattern.

Remember that Type E behavior is a high-risk coping style. Despite the short-term gratifications from both external and internal sources that may accompany and reinforce many everything-to-everybody behaviors, the overall pattern of fragmented, overtaxed resources is not an avenue to success, health, or happiness.

Research on Type A men has revealed that success is attributed to the very behavior that compromises their health. In other words, they frequently believe that their success (read: salary level, amount of material possessions, amount of competitive triumphs) is, in part, due to their ability to get more things done in less time than other people. In this way, Type A men internally reinforce their self-destructive behavioral patterns. It is only when they realize instead that their behavior is the cause of their *stress* and ill health, rather than the cause of their *success*, that they can be motivated to alter their self-destructive behavior.

In addition to positive reinforcement, behavior is also conditioned by negative reinforcement. Negative reinforcement is not the same thing as punishment. Punishment occurs when a behavior results in the experience of a negative stimulus. Negative reinforcement occurs when the negative or aversive stimulus comes first and is removed or ceased when the behavior in question is produced.

The classic example of negative reinforcement is a laboratory rat placed in a divided cage. It is conditioned to escape from the black section into the white section via a white connecting door. When the rat is put into the black section, it receives electric shocks to its feet. Eventually, the pained and panicked rat discovers the door and learns that it can stop the shock by running through the door into the white part of the cage where no shock grids exist. This "white door" behavior is conditioned by negative reinforcement—the shock is removed when the proper behavior is done.

We could also teach a rat to run through the door into the white section of the box by rewarding it with cheese when it reaches its goal, instead of using shock. In this instance, the conditioning would be based on positive reinforcement.

Negative reinforcement is every bit as powerful a form of behavioral control as is reward. Perhaps it is even more potent, since the control can be aversive, insidious, subtle, and highly manipulative.

Type E women often set up "white door" scenarios in their own heads using negative reinforcement to condition their behavior.

Betsy, for example, works full-time as a marketing executive, and is the married mother of two young boys. Her husband, Stu, is an accountant with a large firm, and he is eager to make partner. For both business and social reasons, Betsy and Stu have joined a number of organizations. The problem is that Betsy almost always winds up in charge of organizing something or taking on more responsibility than she really desires.

"I can't say no," she explains. "This conscience of mine is a killer. I start to tell myself that I'll feel guilty if I don't help out, or that—for the sake of my husband's business—I'm letting him down if I don't get more prominent at the Club. So I suppose I keep joining and overvolunteering as a way to shut off the guilt."

Betsy's internal voice is tantamount to the electric shock grids applied to the feet of our experimental rat. Just as the rat learns to escape the shock by running for the white door, Betsy has conditioned herself to volunteer and be a joiner as a way of turning off the negative voices in her head that make her feel guilty and obligated.

Type E women often motivate themselves and shape their behavior through negative reinforcement. Statements like, "I can't stand it if I don't do X," "I'm afraid that So-and-so will be angry with me if I don't do what he/she wants," or "I have to do such-and-such or else I'll feel guilty or inadequate" are good clues into negative reinforcement patterns.

Other people in a Type E woman's life may also control her behavior with negative reinforcement. In this sense, they can be said to have "aversive control" over Type E women by applying negative stimuli (e.g., nagging, criticism, guilt induction) in order to get what they want.

Nan, for example, describes an amusing, albeit frustrating, pattern of negative reinforcement in which her excessive household activity gets reinforced by her husband's "learned helplessness."

"My husband is really sneaky," she says, only half-kidding. "He knows that the best way to get me to do *all* of the cooking or *all* of the cleaning or *all* of the taking care of the kids is to try to do something but to look helpless and eventually mess things up. I just can't stand the process of watching him. It drives me nuts. I feel guilty and irritated at the same time. But the gambit never fails. He winds up looking like a good guy for trying, and I wind up doing everything myself because I can't stand to see him struggle and then do things all wrong."

In fact, Nan's husband didn't really do everything *wrong,* he just didn't do things in the same way that she did. Besides, she had had a lifetime's worth of practice, and she wasn't even giving him a chance to learn by trial and error. Nan turned on the shock grids in her own head when her husband assumed any part of the household operations. But as soon as she took over, the "shock" terminated as her husband's expression of helplessness and incompetence ceased. He then positively reinforced her with his gratitude for letting him stop.

Nan was able to reduce her Type E stress by forcing herself to let her husband do some of the work. As she trained herself to be more patient and less dogmatic about the way things "should be done," he became more competent, less "helpless," and even more willing to hold up his end of the household responsibilities.

Not all Type E women have Nan's "problem." At least her husband was willing to share the load—as soon as Nan gave him permission to help. More often, Type E women feel that no one proffers assistance, and that the interpersonal strain and hassle required to get help may not be worth the trouble.

"Periodically, I just give in and clean up my kid's room," said Donna, a woman who doesn't get enough help. "How long and how much can you nag someone? I literally can't stand the sound of my own voice asking my son to clean up. So I'd just rather do it myself. At least that way I don't have to listen to myself nagging."

A third woman, Louise, explains that her husband says that he is willing to help out around the house as long as she tells him what needs to be done. But when she asks him (or tells him) to do something, he snaps "Get off my back. Don't nag. I'll get around to it when I have time."

It's a classic Catch 22 setup, and Louise capitulates by doing the work herself. "Either he accuses me of nagging or he waits so long to do something that it sends me up the wall. Eventually, I give up and do it myself. The problem is I'm only one person doing the work of two."

In both Louise and Donna's cases, the Type E behavior is negatively reinforced. Nagging and passive resistance are forms of interpersonal electric shock and are common techniques for controlling another's behavior ("You do the behavior, I'll stop the nagging").

*   *   *

For many Type E women, the everything-to-every-body behavioral cycle is so deeply ingrained that they fail to see that more adaptive, alternative coping responses exist. Instead of acceding to demands or requests from others as a way of turning off the negative stimulation, they could negotiate the terms and conditions of the request (such as deadlines, amount of support or assistance, and so on), assertively deny or postpone the request, prioritize and filter demands so that they are ordered and manageable, or delegate tasks to others.

When you examine Type E behavior as a learned habitual response to stressors in your own life, you will probably be able to identify both positive and negative reinforcement patterns for the behavior. Understanding Type E behavior in an interpersonal context will reveal the self-perpetuating nature of the cycle. You condition, shape, reinforce, and control the expectations and behavior of other people in your life by virtue of your own behavior. They, in turn, condition, shape, reinforce, and control your behavior by virtue of what they say or do, or don't do.

The Type E cycle is enigmatic because it is punctuated by positive reinforcements and sustained by negative reinforcements. And because Type E behavior is deeply embedded in interpersonal dynamics, breaking the vicious cycle often involves changing more than just yourself. Others' expectations and responses that contribute to and perpetuate the problem must often be altered as well. While these changes may be slow and difficult, they are necessary. Some of the changes in others will occur in response to the changes you make unilaterally in your own behavior. When you stop reinforcing their demands with your continual attempts to comply or please, you will be reconditioning their expectations.

Diane worked as an investment analyst in an exclusively male environment. Because Diane was married and the mother of a ten-year-old boy, her boss was initially resistant to hiring her. "We have to work late a lot in this office," he warned, "and you'll have to adjust your responsibilities accordingly."

Diane felt that she was continually under her boss's suspicious eye. "It felt like he was just waiting for me to make a false move and leave early so he could climb all over me. So I waited him out. . . . I never left the office before he did. If he stayed until seven, I stayed until seven-ten, if he stayed until nine-thirty, so did I." This pattern worked; it kept the boss off Diane's back for leaving early—but he almost broke her back with more and more work to do, since he could always expect her to stay late. Meanwhile, Diane felt resentful toward her boss, and guilty toward her family for missing so many after-school activities or for getting home late so often.

The big conflict came when her son asked (begged) her to participate in a school program that required monthly meetings at 7:00 in the evening. Diane had conditioned her boss to expect her always to work late, and he had conditioned her into staying. In this instance, though, her priorities were clearly favoring her son, but she was at a loss to know how to change her boss.

Diane decided to bite the bullet. She committed herself to leaving work by 6:00 on the nights of the school meetings, no matter how late the boss worked. The first time she left "early" was an occasion of enormous anxiety and discomfort for Diane. "I worried all night about his reaction," she admitted. But the next day, there were no untoward consequences. The following week, she stayed later than her boss on four nights, but left by 5:00 on one night, even though she didn't have anywhere special to go.

"Breaking his expectation that I would always be the last one to go home was the best thing I could have done," she said later. "I think when he realized that he couldn't take my working late for granted, he started appreciating me and my work more. And he was less inclined to simply throw extra work my way because he knew I'd be willing to forfeit time with my family as a way of 'proving myself.' "

Diane altered her boss's expectations by modifying her own behavior unilaterally. In her case, the cycle was broken relatively easily, and the consequences of leaving earlier than he left were not nearly as dire as Diane had expected. In fact, there were virtually no consequences at all other than her own concern. Of course, Diane was careful not to make a habit out of leaving work before the close of business, but neither did she offer explanations or excuses for those times when she left the boss to close up the office.

Under other circumstances, Type E women may find it necessary to intervene more actively in the reinforcement patterns. For example, Donna's dilemma over her child's messy room was resolved by instituting a "new set of rules" with her son. Donna explained to him that her nagging had become more stressful to her than was his dirty room. So she would no longer be responsible for telling him to clean his room. She would, she explained, heretofore respond to his "pigsty" by closing the door and closing her eyes to the mess inside. If, however, more than three days went by with a closed door and a dirty room, one hour of television watching per week would be forfeited for every day thereafter that the room stayed messy.

Donna stuck by her new rules, despite the fact that the first two weeks were very difficult. But by the third week, her son had adopted a strategy of cleaning his room every three days. He lost no television time, and Donna gained the extra hour or two she had previously spent every week cleaning up after him. In this instance, the interpersonal pattern was broken by changing the Type E behavior and by directly altering the expectations or "rules" between mother and son.

PARTIAL REINFORCEMENT AND EVERYTHING-TO-EVERYBODY BEHAVIOR

Type E women often feel "hooked" on their own behavior. Frequently, I hear comments like, "I know that pushing myself this hard and feeling so pressured isn't good for me, but I can't seem to stop" or "This is the only way I can get things done. If I don't get myself worked up, I won't do all the work I have to do; but it's a hard way to live."

To understand fully how Type E women get hooked on their own stress patterns, it is necessary to understand the concept of partial or intermittent reinforcement. We have reviewed some of the ways in which Type E behavior is conditioned in women, both developmentally and in their current, adult lives, through positive and negative reinforcement. And we have seen that both forms of reinforcement can come from internal or external sources, from inside the woman herself or from factors outside the woman, generally other people.

But behavior is not determined only by the nature of the reinforcement, whether positive or negative. Learned behavior also depends on the *schedule of reinforcement* by which the reinforcement is provided. Schedule means the rate or frequency of the reinforcement.

Again, the best way to grasp the concept of partial reinforcement is from a basic piece of psychological laboratory research. What we are interested in is the comparative *habit strength* of a behavior that is conditioned on a schedule of *continuous* reinforcement versus that conditioned by *partial* reinforcement. The latter schedule is also called intermittent or random reinforcement, or a gambling schedule. If you've ever stood throwing coins into a slot machine waiting for the occasional random jackpot, then you have been the subject of partial reinforcement.

But instead of gambling pigeons, let's consider the laboratory example using real pigeons. In this case, we'll make them two hungry pigeons, each of which is placed in an experimental box.

The "box" in question was designed by Dr. B. F. Skinner of Harvard University for purposes of investigating the nature of operant conditioning with animals. In each pigeon's Skinner box is a lever that, when depressed, results in the delivery of a pellet of pigeon food. Since the experimental subjects are food-deprived, both pigeons learn "lever-pressing behavior" rather quickly. Within minutes, both pigeons acquire a lever-pressing "habit."

The experiment is designed to examine the effects of two different schedules of reinforcement. For Pigeon A, positive reinforcement (food pellets) are delivered on a continuous, 100 percent reinforcement schedule. That is, every time the pigeon presses the lever, it receives a pellet of food—one press, one pellet.

But for Pigeon B, another schedule is used: As soon as the basic lever-pressing habit has been initially taught or conditioned, the frequency of reinforcement is changed. Pigeon B's pellets begin to be delivered on an intermittent, random basis. Perhaps the pigeon presses the lever five times with no delivery of pellets, but is rewarded for the sixth try. Then it may press fifteen times with no pellet, but is reinforced on the sixteenth press. The point is that reinforcement is delivered on a partial schedule that is essentially random.

Now comes the test of habit strength. Psychologically, habit strength is defined as the length of time that the pigeon will continue to press the lever in the absence of any reinforcement. So we stop delivering food pellets to both boxes. And we measure the time that each pigeon spends pressing the lever, even though no pellets are forthcoming.

What we discover is that Pigeon B's habit strength is far greater than that of Pigeon A. Pigeon B was conditioned on a partial reinforcement schedule and, perhaps because hope springs eternal even in a pigeon's breast, it continues pressing the lever without reward far longer than does Pigeon A.

It is a basic principle of human and animal learning that habits conditioned by partial reinforcement are strongest and, therefore, most difficult to extinguish.

Now let's make the leap from the behavior of our pigeons to that of overstressed Type E women. Let's recall the proposition that the Type E woman baits her own stress trap, ironically enough, with the very fact of her competence. Eventually, she becomes the victim of her own dazzling feats. The more that she demonstrates that she can do, the more others expect of her. And because others come to *expect* her behavior, they don't reinforce it all the time. Instead, positive reinforcement tends to come on a partial, intermittent schedule.

In the life of a high-achieving woman, partial reinforcements may come in the form of periodic praise, monetary or promotional reward, or other "pats on the back" in a work environment; on the home front or personal side, partial reinforcements may include expressions of praise, gratitude, admiration, and signs of affection and love from others, as well as strokes of ego gratification that she provides to herself. But whatever the form of positive, or negative, reinforcement, the important point is that a Type E woman is *partially* reinforced for her behavior.

And because of the habit strength that results from

the schedule of partial reinforcement, the pattern becomes deeply ingrained, almost addictive in nature.

The Type E woman, addicted to her own adrenaline rushes (which occur intermittently) or "hooked" on a coping style that works some of the time at a substantial price to her overall health and well-being, does not see an alternative. After all, when behavior of any kind becomes habitual, alternatives, by definition, are eliminated. Type E coping—pushing herself to try to be everything to everybody—becomes the only thing that she can think of to do about the dilemma of wanting to achieve excellence in both personal and career domains, given the level and quantity of demands on her time and resources.

There is a lethal logic to this formula for coping. Pushing the body's physical resources and the mind's mental and emotional energy to the limits, without proper respite and balance, is sheer brinkmanship.

One answer to the problem lies in learning new skills that help you to gain control over the intensity, rate, priority, and response to the demands that are continually made on your time and resources. Of course, as we have seen, changes must come as well in the ways Type E women think about themselves, their achievement drive, and their needs in close relationships.

I have discussed the underlying cognitive issues that fuel the stress cycle of Type E women in preceding chapters. The behavioral focus of this chapter is on emphasizing that building stress resistance is a matter of changing your head *and* changing your behavior. As I have said, one without the other is not sufficient.

By applying basic principles of behavior modification, psychologists successfully change what people actually *do*, not just how they think. Altering your own stress habits depends on identifying the undesirable behaviors that contribute to your dis-stress level, and analyzing and understanding the nature and schedule of the reinforcements that support those undesirable behaviors. But the process doesn't stop with mere understanding and insight. The next phase is critical: More adaptive, less damaging behaviors must be substituted for the poor coping patterns. And the nature and frequency of reinforcements in the environment must be altered to support the healthier behavioral pattern.

Before we turn to the acquisition of better coping skills in the next chapter, let's consider some of the tactics used by behavior modification psychologists that you can learn to apply to your own stress habits.

IDENTIFYING PROBLEM BEHAVIORS

The term everything to everybody is a global, summary term for a whole set of behaviors that lead to chronic overarousal cycles and potentially damaging stress. While the term strikes a frighteningly familiar chord with almost every woman I've known who strives to achieve in a complicated life with multiple role demands, it is not specific with respect to discrete behaviors.

At the outset of this chapter, you will recall, the everything-to-everybody syndrome was defined in behavioral terms. But even this dissection of the global term into its component parts is not sufficiently personalized to apply to the behavorial stress problems of individual Type E women.

In order to identify your own behavioral stress patterns, it is useful to keep track of your stress reactions in terms of their behavioral components. To do this, begin by monitoring your subjective stress level. When you reach a threshold level—that is, when you start to notice that the stress is becoming too high or uncomfortable—take note of the situation that immediately preceded your reaction. What was going on?

What was said to you? What choice were you asked to make? And so on.

Now ask yourself what you *did* in response to the situation. Write it down. What was your actual behavior in response to the situation that elicited a stressful reaction? Be as specific as possible in describing what you did.

Finally, ask yourself what happened in response to your behavior. What was the reinforcement? Was it a positive reward? Was it the cessation of something negative or aversive—negative reinforcement? Or was there no reinforcement that you could see? Perhaps you should look again. What are you waiting for or expecting to happen?

Keep a written record of your stress reactions including their situational antecedents, their behavioral analogues, and their reinforcements.

Psychologists have long recognized the salutary effects of self-observation and record-keeping on reversing or ameliorating self-defeating, destructive behaviors. Raising your awareness of how you respond to stressors—by writing down what you actually *do*—and understanding the consequences of that behavior in reinforcement terms will enhance your stress resistance. In addition, pinpointing problems in behavioral terms suggests concrete avenues for changes and benchmarks against which to evaluate progress.

In identifying the behavior patterns that cause, perpetuate, and exacerbate your stress problems, try to be specific. Breaking long-standing, deeply ingrained patterns of thought and behavior, like the Type E syndrome, is best accomplished by dissection into component parts and attacking one piece of problematic behavior at a time. You can't beat a stress problem overnight. But you can start to deal with the problem strategically right now by identifying the chain of events that comprise your own Type E behavioral stress problems.

CHANGING BEHAVIORAL CYCLES

Once you train yourself to be a good internal observer of your feelings and behaviors, you will begin to see how to interrupt your stress cycles by altering either the *stressor*, or the *behavioral response*, or the *reinforcement*—or perhaps all three.

I have emphasized throughout this book that Type E is a stress *cycle*. The concept of a cycle, in behavioral terms, is that each stimulus-response chain elicits the next. One stimulus elicits a response, which in turn becomes the next stimulus for another response, and so on.

Stress problems are generally embedded in complex chains of events that revolve in cyclical fashion. That is why they appear to be so ingrained and so difficult to solve or change. But from a behavioral perspective, you can affect the entire cycle by changing just a few significant stimulus-response links.

Let's examine Anne's stress problems to see how a behavioral analysis and change strategy can effectively alter self-destructive patterns.

Anne was referred to me by her doctor after organic explanations for Anne's severe headaches were ruled out. The doctor believed that Anne's headaches were stress-related.

First, I taught Anne how to be a good observer and meticulous recorder of her own behavior and stress patterns. Whenever Anne felt a headache coming on, I told her to use the pain as a cue to begin recording what was going on from a behavioral perspective.

On the basis of her carefully maintained records, within about ten days we had a good picture of Anne's stress cycle and of how the headaches were "functioning" in her life.

The basic problem stemmed from Anne's feeling that she could "never relax." Anne began her day early as an office administrator for a large law firm, rising at 5:30 A.M. and arriving at her desk by 7:30. Anne's day typically involved managing and responding to a myriad of demands and inputs from attorneys, clients, and office staff.

When Anne got home at 5:00 P.M., she would immediately change clothes, start straightening the house, and begin to make dinner for her two teenage girls. Anne's husband, Fred, would arrive home at 7:30, but her routine was first to serve her daughters dinner by about 6:00 and then to cook again (or heat things up) for herself and her husband for an 8:00 meal.

The headaches seemed to start sometime between 5:00 and 8:00 P.M.

"At first I started to worry that it was something about my husband that was causing the headaches . . . like I didn't want to see him, or that he made me nervous. But we have a good marriage. We love each other," Anne explained. In fact, she admitted to being initially reluctant to follow her doctor's recommendation to see a psychologist for fear that the "shrink would say that I hated my husband or something."

Our behavioral analysis revealed the trigger for Anne's tension headaches. Somewhere between cooking dinner for her daughters, talking with them while they ate, and waiting to sit down with Fred, Anne found that she had some "time on her hands." Not a lot of time, mind you, maybe an hour or so.

This is where the stress cycle was exposed. During these unoccupied minutes, Anne would begin thinking about all the things that she had to do either around the house or at work. She would construct mental "To Do" lists and she would push herself to "do something productive with the time, since I have so little." She would start cleaning out drawers, or do some ironing, or pay some bills. She couldn't seem to just sit down and put up her feet.

"I can't relax. It's really frustrating. As soon as I sit

down, this nagging voice starts playing in my head that I should be doing *something*, that I have so many things to do as a working wife and mother, that I shouldn't waste time. Then, the worst part is when I actually start doing one thing, my mind jumps to something else that I have to do, and maybe I'll even start doing the other thing. Then I begin feeling overwhelmed by *all* the things I have to do and how little time I have to get them done. That's when the headaches start."

As Anne and I dissected the patterns of behavior and reinforcements in her life, we discovered some fascinating connections. First, Anne could see that the "tapes" to "be productive" that played in her head were like the electric shock in the negative reinforcement experiment with the rat and the white door. She, in effect, trained herself to be constantly active so that she could turn off the "nagging" inside her own head. Every jump from one activity to another was an "escape" leap through a mental white door.

When Anne's headaches intensified, she eventually would "have to go to bed." Anne recognized that her headaches were the only "excuse" she had for stopping her incessant activity and becoming passive. Moreover, the positive reward value of finally lying down also reinforced Anne's headaches; the escape that the headache afforded her from the demands of the household was a potent *negative* reinforcement.

Together, Anne and I developed a behavior modification strategy that effectively reduced the frequency and intensity of her headaches.

Every other day (Monday, Wednesday, and Friday), Anne would arrive home from work at 5:00 and would proceed immediately to draw a hot bath for herself. She would immerse herself in the soothing tub for about twenty minutes and then spend forty minutes either napping or just lying on the bed, perhaps with quiet music on her headphones.

Anne's daughters were enlisted to let their mother

be alone until 6:00, at which point they were asked to wake her and to help set the table and get ready for dinner. Fred agreed to start coming home by 7:00 and to eat dinner with the whole family before going into his regular evening habits of reviewing his mail and returning phone calls.

On Tuesdays and Thursdays, the family's routine was the same, but Anne's behavior was different. On these days, Anne was to choose one activity that would require an hour to do, or two activities that would require an hour in total to accomplish. Anne was encouraged to construct a weekly "To Do" list for her activity days, and to focus on accomplishing the limited number of tasks on the list. While she worked, she was taught to reinforce herself for getting something productive done and to train herself to stop thinking about other tasks at the same time. Focusing her concentration on the task at hand had a relaxing effect on Anne, and actually helped to calm her down, much like a form of Zen meditation.

And she was able to give herself permission to relax once she saw the "productive" value of relaxation as a necessary condition for self-preservation.

"I feel so much better now that I can let myself unwind without feeling guilty or hassled, and without having to get a bad headache," she said. "And because you made the relaxation an 'assignment,' I was able to do it because it actually felt productive."

Several factors surrounding and contributing to Anne's overarousal cycle were modified and, therefore, allowed her to gain control of her stress problems. The behavior of the rest of the family, for example, was changed, and that, in turn, simplified the demands on Anne to prepare and eat dinner. By preparing only one meal in the evening and eating together as a family, Anne enjoyed dinner more, and she, in turn, rewarded her family with lots of verbal praise and words of appreciation for their help and support.

Anne learned from the changes in her family's behavior that she didn't "need" to get a headache in order to get some time to herself to be alone and unwind. She also observed an improvement in the quality of the time that she spent with her family.

"Before my structured activity days, I felt like I was being pulled in five directions at once. My kids seemed to always need something, and I resented their getting in the way of my accomplishing chores. But if I didn't stop to deal with them, I felt guilty. Now they know that that one hour is my time to concentrate, and they hold their problems until I'm through . . . unless, of course, it's an emergency. And I'm much better at handling emergencies, too, now that my stress level is lower."

Anne's case illustrates many of the principles of behavior modification that I have discussed. The focus on one hour, in particular, out of Anne's day demonstrates the effectiveness of interrupting the stress cycle at the level of concrete, specific behaviors. Anne's analysis directed her toward changing some of the situational stressors that were eliciting her tension response: the family's complex dinner schedule, her own internal "tapes" that propelled her constant activity, her children's demands on her time, and so on.

In addition to altering the stressors, Anne made some significant changes in her own response and behavior patterns. She taught herself relaxation skills, and trained herself to build time off into her hectic schedule so that tension headaches could be headed off before they became intense. Anne also learned to stop fragmenting her energies, and to focus on one behavioral task at a time.

Finally, the reinforcement contingencies for Anne's stress behaviors were changed. As Anne learned more about her Type E behavior patterns, she became sensitive to negative reinforcement patterns, partial reinforcement schedules, and positive reinforcement sources that operated to support her everything-to-everybody behavior. Since she came to see the negative consequences of her over-arousal cycles (in her case, tension headaches), she changed her internal evaluation of the behavior. In other words, Anne stopped rewarding herself for pushing to the limits of her resources, and began to reinforce herself instead for new coping skills that gave her a better sense of control over the demands in her life.

Anne's story also illustrates the value of both passive and active relaxation in reducing stress levels. A central concept of behavior modification is that an undesirable behavior can be "unlearned" by substituting another behavior that is incompatible with the first.

You cannot, for example, be relaxed and anxious at the same time. Anne was encouraged to identify or discover things that were relaxing to her—warm baths, quiet music, napping, glancing at magazines. Then she was taught to do the relaxation behavior during the period of time when she typically began experiencing tension. She found that the incongruous relaxation behavior effectively substituted for the arousing thoughts and compulsive activity.

But Anne was also given a form of active relaxation: mundane tasks that she identified for her activity days. These included jobs like sewing, cleaning out boxes, closets or drawers, or giving herself a manicure. Once she learned to concentrate on one activity at a time, Anne was able to let her mind passively wander to pleasant thoughts and she found the experience calming and reinforcing. Once again, she had substituted focused, quiet activity for her previously fragmented, aroused, conflicted behavioral style.

Mental imagery is another powerful form of interrupting and controlling negative stress cycles. Again, on the basis that your mind's behavior cannot be both agitated and peaceful, the concept is to conjure pleasing, relaxing, or calming images in your mind—a stress-reduction movie in your head—as a behavioral substitute for getting worked up and upset.

Passive forms of relaxation are only a part of the solution to the stress problems of Type E women. They must learn active fight-back strategies as a way to gain control over the external demands and internal beliefs, expectations, conflicts, and pressures that comprise the Type E dilemma. The next chapter offers a set of exercises designed to build stress resistance by teaching Type E women better active coping skills.

CHAPTER TEN

Exercises and Tactics for Reducing Type E Stress and Building Stress Resistance

TYPE E stress is a vicious cycle. And vicious cycles don't get their names for nothing!

But cycles, even vicious ones, can be interrupted. The effective strategy for interrupting a destructive cognitive and behavioral cycle is a three-step process.

First, a specific problem area must be identified, and concrete behaviors targeted for change. The next step is to learn a new, more adaptive coping skill to substitute for the target behavior problem. Finally, the most important step: implementation. The new coping behavior *must* be substituted for the old patterns. By altering the behavioral link in the stress cycle, the interlocking web of factors—both cognitive and interpersonal—that serve to elicit and reinforce the Type E pattern will themselves be altered.

There is a way out of the Type E stress trap. But to spring yourself loose requires a proactive rather than a reactive attitude. There are tangible things you can do—*must* do—if the stress cycle is to be broken.

The prescription for treating stress problems of Type E women is different from treatment for Type A men. In the case of Type A stress, passive forms of stress management are generally emphasized. But this traditional "go limp" approach—deep breathing, self-hypnosis, and so on—is of limited value in the treatment of what ails Type E women. Ten minutes a day of deep breathing as the *only* way of dealing with the stress in a Type E woman's life is woefully inadequate. In fact, many women admit to having a strong resistance to the passive approach. The "letting go" relaxation emphasis is apparently too reminiscent of women's historically based fears of helplessness and passivity. Still, as we will see, there is a value to passive relaxation in alleviating Type E stress, but active coping skills are necessary as well.

Conquering Type E stress does not require forfeiting a full and complex life that is enriched by the multiple roles a high-achieving woman plays. Nor does it mean giving up the positive drive and energy that fuel the engine of achievement motivation. But learning to reduce and manage Type E stress does require a reexamination and reevaluation of the behaviors and reaction patterns that are considered necessary to fulfill those multiple roles satisfactorily.

Getting a grip on your stress problem requires learning and implementing a new set of behaviors, and it requires working on your head in order to straighten out anxiety-laden, unresolved issues, self-esteem problems, and erroneous, self-defeating ways of thinking.

This chapter details ten exercises for learning new coping behaviors. Together, these exercises and tactics for their implementation constitute a behavioral armory for assaulting your own stress cycle. The emphasis here is not passive; it is an active fight-back approach. Type E women need a strong, assertive strategy for regaining control of their lives.

HOW TO READ AND USE THIS CHAPTER

I can almost imagine your reaction at this point. "Just what I need. Ten more things to do!"

The short answer to this objection is a resounding "Yes." You *do* have some new skills to learn and develop. You have some tactics to formulate for keeping the demands of your life from overwhelming you.

But you won't be doing all the exercises at once or in timed sequence. And you don't need to worry about how to do the exercises, or in what order to do them, or when to implement them in your daily routine. This will all be spelled out for you.

Each exercise is focused on a specific target behavior problem. Then the exercise process itself is explained in clear, step-by-step instructions. Third, specific how-to recommendations for implementing the exercise as a workable coping skill in your daily life are provided.

In the next chapter, the stress of deciding when to do the exercises or how to get on a behavior modification program will be alleviated. A 21-Day Program—a mental workout—for changing Type E patterns and building stress resistance is provided.

All you need to do now is make one choice: You can continue trying to be everything to everybody (for as long as you can last), or you can make some changes in the direction of self-preservation, enhanced quality of life, and lower stress.

Doing something about your stress problem is like doing something about your weight. Reading all the diet books in the world won't help you to shed a pound if you don't follow the diet *behaviorally* on a day-to-day basis. Reading workout books won't help you tone an inch if all the exercise you really get is turning the pages.

What follows is a stress-reduction diet and mental workout program that works for Type E women. If you stick with the program, you'll reap the benefits.

I recommend that you read through the remainder of the chapter for content and approach before you actually begin doing any one exercise. Then proceed to Chapter 11 for the full 21-Day Mental Workout program.

EXERCISES FOR LEARNING BETTER COPING SKILLS

Exercise 1:
Redefining Role Requirements

Focus: The purpose of this exercise is to examine your various roles from the perspective of the actual behaviors that each role encompasses. The issue here is that Type E women simply try to do too much themselves. They are poor delegators, in part because they are often not sure which behaviors are appropriate to delegate.

High-achieving women are concerned with excellence in all their roles. The dilemma lies in the arithmetic of adding up all the activities and behaviors that could be said to encompass or define the role "wife," for example, or "businesswoman" or "professional woman" or "mother." Then throw in, for good measure, the list of behaviors that comprise the roles of "friend," "community member," or "girlfriend/lover." A clear picture begins to emerge of an impossible calculus. How can one woman, no matter how energetic and talented, do all these behaviors herself?

The answer: She can't. And she shouldn't even try. But what can she do, given that she has chosen not only to define her life by multiple roles but to excel in each of those roles to boot?

The Type E woman needs to redefine the set of behaviors that she *herself* must actually do in order to satisfy her own standards for fulfillment and excellence in her various roles. And at the same time, she needs to decide which behaviors that may traditionally or conventionally be assigned to a certain role can be effectively delegated.

Exercise Process: Begin by making a list of all the roles that comprise your life. Then, using a separate piece of paper for each role, make a list going down the left side of the page of the behaviors that comprise the role.

To the right of your list, divide the sheet into three columns labeled, respectively, "Must do myself," "Can delegate with supervision," and "Can delegate completely."

Now go through the lists of behaviors asking yourself whether you actually need, or want, to do the behavior yourself in order to feel satisfied that the task has been accomplished. Your goal is to reduce the amount of activities you actually do with your own time and resources, thereby focusing your energies on those tasks that are most clearly related to making you feel successful in your role.

For those tasks that you are able to assign to the second column—Can delegate with supervision—a certain amount of your own resources will be diverted merely by virtue of the required supervision. Where it is possible to delegate completely (column three), the task will be turned over to someone else and your responsibility will be relinquished.

This exercise is the first step toward a delegation system that will assist you in getting the amount of demands that arise from multiple and competing roles under manageable control.

Implementation: In order to build delegation into your life, you must first give up the compulsion—or more accurately, the illusion—of maintaining control and quality standards by doing everything yourself. Then implementation of this exercise requires turning over the appropriate tasks in column three to the selected delegates, with clear communication as to the fact that the task is expected to be *entirely* their responsibility. To benefit from complete delegation, you must remove yourself from all further involvement.

If total removal is not possible, keep supervision to a minimum. Answer questions when required, check on behavior as necessary, but remember to give the person to whom you have delegated the task enough independence and autonomy to make his/her own mistakes and to learn by doing so. Patience is a mandatory virtue if you are going to turn over to someone else things that you are accustomed to doing *your* way. Bear in mind that the effective manager is someone who makes sure that the work gets done, not someone who does everything herself. As the stress manager of your own life, keep the appropriate distance from those to whom you delegate. Guard against the tendencies to nag, oversupervise, assume too much responsibility or control, or criticize.

In delegating tasks to others, don't apologize. Too often, Type E women feel compelled to explain why they are not able to do everything themselves, as if they somehow *should* be able to do so. Simply state your requests or instructions clearly and respectfully. Expressions of gratitude, appreciation, or reinforcement are appropriate, in general, after the task has been completed.

Exercise 2:
Rank-Ordering for Prioritizing Activities

Focus: One of the most common sources of Type E stress is an unorganized, cacophonous stream of demands that tax the finite supply of time in a woman's life. The problematic Type E behavior that is targeted for change in this exercise is the creation of unprioritized "To Do" lists.

Failing to set priorities and concentrate your energies can result in a subjective sense of fragmentation, "running around in circles," or "not knowing where to turn or what to do first." The perception of too much to do in too little time is the essence of stress. The correction lies in applying a tactical method for putting the "things to do" list in priority order.

Exercise Process: Begin by making a list of *everything* that you feel you *must* do today as well as things that you *want* to do.

Now force yourself to put the list in rank order, with number one being the activity that will have the worst consequences if you don't do it *today*. Assign the rank of "two" to the task or activity that will have the next worst consequences for noncompletion. Continue until you have a fully ordered list. Every activity must have a number.

Implementation: Once you have ranked the list of things to do in order of importance, you will no longer feel like you are fragmented or running hither and yon trying to decide what to do first. You will *know* what to do first: number one. Concentrate your attention and energy on accomplishing *only* the first thing on the list. Turn your attention to number two *only* after you have completed task number one, or gone as far as possible for that day.

Type E women are notorious for Herculean "To Do" lists. These lists typically reflect the excessive burdens they place on themselves and the erroneous thinking that sets them up to feel like they're not accomplishing enough.

Using the prioritizing technique, do as many of the tasks *in order* as is possible in one day without pushing yourself to the point of exhaustion. As a rule of thumb, if you can accomplish the three to five most pressing things on your list, you will have put a comfortable enough buffer between your list and the consequences of not getting something done to sleep easily at night. In other words, by rank-ordering according to a standard of priority for things that will cause more stress if they are not accomplished, you will have set up a system for acting on and removing a finite but important number of stressors each day.

Make the list a rotating and continually updated tactic for managing the demands of your life. Cross off the things you accomplish. The next day, create a new list according to the same criterion for assessing how bad or serious the consequences will be for *not* doing the task or activity.

Another implementation of this exercise is to transfer completed items from the "To Do" list to a list of accomplishments. Make the second list a compiled account of all the important things that you did during the period of one week. At the end of the week, look over the list and reward yourself for how much you got done, and how efficiently you ordered the stream of demands and kept the stressful consequences of letting things pile up to a minimum.

Exercise 3:
Creating and Rehearsing "No" Scripts

Focus: As I have discussed throughout this book, Type E stress is characterized by taking on more than you can do and acceding to an unrealistic number of demands from others.

The central problem or target behavior is the inability or reticence to deny a request or need of another. Conditioned to take care of others, women are often uncomfortable setting limits on their own capacity or resources for nurturance.

In a word, the problem boils down to the inability to just plain say "No."

The purpose of this exercise is literally to learn *how* to say "No." More specifically, the exercise is designed to teach you to create "No" scripts, to turn

down requests or demands in ways that sound acceptable to your ear. Many women, for example, fear that
a refusal of a request or demand will be interpreted as
hostility, or they may be wary of their real resentment
showing through, so they say nothing at all and meekly
comply. And the resentment, of course, compounds.

Managing Type E stress means learning effective
tactics for filtering the stream of demands and selecting channels in which to direct time, energy, effort,
and attention. This process requires, therefore, the
verbal skills to communicate the decision not to act,
and the technique to implement that decision accordingly. To reduce the unregulated outflow of energy,
Type E women must learn to control the rate and
intensity of demands verbally.

To most Type E women, the phrases that verbally
convey denial, refusal, rejection, withdrawal, inacces-
sibility, or simply a negative response do not come
easily. They are speaking a foreign language. Type E
women lack a facile or effective vocabulary for protecting themselves against the onslaught of demands
on, or expectations of, their resources.

The problem is often compounded by the source of
the demand or request. It is especially difficult to deny
the needs, requests, or expectations of people whom
you love and need; it is risky and problematic to say
"No" to individuals who are superiors and who therefore wield control of your career.

But the risks of *not* saying "No"—in the most diplo-
matic, appropriate, and effective manner—have a
steeper and more dire downside slope. Not saying
"No" to some of the people some of the time is a
setup for failure. You will necessarily fail in trying to
be Superwoman for an extended period of time, so
learning how to say "No" sometimes is necessary if
you are to reach your most important achievement goals.

This exercise is designed directly to build the verbal
and nonverbal skills for saying "No" effectively.

Exercise Process: Begin by making a list of five to ten people in your life who are the sources of demands (needs, expectations, requests, and so on) on your time and energy. Write out some typical examples of the stressful requests or expectations from each of them.

For each person on the list, write a script of how you could say "No" to his/her request or expectation. For example, you might say, "I'd love to be able to help you out, but I won't be able to today," or perhaps, "I don't have time to do that for you, but I can help you figure out some other way to get it done," or even, "No, I'm sorry; I wish I could, but I can't."

You can, of course, use the same responses for different people if that feels appropriate. The purpose of writing different scripts for different sources is to emphasize the tone or emotional shading of your response. You would, for example, say "No" very differently to your four-year-old than you would to your boss. By the same token, it is appropriate to use humor with some people; others require the essence of solemnity and tact. Shape your responses accordingly.

The best way to practice these scripts is with a tape recorder, but a mirror or a good friend will do nicely. Say the phrases, imagining the scene. Listen carefully: Do you sound apologetic? Aggressive? Defensive? Reasonable? Persuasive? Assertive?

Decide how you *want* to sound to each of the sources. Work on being assertive—but not aggressive—when you say "No."

Implementation: The criteria for saying "No" for Type E women is twofold. In some cases, both criteria will apply; in others, one or the other will be mostly or exclusively applicable.

The first decision criterion is your ability to comply with the request. Sometimes the constraints of reality prevent you from saying "Yes."

The second criterion is choice. You may be able to

fit the activity into your schedule, but the fact of the matter is that you don't *want* to do it. That's your perfect right. You may, however, choose to do the behavior in spite of the fact that you don't want to, perhaps because of a sense of responsibility or even moral obligation.

But sometimes the reason for acquiescing to requests, invitations, suggestions, or demands is no more compelling than wanting to "look like a nice person," "not wanting to seem mean or rude," or "not wanting to hurt someone's feelings." The point is that Type E women frequently sacrifice their precious time doing things that they don't have to do and don't want to do merely because they do not readily and forthrightly say "No."

In order to do many things well, a high-achieving woman must exercise her prerogative to filter requests and allocate her time and energy according to her values and preferences. Learning how to say "No," by mechanically beginning with scripts and advancing to the level of natural and effective communication, will go a long way toward interrupting the Type E stress cycle.

Exercise 4:
Pleasurable Activities Schedule

Focus: Type E women, as a group, do more things in a day that are unpleasurable or obligatory than they do pleasurable things. This simple observation accounts for their feeling subjectively stressed, tired, and periodically depressed. Burdened by responsibilities and obligations, most Type E women have lost the art of playing.

Raising the proportion of pleasurable activities relative to unpleasurable or mandatory activities has demonstrable value in the short-term treatment and amelioration of depression. Since depression is one of the most common psychological disorders that arise from excessive negative stress, the application of a simple pleasurable activities regimen as a treatment for Type E stress is often highly effective.

The purpose of this exercise is to build stress resistance by altering your mood, raising it to a more pleasurable plateau. Depression or great sadness, and the sensation of subjective stress and pressure—two psychologically uncomfortable and even painful states—feed on each other. When you are depressed or "down," things that might otherwise merely graze your ego can demolish your self-esteem and blow your stress level sky high. For example, many Type E women experience elevations in their stress level during the premenstrual days of their cycle when PMS-induced depression may color their thinking and responses. And conversely, chronic stress will erode the best of moods and the happiest of spirits if left unchecked. Then depressed mood states creep in and insidiously inject conflict, irritability, or hostility into life's "good times."

Stress and depression are inextricably interwoven. As mentioned earlier, however, vicious cycles can be broken by interrupting the connections: Attack the negative or depressed mood and the underlying stress will be positively affected.

This exercise is emphatically *not* a thorough or sufficient treatment for clinical depression, which requires competent professional help, and sometimes antidepressant drug therapy. But low or depressed mood states that often arise or result from chronic Type E stress can be substantially improved by building pleasurable activities daily into your schedule that is otherwise overcrowded with obligatory and unpleasant jobs.

Exercise Process: Often, when I tell stressed and depressed patients that I want them to start doing two pleasurable activities every day as an antidote to what ails them, they are not only dumbfounded by the sheer simplicity of the approach, but they are also frequently stumped.

"I can't even think of anything that I really like to do," one flattened-out Type E woman responded.

So the first step in this process is to construct a pleasurable activities list. The minimum number of items on your list is *fifteen*. There is no maximum number—you can never think of too many ways to have fun.

Write down things that make you—or would probably make you—feel happy, relaxed, peaceful, mellow, pleasantly stimulated, excited, playful, and so on. Next to each item, note the approximate amount of time required, and whether any advance plans or preparations are necessary.

The pleasurable activities on your list don't have to be exotic, erotic, immoral, fattening, complicated, or time-consuming. They can include simple things like reading a magazine, taking a hot bath, listening to music, watching television, going to a movie, or just looking at the moon and stars, watching people, children, or animals play, or smelling and admiring flowers. Of course, depending on your schedule and budget, your activities might include going to plays, concerts, or other live events, or even going on short weekend trips out of town, or longer vacations.

Include things that you used to enjoy but never seem to have or *make* the time to do anymore: shopping or browsing, a day at the zoo or a museum, lunch at a favorite restaurant, a game of tennis or racquetball, a walk. The list can be endless.

One pleasurable activity that is popular among my Type E patients is something I call "refoxing"—buying some new clothes, getting a new haircut, a manicure, pedicure, and facial, and so on. Refoxification can rejuvenate the faded feminine soul of a stressed-out Type E woman.

You don't have to do the activities alone. By all

means ask a friend, husband, boyfriend, or someone else to join you—provided the inclusion of others enhance the quality of the experience *for you*.

The most important thing about your pleasurable activities list is that it be extensive and varied. Make sure that the list is adaptable to your busy life. Weekends generally allow for more time-consuming activities, whereas your weekday regimen is likely to require pleasurable activities that require mere moments. If your list is creative, varied with respect to time and complexity of the activities, and highly tailored to what *you* really enjoy or want to do, there will be absolutely no acceptable excuses for not fulfilling your pleasurable activities assignment every day.

You'll be amazed at the positive difference just being aware of and including pleasurable activities intentionally and deliberately in your life makes on your mood and overall stress level.

Implementation: Do two pleasurable activities from your list *every* day. Some people choose two behaviors for the next day on the evening before; some like to wait until they begin to feel stressed or low before they turn to their lists and select the "right" activity for the moment. The critical thing is to *do* two pleasurable activities per day. This is the Type E woman's replacement for the old "apple-a-day" saw: Two pleasurable activities a day help keep stress and depression away.

The reasons that doing pleasurable activities has a positive effect on mood are both obvious and complex. On the surface, doing things that are fun or relaxing ought to make you feel better. This is the kind of psychology wise grandmothers promulgated. And they were right. If you're feeling bad, do something that makes you feel good—airtight logic. The problem is that it's exactly when you feel down or depressed that you normally lack the energy or enthusiasm for doing *anything,* let alone anything pleasurable.

But that is exactly when you should force yourself to act. Depression can be enervating, vegetative, even paralyzing. But these debilitating effects can be counteracted, at least partially, by the benefits of activity, especially pleasurable activity.

There are a number of theories to account for why activity has a beneficial effect on depression and stress. One is that activity in general, and pleasurable activities in particular, involve the release of brain chemicals, including endorphins and encephalons, that are natural painkillers and mood elevators.

Another theory is that pleasurable activities relieve depression and stress through distraction. By diverting attention from negative or stressful thoughts your mood can be temporarily improved. And perhaps the distractions then have a cumulative effect so that spending time on pleasurable activities adds up, leaving less time available for negative thinking.

Another explanation for the salutary effects of exercise and activity on stress levels generally is that activation of one system—the physical—functions to relax the other—in this case, the mental. In more concrete terms, a good workout or vigorous tennis match may be more beneficial in reducing stress after a solid day of intense mental concentration and productivity than a nap might be. Use this relationship between system activations to balance *active* and *passive*, *physical* and *mental*, pleasurable activities with the kinds of stressors that characterize your days.

The key implementation of this exercise is to include, by intention, at least two pleasurable activities a day, and watch your stress level come down as your mood improves.

Exercise 5:
Brainstorming and Problem-Solving Sessions

Focus: One of the most common and dangerous effects of stress on the quality of decision making is something psychologists call "premature closure." Under conditions of stress, people tend to close off the process of searching for alternative solutions to problems after coming up with only the most obvious ideas.

Generally, problems have more than just a few solutions, though some may be impractical, undesirable, or just plain novel. But when you fail to see alternatives, your stress level is aggravated by the perception that you are "trapped" or that you have "no way out" of your present situation or behavioral cycle.

The purpose of this exercise is to train you in the process of brainstorming solutions to problems in your personal and/or career life. Unresolved problems are significant sources of chronic stress. Even seemingly "small" problems can erode your sense of well-being and lower your resistance to stress. Life's big problems, of course, are the stressful events that make up the human condition.

But the stress that arises from any problem, large or small, is best handled by seeking and implementing a viable solution through a process of vigilant decision making.

Paradoxically, some of the "solutions" offered in this book may present new problems for Type E women. For example, recognizing the wisdom and value of delegation may raise new questions regarding to whom one can and should delegate certain responsibilities. This exercise is focused on learning an active, effective method for problem solving.

Exercise Process: The first step in the problem-solving process is, of course, to identify the problem. Select any specific issue that is contributing to your current stress level. Perhaps it is a problem with somebody or something at work; perhaps there is a household issue to work out with the family, or a conversation to be had with a boyfriend. Maybe financial responsibilities are breathing down your neck.

Whatever the problem, large or small, write a few sentences or a short paragraph to define the issue clearly.

The next step is critical to counteracting the tendency of people under stress to close off the alternative search process prematurely. As a Type E woman, assume that your tendency is to do just that. The correction for this premature closure tendency is to engage in a brainstorming session, either by yourself, with your spouse, a trusted friend, or any supportive person whose input you value.

The purpose of the brainstorming session is to come up with every possible solution to the problem. The only limits are your creativity, your ingenuity, and your imagination.

Don't limit yourself to "reasonable" or "acceptable" solutions. Sometimes ideas that seem at first to be undesirable or impossible become the preference after a thorough, vigilant decision-making process has taken place. Remember to include the alternatives of "doing nothing," since that stance represents a decision itself, or to keep on doing what you are already doing, since this, too, is a possible solution.

When you are satisfied that you have identified every alternative, stop; turn your attention to the next phase, the decision-making process itself.

Vigilant decision making requires that you now commit yourself to one of the solutions that you have identified. After a careful, deliberate process of information-gathering and weighing of pros and cons, *decide to decide*.

Take each identified alternative one at a time. Evaluate the costs and benefits of each. Decide if you need more information and/or whether there is sufficient time or the possibility of gathering such information.

After you have considered each alternative—reassured that your list represents the product of a thorough brainstorming session—make a reasoned choice. There may be a clearly preferable alternative. In many cases, however, problems, by their very nature, are amenable either to few solutions, or to solutions that involve considerable downside costs.

But keep in mind that unresolved problems are fertile breeding grounds in which stress-related illnesses and other problems incubate and eventually hatch. You are better off selecting and implementing the most desirable or, if necessary, the least undesirable alternative, than letting the problem linger to fester and burrow deeper.

Implementation: There is an old Japanese proverb: "To know and not to act is not to know at all." Clearly, problems are solved by *implementing* the solutions, not just by *knowing* what to do. However, *knowing* (through the process of vigilant decision making detailed above) *will* go a certain portion of the way toward bringing down your stress level.

The skills of identifying the problem, brainstorming alternative solutions, collecting information, weighing pros and cons, selecting, and implementing a solution are invaluable coping skills for Type E women.

Whenever problems start to "close in" and you feel stressed to find an answer, use the brainstorming and problem-solving techniques to manage your problems more efficiently and effectively.

And don't forget to reassess the situation periodically. Is the solution that you implemented working successfully? Does the plan require some fine tuning? Periodic assessments help you to do what politicians and managers call "mid-course corrections" in order to respond to the fluid nature of most real problem situations.

Exercise 6:
Stress Desensitization via
Guided Imagery and Relaxation

Focus: The purpose of this exercise is to reduce the intensity of anxiety reactions associated with stressful experiences. Our minds, the way we talk to ourselves, our cognitive tapes, the images we conjure, and the associations we connect all have an enormous impact on the level of subjective stress that we experience.

Before the occurrence of an event that you anticipate will be difficult, unpleasant, anxiety-producing, or otherwise stressful, your body begins reacting. As you approach the dread day of the event in question—be it a meeting with your boss, a confrontation with a difficult client, a candid tête-à-tête with your husband or boyfriend about the state or status of your relationship—your mind begins rehearsing the scene.

And as the images are conjured—consciously or unconsciously, in states of awareness or in dreams—the body's stress reactions become cumulative. That is why you may feel exhausted and "stressed out" on the morning *before* an important meeting. Your mind has gone over the event innumerable times, and with each rehearsal the stress reaction is being conditioned to the upcoming experience. This, of course, becomes a vicious cycle itself as the stress reactions create even greater mental worry, which, in turn, exacerbates the stress.

Instead of being victimized by your mind's undirected worry, you can apply your mental capacities to *reduce* the amount of stress that can accumulate as you approach an event.

It is an established principle of behavioral conditioning that two incongruous responses—such as anxiety and relaxation—cannot occur simultaneously. So this mental exercise associates the relaxation response with the mental imagery of the anticipated event. By substituting the relaxation response for the anxiety or stress reaction, while thinking about the experience, the mind-body connections are rewired. In other words, you will "desensitize" the conditioned reaction of anxiety and stress whenever you think about the event, and replace the arousal reaction with a more adaptive relaxation or calming response.

Exercise Process: The first step in this process is to learn a rhythmic breathing, relaxation technique. There are several versions of this technique, known by several names—deep muscle relaxation, self-hypnosis, deep breathing, autogenics, and so on. The quickest, easiest and, I believe, best instruction on the technique is in Dr. Herbert Benson's book, *The Relaxation Response.*[1]

The important point is not to burden yourself with the pressure of *mastering* yogic breathing or perfectly controlled biofeedback. The requirement is simply to discipline yourself enough to lie down in a quiet place for five or ten minutes and, without trying too hard, "let go" and relax your muscles. Imagining your arms and legs feeling heavy and warm is helpful for inducing relaxation.

While you relax your muscles, regulate your breathing so that you inhale through your nose, inflating your diaphragm as you do so, and exhale through your mouth. You can learn to monitor this technique by placing one hand on your diaphragm (just above your stomach) and feeling it rise and fall as you inhale through your nose and exhale through your mouth. Many people find that imagining the rhythmic motion of the ocean's waves gently washing up on shore and lazily rolling back to sea is evocative and effective in promoting the proper rhythmic breathing.

Don't try to be perfect about relaxing. In fact, the harder you try on this exercise, the less successful you're likely to be. Your muscles know how to relax, even though you may think that *you* don't. It's a matter of gaining conscious control over the response and letting your body instinctively release its tension.

With practice, you will be able to develop your own version of a "relaxation response." Some women put on headphones and relax to music; some close their eyes and think about how good it feels to let the tension flow out of their bodies. Others focus on a meditation word using slow and rhythmic breathing.

Having learned a relaxation response, you're already ahead of the stress game. But now we will actively apply the relaxation behavior to desensitize and reduce the stress reactions created by difficult interpersonal or other tense situations.

Desensitization always begins with adopting the relaxation posture that you have learned, and giving yourself a few minutes to get into the relaxed mode. Practice your relaxation response for five to ten minutes. Then, when you feel relaxed, apply your mental imagery capacities to conjure the picture of the scene you are anticipating. If, for example, you are worried about an upcoming important meeting with a business associate, envision yourself walking into the meeting. What are you wearing? What do you say? Can you see yourself looking confident and calm? Try to envision the best and worst things that could happen.

Now check on your relaxation state. Are you still relaxed and breathing rhythmically? If so, you have successfully paired a relaxation response with the imagery of an impending stressful event.

But if you begin to feel anxious, stop imagining the scene and refocus your consciousness on relaxing your muscles and breathing deeply. Continue until you feel relaxed once again.

Then repeat the imagery while seeking to maintain your relaxed posture and breathing. With repetition, you will eventually be able to think about the scene or imagine yourself in the event and remain relaxed. Desensitization is a powerful technique, one that is well worth the time and discipline required to learn it.

Implementation: The techniques of stress desensitization, guided imagery, and relaxation are among the most effective tools in the psychologist's armory for behavior modification of anxiety and stress reactions. Use them to desensitize your stress response to any work-related or personal situations about which you feel anxious.

Remember, you don't have to do the technique perfectly. Nor should you expect miracle cures. If the technique gives you a break from the dis-stress cycle, you've accomplished your purpose. If the guided imagery with relaxation work successfully to reduce—not necessarily eliminate—your stress level, you have reached your goal.

Be realistic. Difficult situations in your work or personal life are likely to continue to cause a certain degree of anxiety, stress, and arousal. That is appropriate when the situation is indeed one that could have important or valuable consequences to you. Don't aim toward eliminating stress completely or toward trying to react like you're not reacting at all. That would be unnatural and unrealistic. Your purpose in implementing these techniques is to use better coping skills to handle the cumulative effects of stress that can build as you mentally rehearse and approach a difficult situation. Your goal is to keep stress contained within optimal boundaries so that you are aroused enough to do a good job, but not so overaroused as to interfere with your own performance.

Exercise 7:
Stress Inoculation via
Role-Playing and Script Rehearsal

Focus: Like Exercise 6, this exercise focuses on situational problems that are particularly stressful for

Type E women. The specific target problems include communication about delegation of responsibility, negotiation of deadlines, and asking for assistance or support. These three areas of communication skills are essential for Type E women to develop and refine if they are to reduce the avalanche of demands on their limited time schedules.

The rationale behind this inoculation exercise process is analogous to medicine. In medicine, an inoculation involves giving the patient a small, benign amount of a potentially dangerous virus or bacteria, thereby stimulating the production of the body's natural immune antibodies. In this way, the person is said to be inoculated against the ravages of the disease.

In *stress inoculation,* a "small dose" of the stressful event is presented in the form of a role-playing exercise with a trusted friend or partner in a neutral, comfortable setting. By practicing the verbal skills required to delegate, seek support, or negotiate a deadline extension effectively, you will build psychological resistance to the stress associated with these necessary coping behaviors.

Exercise Process: The first step in this exercise is creating scripts. On one sheet of paper, write three to five "lines" of dialogue that would be appropriate if you were delegating a job or responsibility to another person. Work on making the lines clear and free of apology. Make certain that the point is unmistakable that when you are delegating responsibility, you mean just that: You will no longer assume responsibility for the decision making or implementation of the task. Devise delegation scripts that most clearly and effectively communicate your intention. Write some for work, some for home, some for your organizational work, and so on.

Now write a set of scripts titled "negotiating deadlines." Too often, the Type E woman responds to requests or deadlines from family and/or employers and others as if the requests were immutable, as if she had no input or control of the process that structures her time or expenditure of resources. Write some scripts that try to "buy time," or that get a reading on how much of a priority a particular project really is.

Finally, write three to five scripted lines requesting support—emotional, work-related, financial, or whatever form of assistance that you might need. As you will recall from the chapter on excessive self-reliance, Type E women are not skilled at asking for what they need; instead, they tend to defend against needing anything from anyone as a way of avoiding vulnerability. As we have seen, however, the strategy generally backfires, and the stress of being overly self-reliant is burdensome and undesirable.

The second step of the exercise involves role-playing. You will need a friend, coworker, or your husband or boyfriend to participate. The criteria for choosing a role-playing partner are (a) that you feel comfortable, relaxed, and safe in his/her presence; and (b) that the person understands the purpose and value of the exercise and is willing to participate in earnest.

Together, create scenarios of situations in which you would use one of your scripted lines. Perhaps you want to rehearse delegation scripts. Your partner might play the role of a secretary, housekeeper, child, mother's helper, fellow employee, and so on.

Rehearse your scripts until the lines feel natural and you can say them without feeling unduly aroused, angry, or stressed. Ask your role-playing partner (with your guidance) to respond in some ways that you predict are likely or possible. Role-play what you would say to a resistant delegate; practice how to respond to a rigid superior about an unachievable, unrealistic deadline; ask your spouse for the *sharing* of responsibility that you really need.

The purpose of the exercise is to practice delegation, negotiation, and requesting support in a context that is relatively safe and relaxing. If you role-play with your husband or boyfriend in the comfort of your own living room a negotiation script designed for your boss, you will not be exposed to the physical cues of your boss's office that may increase arousal levels. So role-playing in a safe, relaxed context is a form of desensitization, since the stressful communication is associated with a pleasant environment. And the repeated exposure to the scripts will inoculate you against an intense stress reaction when the actual opportunities arise for implementing the scripts.

Ask your role-playing partner to critique both your lines and your delivery. Practice until you have removed any notes of apology or defensiveness from your voice or words; rehearse your lines so that they sound natural; check your intonations for shades of complaining or whining. Ask your partner to describe what effect your words and tone have on her/his feelings, thoughts, and reactions.

Implementation: The coping skills of delegation, negotiation, and requesting support are the basis of the proactive approach to stress management. These skills allow you to act on your environment by organizing, limiting, and reallocating your resources.

Obviously, to be maximally effective you must implement the scripts in the form of actual conversation in real settings. Role-playing is not a substitute for action in reality. But the exercise will make the real-life implementation far easier and smoother. The effort you expend making your communications as "clean" and straightforward as possible—without detracting apologies, aggressiveness, defensiveness, and so on—will increase the effectiveness of these coping skills.

Exercise 8:
Talking Yourself Down

Focus: Anybody who has ever witnessed a masterful nursery school teacher at work calming down a hysterical child, or a skilled psychiatrist or psychologist quieting an agitated patient merely by speaking calmly and logically, has seen the powerful effect of words. Language hath charms to soothe the savage mind.

As I noted earlier, Type E stress can be compounded by dysfunctional ways of talking to yourself that only serve to keep you aroused, to replay the upsetting event, and to distract your energy and attention from effective problem solving. Since stress incubates where problems remain unsolved, negative ways of talking to yourself that interfere with adaptive problem solving are a surefire method for perpetuating the stress cycle.

Or language and self-talk can be used as a potent method for interrupting the stress cycle and focusing on adaptive problem solving. All you need to do is assume the attitude that when stress hits, you can be your own best ally by calming yourself down instead of riling yourself up further.

The purpose of this exercise is to train you to monitor the internal monologues or tapes that play in your head as stress strikes. It is similar to the sentence-completion exercise in Chapter 8, only now you will be more freely recording your stressful thoughts flawed by cognitive errors. Making your self-talk explicit by writing it down permits you to evaluate your thinking analytically in order to clean up errors, distortions, exaggerations, and other aspects that perpetuate the Type E process, and to substitute more rational ways of talking to yourself that reduce stress and promote better coping.

Exercise Process: Keep a journal of your self-talk when you feel stressed. Divide a sheet of paper into two columns. At the top of one, write "Stressful Thoughts," and at the top of the other, write "Corrective Responses." In the "Stressful Thoughts" column, write your uncensored thoughts about your situation, mood, or feelings at the present time. Make as accurate a written record as possible of what you are saying to yourself.

After you have decoded your internal self-talk into journal format, you can systematically examine the stream of thought for evidence of faulty reasoning, exaggeration, erroneous expectations, and the like. Are you labeling yourself and overemphasizing your shortcomings and mistakes to the exclusion of your strong points and successes? Perhaps your thinking is polarized, cast in unrealistically framed, extreme language. "This is the worst thing I've ever done," "I'm going crazy, I'm coming apart," and "There's no way out of this catastrophe" are common examples of stressful, erroneous thinking. Type E women tend to talk themselves "up" into further stress, rather than to talk themselves down.

After you have examined your journal of self-talk under conditions of feeling stressed, your next step is to engage in a constructive dialogue with yourself. In the "Corrective Response" column, respond to each erroneous thought by writing a more rational, less polarized, less dramatized, nonexaggerated statement. In short, write down the sentences that will "talk you down."

Reformulating your self-talk in language that is more accurate and less emotionally loaded will interrupt the stress cycle. Your rational responses should be aimed at problem-solving whenever possible. Sometimes, though, your rational response might just be corrections of your uncensored, automatic thoughts.

For example, you might write as a corrective response, "This is an unfortunate turn of events, but it's not the worst thing that ever happened. Now that I accept that this has happened, what can I do about it?" Or your rational response might be self-protective in the sense that it defends against your own uncontrolled self-talk's name-calling. "I'm not an incompetent bimbo. I'm a busy woman who made a mistake that can be corrected."

Implementation: Recall that the techniques of writing down your uncensored automatic thoughts, identifying the errors, and designing corrective responses are the key methods in Cognitive Therapy. These techniques have application to managing not only stress reactions, but also mood swings or even extreme anxiety states, including phobias. Accessing your internal "tapes" and "cleaning" them by correcting maladaptive and self-defeating thinking are important coping skills for Type E women to practice and master. Eventually, the process of internal monitoring will become second nature, so that incipient stress reactions will automatically trigger your careful scrutiny.

Exercise 9:
Mental Minivacations

Focus: This exercise is targeted at the most common and debilitating symptoms of chronic stress: physiological overarousal, mental and physical fatigue, fragmented concentration, and depressed or flattened mood state.

Because Type E women have overcrowded schedules and multiple goals and ambitions, they often have overcrowded minds, too. There are so many things to do or to keep track of that concentration can become diluted, fragmented, or blunted. Obviously, the damaging effects of chronic overarousal on concentration are dangerous when considered in light of their threat to work productivity and quality. It is exceedingly frustrating to be the victim of a wandering mind when you're attempting to muster your discipline and concentration for a specific task, especially when you're working under a deadline.

One purpose of Exercise 9 is to improve and increase conscious control and discipline over your mind's concentration and direction. Paradoxically, the exercise trains you to regain control of concentration by intentionally letting your mind wander, by using your extraordinary powers of imagery to take yourself on a mental minivacation.

The second purpose is to learn to integrate short periods of relaxation, rest, and rejuvenation into your day.

To be effective, mental minivacations require commitment, creativity, and practice. For your efforts, you will possess a precious coping skill for interrupting the Type E cycle.

Any doctor will tell you that taking vacations and naps is good for your health. But in realistic terms, both are often unhealthy or unfeasible for your pocketbook or schedule.

However, there is a ten-minute period during each day that you *can* set aside to take a vacation in your mind. Make it a priority. Use this exercise selectively to refresh your overworked mind, depending on the nature of your feelings at the time that you begin your imagery work.

Do you feel nervous, agitated, overwrought? If so, the right "vacation" for you is one that is associated with feelings of serenity, peacefulness, and calm.

On the other hand, your mental symptoms may be more like burnout—low energy, boredom, fatigue, flatness. The right prescription is a mental minivacation associated with experiences of exhilaration, revitalization, motivation, and euphoria.

Or stress might be making you feel anxious, insecure, unconfident, or threatened in some pervasive but perhaps indescribable or inexplicable way. The needed mental imagery here is associated with feelings of comfort, reassurance, security, and safety.

Imagery is a powerful, almost magical, mental coping skill. Tangible, positive alterations in blood pressure, muscle tension, and even brain waves have been demonstrated to respond to the mind's images. Many Olympic athletes, especially Russians and Italians, rely heavily on imagery as an integral part of their training programs: They *see* themselves beating a record or winning a race. The positive consequences are impressive.

In a similar vein, you can recondition your mind and body to deal better with the inevitable stress of your complicated life. Mental minivacations can and should be used daily (or more often, time permitting) to alter the over-arousal cycle and allow you to call "Time Out" for yourself.

Exercise Process: The first step is to write three scenarios, each designed to elicit a specific set of feelings. First, write a description of a setting, place, person, or sensory experience—from memory or pure imagination—that you associate with feelings of serenity, peacefulness, and calm. Perhaps you see yourself on a sailboat. Maybe you envision the lush green expanse of a park or meadow. Or your image might be of a place you treasured as a child because of its tranquility.

Make your scenario individually tailored to you—to your personality, your fantasies, your personal history and experiences, your responses. In your mind you can go anyplace and do anything. Whatever comes to your mind is legitimate and valid for our purposes. This exercise is imagery, not action. It is private and personal, for your mind only.

Second, being as free, creative, and inspired as possible, write a scenario describing yourself doing something that you associate with feelings of exhilaration, revitalization, motivation, or euphoria. Are you galloping on horseback along the surf? Is it a sexual image or fantasy? How about snow or water skiing? Or going on a great adventure? Conjure your own personalized image of something that makes you feel "pumped up."

Third, imagine and write in descriptive detail a setting or sensory experience that you associate with sensations of comfort, reassurance, security, and safety. This time the image might be the warmth of a cozy bed with a goosedown comforter and a glowing fireplace. Of course, you don't have to be solo in these movies; include whomever you want in your fantasies. Maybe you see yourself on a beach soaking up the sun's warm, reassuring rays. Again, whatever makes you feel sensations of comfort, reassurance, security, and safety is what your scenario should embody.

The next step is to record your scenarios onto a cassette tape. Read each scenario relatively slowly, trying to use the appropriate feeling and intonation in your voice. Just do this recording as well as you can; don't try to be perfect or mesmerizing. And do overlook the oddity of hearing your own voice on tape. This is jarring to almost everyone. It doesn't matter how you sound. The purpose of the tape is merely to talk the imagery into your own head.

Next step: Get into a relaxed position—lying down or sitting in a reclining chair—and listen to your first scenario. The best way to do this is with headphones, but a regular tape recorder playback mechanism will do the trick.

What you will be listening to is yourself saying something like, "I am sitting in a lush, green park . . . ," or "I am immersed in a perfectly warm bubble bath, listening to my favorite jazz . . . ," and so forth.

As you listen to your self-hypnotic tape (yes, this *is* self-hypnosis), concentrate on the feeling that you intended to create with your scenario. Breathe slowly and rhythmically—inhaling through your nose and exhaling through your mouth, as you did in Exercise 6. Focus on feelings of serenity, peacefulness, and calm.

While your tape can last as long as your creativity and scenario provide, an effective mental minivacation can be accomplished in only ten minutes. This doesn't mean that your tape-recorded imagery-induction scenario has to be ten minutes long. You can use a three- or four-minute induction, and then merely continue rhythmic breathing and imagery, letting your mind's semiconscious dreamstate do the work. Your assignment is to sit or lie back and enjoy the movie in your mind, letting yourself be transported to another place and another experience.

Once you have mastered the imagery technique, you'll want to stay away longer than ten minutes. But if time really won't allow, use an alarm clock or kitchen timer to awaken you from your miniature departure from reality.

At first, practice each of your scenarios for at least ten minutes per day (a regimen is outlined in the next chapter). Later, your choice of scenario will be determined by the nature of your stress state at the time of your practice.

Implementation: After you have spent a few weeks practicing this exercise, your mind will elicit a conditioned reaction. The first few words on the tape designed to produce peacefulness and serenity will elicit a relaxation response. Eventually, you'll get so good at this that you won't even need the tape. When the pressure builds at work, for example, you can lean back, close your eyes, and recall the imagery of peacefulness for a minute or so. When you feel haggard and run down, you can elicit your mental movie of an exhilarating and energizing image; and when your self-doubts and fears get the better of you, you can respond by eliciting the imagery associated with comfort and security.

You should, of course, continue taking your full

ten-minute vacation breaks daily for purposes of rest and rejuvenation. Use your newly acquired imagery skills like a behavioral tranquilizer. You can't make all the pressures of your busy life disappear, but you can build mental skills that enable your body to respond in accordance with the mind's imagery.

The extraordinary mind-body relationship, which this exercise is designed to enhance, gives you an alternative to *chronic* arousal. You can't get away for enough vacations or take enough naps during your hectic life, but you can arrange for a short mental break in order to recenter your mind and concentration, or lift your energy.

Of course, after your mental minivacation, you're going to return to the same onslaught of demands that sent you packing in the first place. But you'll be refreshed, even after only a ten-minute break. In the fight against debilitating stress, your mind can be your best ally—or your worst enemy.

Exercise 10:
Efficiency and
Time-Management Analysis

Focus: The essence of Type E stress is feeling that there is not enough of you to go around. There are so many demands, so many things to do, and not enough time to do them well.

As I covered in Chapter 8, Type E women often feel that they have failed to live up to their erroneous expectations of what they should be required to accomplish in a day. They have a chronic case of overcrowded schedule.

The reasons for the overcrowding are several, including real demands from valid sources and persons, inadequate delegation, lack of assertiveness in negotiating deadlines and, importantly, underestimation of the amount of time that certain activities necessarily require. The consequences of poor time management are a sense of inadequacy and mounting stress.

This exercise is designed to correct faulty time allocations that contribute to the unrealistic schedules of Type E women.

Exercise Process: The first step is to write down three activities that you have scheduled for tomorrow. Next to each, predict the amount of time—in hours and minutes—that you think the activity will require.

You may choose any three activities. It is useful to select three things that generally take longer than you expect, and therefore cause delays that compound your stress cycle. Or you might want to select activities about which you have the least clarity or certainty with respect to how much time they actually will require to accomplish. Perhaps you will select the three activities on tomorrow's agenda that are the most negative and stressful, or the ones that are most positive, or a combination of these.

The important point is to increase your awareness of how you actually spend your time.

Implementation: To get the maximum benefit from this exercise, adopt a neutral attitude; do not try to prove yourself right or wrong in your time estimates. Since you are the participant-observer in this exercise, your attitude should be as unbiased as possible.

The next day, you will have the list of the three activities and their expected time allocations. Leave the list at home.

During the day, keep a careful log (to the minute) of exactly how long each activity took. Don't try to rush or slow down. The fact that you are observing your time allocations will alter your behavior to a certain degree. That is a well-documented psychological fact called "observer bias." Once you start watching a behavior, the behavior is somewhat altered. Notwithstanding the observer bias, try to behave naturally. Just keep an honest, accurate record.

When you get home, having completed your three activities, take out yesterday's time predictions. Compare your predictions with the actual times.

If you underallocated time, you will have uncovered an important source of stress: When you underestimate the time required for tasks, your schedule is likely to be perpetually overcrowded, with the consequence of making you feel like a chronic underachiever.

Moreover, if your timekeeping records surprise you in terms of the high amount of time that an activity requires, perhaps you should examine your behavior in order to see whether there are possibilities for delegation, being more efficient, ending perfectionism, and so on.

If you overestimated the times, look at that carefully, too. If you think that things will take much longer than they actually do, you may not be maximizing your time with efficiently planned schedules. You may be underutilizing the most productive parts of your day by not doing enough minor activities. Or perhaps your predictions reflect some unnecessary worry or stressful anticipation of "problems" or "complications" that you thought would happen but did not, in fact, occur.

If your estimates and time records jibe fairly well, then your problem is not in misestimation of time, at least not for the activities you selected to observe. But, if your schedule is overcrowded—as most Type E women's are—your problem probably lies in an arithmetic error. Add up the amount of time that all the activities on your typical "To Do" list really ought to require. If your individual time estimates are accurate, the safest assumption is that your arithmetic adds up to a day that is longer than twenty-four hours, taking into account the time required for sleeping.

This kind of personal time analysis raises the awareness of Type E women and helps them gain a better sense of control over their time and their schedules. When you have completed your analysis, integrate your newly gained skills in time prediction to amend your schedule so that it becomes more realistic and attainable. More efficient and realistic schedules result in feelings of accomplishment, satisfaction, and heightened self-esteem.

It is better to do fewer things at a reasonable pace and to accomplish them all, than to plan to do an unreasonable number of activities that will necessarily result in failure to finish.

WHAT TO DO FROM HERE

You now know about several things that you can proactively do to interrupt the vicious Type E stress cycle.

But reading isn't enough; action is required. What to do now is ask yourself these obviously loaded questions: Do I want to continue feeling overwhelmed and unable to control my Type E stress cycle? Or do I want to get on a program that will alter that cycle?

If you opt to change, get yourself ready for a 21-Day commitment to breaking your long-standing stress habits and learning better coping skills.

CHAPTER ELEVEN

The 21-Day Mental Workout: A Training Program for Building Type E Stress Resistance

LIKE breaking other bad habits that have self-destructive consequences—such as overeating or under exercising—the solution to Type E stress requires mustering your willpower, discipline, and commitment to change. But to attain your goal of breaking the vicious Type E stress cycle and building your resistance to the potential ravages of Type E stress, you have to know *what* to do.

In the last chapter, ten exercises designed to develop coping skills were explained in terms both of their justifications—*why* and *how* each exercise or coping skill is relevant to Type E stress—and their implementations.

In this chapter, the exercises are translated into a 21-day training program designed to alter the Type E stress cycle. More specifically, the program is designed to increase your subjective sense of control over stress.

The program outlines, in step-by-step fashion, what to do each day in the form of concrete *behavioral* and *paper-and-pencil* exercises. It is a self-study course in proactive stress management.

As you will see, some passive forms of stress management, like relaxation practice, are included in the program. But the strong emphasis is on a *proactive* attitude about responding to your Type E stress dilemma by learning new techniques, skills, or tools that you can actively integrate into your daily life and relationships.

THE RIGHT MINDSET

Since Type E stress is a cognitive-behavioral syndrome —a problem with how you think and about what you do—the training program must include mental retraining and conditioning, as well as behavior change. To this end, it is important to take some time before beginning the program to prepare yourself mentally for the training experience.

First, be clear that the basic answer to Type E stress is to change your behavior and stop wanting and needing to be everything to everybody. Your new focus should be on regaining a sense of mastery so that you feel less like your life is in control of you, and more like you are in control of your life.

The next mindset adjustment is to accept that no high-achieving woman can eliminate all stress from her life. What you are striving toward is building mental skills for containing stress and for balancing the negative effects of dis-stress with the motivational and relaxation value of positive stressors.

Next, get yourself "psyched up" and properly motivated for the program. Make a three-week contract with yourself. Stick with the program, and the benefits will be returned. But the benefits of training never come without effort, time, and energy. As athletes say: no pain, no gain.

This *is* a mental workout and, consequently, you must be of the mind to do something positive about your stress problem—before it does anything else negative to you. The program involves new behaviors designed to break the vicious Type E stress cycle, and it includes periodic self-assessment measures to help you evaluate your progress.

A stress management plan cannot last for only three weeks. Stress management must become a way of life, just like changing eating habits immediately and permanently is the path toward solving long-term weight problems. But in three weeks, by sticking with the program, you can master a number of tools that, when implemented appropriately in your life, will be your best buffer against the Type E stress cycle.

Be patient. Don't expect change overnight, or even expect to be "finished" in twenty-one days. The twenty-one days are for *training;* the long-term implementation of the skills, tools, and techniques is up to you. Therefore, a maintenance program for long-term success is included at the end of the 21-day training schedule.

HOW TO MEASURE YOUR PROGRESS

Three times during the program, you will rate yourself on five separate scales. The self-assessment scales measure overall Type E stress, as well as general mood, achievement (both qualitative and quantitative), and self-esteem.

The baseline measurements are made on Day 1 of the program; the final assessment of the program's effectiveness is measured on Day 22, or the first day of maintenance. At the midpoint of the 21-Day Workout, there is also an opportunity to evaluate your progress and to establish a picture of the trends in your change process.

The scales are simple ten-point ratings. Seeing the evidence and extent of the program's effectiveness—assuming you are properly implementing your newly acquired coping skills—will be easy and clear.

Three assessments over the span of twenty-one days does not contradict the earlier injunction to avoid overly frequent self-evaluations. An exception pertains to self-improvement programs. Any self-improvement regimen, be it stress management, weight reduction, exercise, or time management, requires a method for evaluating progress and assessing the nature of your improvements. But note that the assessments should still be kept to only weekly or so evaluations.

SEQUENCING OF THE PROGRAM

The training program begins on a Saturday rather than on a Monday, unlike many self-help plans. As you will see, the weekends are used as preparatory time for many of the exercises that you will implement later in the week.

I recommend using a spiral notebook so that all written material is kept in one place.

A Note on Changes and Substitutions: A general rule of thumb is not to change or substitute anything, if possible. But if it is absolutely necessary to move something around—say, to change Tuesday's exercise to Thursday—be sure that you do not skip anything. It is not necessary, however, to stick strictly to the precise order of exercises within any particular day. Obviously, no general program will fit the unique time constraints and daily regimen of every Type E woman. Therefore, it may be necessary to make a few changes in order to accommodate peculiarities of your calendar. Just double check and make the required adjustments so that the full training program gets accomplished. If you must miss a day, or more, of the training—due to illness or emergency—simply resume where you left off and continue doing all twenty-one days.

Try to keep the changes to a bare minimum. The success of structured behavioral programs is largely due to *the structure*. Once you start moving things around, substituting your own version of the program, the effectiveness may diminish, due to the loosening of the structure.

Approach this regimen with the mindset of someone going into training, with the optimistic expectation that you can and will pop loose from the Type E trap. If you stick with the program, your ability to handle the demands of your high-achieving life will be enhanced while reducing your vulnerability to the negative effects of chronic dis-stress.

THE 21-DAY PROGRAM

Day 1: Saturday

1. *Baseline Self-Assessment Measures:* Rate yourself on the following scales based on how you are feeling *today*. These ratings will serve as your baseline, or starting point, against which to measure your progress and improvements.

1. Rate your level of Type E stress:

low stress   high stress

1   2   3   4   5   6   7   8   9   10

2. Rate your mood today:

depressed,   happy, up,
low, blue   euphoric

1   2   3   4   5   6   7   8   9   10

3. Rate the *quantity* of your achievements or accomplishments during the past week:

low amount achieved								high amount achieved	
1	2	3	4	5	6	7	8	9	10

4. Rate the *quality* of your achievements or accomplishments during the past week:

poor-quality achievements								high-quality achievements	
1	2	3	4	5	6	7	8	9	10

5. Rate your overall feelings about yourself:

very negative								very positive	
1	2	3	4	5	6	7	8	9	10

2. *Redefine Role Requirements:* Follow the detailed explanation and instructions for doing Exercise 1 in Chapter 10, pages 223–25.

After completing your delegation analysis, study your decisions. Your goal is to reduce the number of things that you feel you *must* do by yourself, and to increase the number of things that can be delegated, with or without supervision.

This exercise is a redefinition in more workable terms of what each of your roles involves, given the presence of your other roles. It should direct you toward finding appropriate persons to whom you can delegate, and toward identifying what needs to be said to whom in order for the delegation to occur effectively.

Day Two: Sunday

1. *Delegation Scripts:* Based on yesterday's exercise in analyzing role definitions, you will work today on

scripting delegation techniques. Review Exercise 7, pages 241–44.

Write out five sentences, based on yesterday's analysis of your responsibilities, that communicate delegation and accurately convey the level of involvement and/or supervision that you will or will not maintain.

Say the sentences out loud to yourself or to a partner, and check your tone, intonation, and other nonverbal modes of communication that may sabotage your message. Work toward good, clear, assertive sentences that are not qualified by apologies, aggressiveness, defensiveness.

2. *Writing Scenarios for Mental Minivacations:* Review Exercise 9, pages 247–52. Write the three mental minivacation scenarios as detailed in the instructions. Record your scenarios onto cassette tape. The actual minivacations will be practiced during the coming week.

3. *Relaxation Practice:* Spend ten minutes lying down with your eyes closed, breathing rhythmically and deeply. Review the instructions in Exercise 6, pages 238–41, on rhythmic breathing and muscle relaxation. Don't worry about how well you are able to do this. Today is your first day of practice; with continued daily practice, you will become adept at eliciting a relaxation response.

Day 3: Monday

1. *Rank Ordering:* Since this is the top of the workweek, do the rank-ordering exercise on pages 225–27 early in your day. Make a list of everything you have to do today. Then rank order the list, giving highest priority to those list items with the worst consequences if not finished today. Then focus on going to work, doing what you have to do, one activity at a time, in rank order.

2. *Efficiency and Time-Management Analysis:* Re-

view Exercise 10, pages 252–55. Take the first three items on your rank-ordered "To Do" list. Estimate, in hours and minutes, the amount of time you think it will take you to accomplish or complete each item. Write down your estimates and put them away in a drawer.

As you do the three items that you selected, record the actual time, in hours and minutes, that the activity required. Remember to remain as unbiased as possible. Don't rush, and don't slow down intentionally just to make your estimates accurate. Analyze your efficiency and time-management predictions by comparing your estimates to the actual recorded data.

3. *Talk Yourself Down and Clean Your "Tapes"*: Review Exercise 8, pages 245–47. Think about the events that occurred today or over the last week. Focus on an occurrence to which you responded negatively and which, therefore, "caused" you stress.

Write down the automatic thoughts that came to your mind about the incident at the time, and the thoughts that you still have about what happened.

Review and analyze the quality of the logic in your thinking. Is it appropriate? Or is it overgeneralized? Polarized and extreme? Dramatized, or in some other way fraught with cognitive errors? Try to identify every logical error.

Next to each erroneous automatic thought, write a corrective, more rational response. This is the process of *talking* yourself down. Use it from now on whenever you find yourself tensing up and starting to feel stressed.

4. *Practice deep, rhythmic breathing, with muscle relaxation,* for ten minutes. *Make the time* for relaxation. Relaxation is a learned response, and practice is necessary to achieve the conditioned response.

Day 4: Tuesday

1. *Update your rank-ordered list:* Cross off yesterday's accomplishments and reorder your priorities, given whatever additional items have come up in your schedule today. See Exercise 2, pages 225–27, for details on updating your list.

2. *Using Guided Imagery with Relaxation:* Today you will integrate the ten-minute relaxation break with a mental minivacation. Select the one of your three scenarios that is best suited to how you are feeling today. Lie down at home (or at work, if possible) and breathe rhythmically and deeply, relaxing your muscles as much as you can. Put on your headphones and turn on your recorded scenario. Try to focus your concentration on the mental imagery your scenario conjures. When the ten minutes are over, open your eyes and think about how rested and rejuvenated you feel.

3. *Preparation for Role-Playing:* Make arrangements with a friend, spouse, or other person to help you role-play your scripts for delegation. Try to coordinate the exercise practice for this coming Saturday; if a person-to-person session is impossible, the telephone is an acceptable substitute.

Day 5: Wednesday

1. *Update your rank-ordered list.*

2. *Write "No" Scripts:* Review Exercise 3, pages 227–30. Identify three people (organizations) in your life who make demands on your time and resources. Think of the kinds of things they ask you to do, or expect you to do, that you would like to refuse.

For each example, write a sentence or two that conveys that you are *not* going to fulfill the request or expectation. Be assertive, not aggressive. Remember that saying "No" some of the time is necessary for self-preservation.

Practice saying the lines aloud, either by yourself or, preferably, with a tape recorder so that you can play back the tape and see how you sound. Work on becoming more fluent with denials, refusals, and other negative answers.

3. *Clean your tapes.* Review the quality and content of your thinking regarding people, events, or things over the past few days that have stressed you. Write down your automatic thoughts; identify cognitive errors. Write corrective, rational responses and replace your negative thinking with more stress-resistant thoughts.

4. *Take a ten-minute mental minivacation* following yesterday's instructions.

Day 6: Thursday

1. *Update your rank-ordered list.*

2. *Do an efficiency and time-management analysis* using any three items from today's prioritized "To Do" list. Estimate the time you anticipate will be required; record the actual time necessary for completion. Compare your estimates and adjust your time management plans and "To Do" lists accordingly. In other words, increase or decrease your time allocations based on whether you have been under- or overestimating time.

3. *Take a mental minivacation* for ten minutes.

Day 7: Friday

1. *Update your rank-ordered list.* Include weekend items; amend and refine your planning based on your efficiency and time analyses from yesterday and Mon-

day. Use the data you have collected to make your "To Do" lists more achievable.

2. *Make a separate list of all the items since Monday that you have crossed off.* Look over the list of the week's accomplishments, and reward yourself for the amount of work you got done.

3. *Take a peaceful and serene mental minivacation.*

Day 8: Saturday

1. *Update your rank-ordered list.* Include one additional assignment for the day: Role-play for at least twenty minutes as described in the stress inoculation exercise on pages 241–44.

2. *Role-Playing and Stress Inoculation:* Locate the delegation scripts you wrote last Sunday and review them carefully. With your role-playing partner, try to anticipate the likely responses of the person whose role is being played. For example, if the delegation script is directed toward a child, ask your partner to say what the child would be likely to say. If the delegate in question is a fellow worker or employee, ask the partner to role-play responses for that person. Also use your partner as a critic for your presentation. Ask him or her to critique and improve your tone of voice, wording, or other aspects of the delegation scripts as necessary.

Practice each script at least three times. With your partner, develop acceptable responses to the anticipated replies. Your goal is to be assertive, clear, and *unmovable* in your delegation. Rehearse attempts on the part of the delegate to argue with you, and construct verbal parrying methods to avoid an argument while still getting your point across. Assertiveness sounds like a broken record. Once you get your main message well formulated, stick with it, repeat it, and don't get sucked into the other person's agenda for the conversation.

Be aware of how your stress level diminishes as you repeatedly practice your scripts.

Note: This exercise can be practiced alone, if absolutely necessary. You will have to play both roles, doing the best job you can of scripting anticipated and effective responses of both participants in the conversation.

3. *Clean your tapes.* Select anything that has happened during the week that caused you to feel tense, stressed, worried, or depressed. Write down your automatic thinking about the event. Carefully scrutinize your written thoughts for the presence of cognitive errors. If necessary, review Exercise 8, pages 245–47. Write corrective responses to your erroneous thinking; focus on these stress-resistant thoughts.

Repeat this exercise any time you start to feel tense or aroused. The earlier you can correct negative thinking, before it takes over and shades your whole thought process gray, the better for stress control.

Day 9: Sunday

1. *Pleasurable Activities List:* Review Exercise 4, pages 230–34. Compose your list of pleasurable mental and physical activities. Remember, the list should be extensive and varied. It should also be flexible and broad enough to include both time-consuming activities as well as those that require minimal time. Include activities that require advance planning, and those that can be done with no planning whatsoever. You will be implementing the pleasurable activities list during the coming week.

2. *Writing "What I Need" Scripts:* See Exercise 7, pages 241–44. As you did last Sunday and last Wednesday, you will be writing scripts. This time, select three subjects to whom your scripted lines will be addressed.

Write three scripts that *ask for something* from these people—affection, help, more resources and support, understanding, or anything else you feel that you need. Write scripts that are as close as possible to your natural way of speaking. You will use these scripts in the coming week.

3. *Take a mental minivacation* for fifteen to twenty minutes. You've earned it!

Day 10: Monday

1. *Do a new rank-ordered list* of everything you have to do today, updating from your previous list.

2. *Include two pleasurable activities in your day's schedule.* Select any two activities from your pleasurable activities list, and *do them.*

3. *Take a mental minivacation* for ten minutes.

Day 11: Tuesday

1. *Midpoint Self-Assessment Measures:* Rate yourself on the following scales based on how you are feeling *today.*

1. Rate your level of Type E stress:

low stress   high stress

  1   2   3   4   5   6   7   8   9   10

2. Rate your mood today:

depressed,   happy, up,
low, blue   euphoric

  1   2   3   4   5   6   7   8   9   10

3. Rate the *quantity* of your achievements or accomplishments during the past week:

low amount   high amount
achieved   achieved

1   2   3   4   5   6   7   8   9   10

4. Rate the *quality* of your achievements or accomplishments during the past week:

poor-quality   high-quality
achievements   achievements

1   2   3   4   5   6   7   8   9   10

5. Rate your overall feelings about yourself:

very negative   very positive

1   2   3   4   5   6   7   8   9   10

Think about what you are learning about yourself. Review in your mind how the exercises relate to Type E stress and to its related components of achievement, self-esteem, and mood. Reward yourself for following the workout program.

2. *Update your rank-ordered list.*

3. *Do two pleasurable activities.*

4. *Clean your tapes.* Review your stress reactions and the automatic thinking associated with them. Clean your mental tapes of cognitive errors by writing the corrective responses and using them to replace your negative thinking.

5. *Take a mental minivacation* for ten minutes.

Day 12: Wednesday

1. *Update your rank-ordered list.*
2. *Do two pleasurable activities.*

3. *Rehearse your "What I Need" scripts* aloud, either alone or with a supportive friend or partner. Focus on getting prepared to implement the scripts in actual conversations when you will assertively and clearly ask for what you need.

4. *Take a mental minivacation* for ten minutes.

Day 13: Thursday

1. *Update your rank-ordered list.*

2. *Do two pleasurable activities.*

3. *Do a time and efficiency analysis* on three items from today's rank-ordered list. Estimate your time allocations; record the actual data. Compare the two, and work on adjusting your schedule so that you are better able to accomplish what you set out to do within realistic time parameters.

4. *Take a mental minivacation* for ten minutes.

Day 14: Friday

1. *Update your rank-ordered list.* Revise your list to include weekend items.

2. *Do two pleasurable activities.*

3. *Review and analyze your rank-ordered "To Do" lists* for the last week; analyze them in the context of what you have learned about your efficiency and time allocations. Notice how many things you *did* get accomplished.

4. *Take a serene and peaceful mental minivacation* for fifteen minutes and clear your mind of the clutter by centering your concentration on the pleasant imagery.

Day 15: Saturday

1. *Update your rank-ordered list.*
2. *Do two pleasurable activities.*
3. *Problem-Solving Session:* See Exercise 5, pages 235–37. Stress arises from unresolved problems. Select one nagging problem in your current life situation. It can be a big problem or a minor but irritating hassle. Cumulative stress from common, daily hassles, in fact, can be quite destructive even though the problems themselves are nothing more than trifling nuisances.

First, *identify* the problem. Then *brainstorm* (by yourself or with a friend or partner) as many alternative solutions as you can think of, no matter how improbable or patently undesirable a solution might initially seem.

After brainstorming, turn to evaluating and weighing alternatives. Remember, even the "best" solution may still be somewhat undesirable or entail some cost or other, but that is the nature of nagging problems: their solutions often are an array of undesirable alternatives, so decisions are frequently deferred or altogether avoided.

In the evaluation process, assume the attitude of a vigilant decision maker. Get the information you need and evaluate the pros and cons, the benefits and costs, of each alternative.

Then, having satisfied yourself that you have carefully considered each alternative (including doing nothing, or continuing to do what you are now doing), turn to the step of *selection.* Make the best, or the least undesirable, available choice.

Make a plan to implement the solution during the coming week. Then stick with your plan. If the solution to your problem includes the need to delegate, say "No," or ask for something that you need, remembering that you have been practicing these skills. Use your new tools to implement the solution to your problem.

4. *Practice your "No" scripts, delegation scripts, and "What I Need" scripts.* Use a tape recorder or a role-playing partner to rehearse. Work on feeling natural and self-assured with your communications. Rehearse the phrases for at least ten to twenty minutes.

Think about the opportunities you will have in the coming week to implement some of your scripts. Be aware that the choice is now yours: If you start to feel overloaded, think about the tools you have to fight back against the deluge of demands.

Day 16: Sunday

1. *Update your rank-ordered list, as necessary.*
2. *Do two pleasurable activities.*
3. *Negotiation Scripts:* Not all deadlines can be met. When a choice must be made between competing demands for your time, you must know how to negotiate effectively for schedule changes or adjustments in others' expectations of you.

Write five scripts that would be appropriate for various sources of demands on your time. Include work, family, organizational, social, and other stressors. In your script writing, remember that the concept of negotiation embodies an attitude of *flexibility,* not rigidity, as well as compromise.

Construct realistic, or imaginary but plausible, scenarios of deadline demands, or requests that imply a deadline, and write a script to bargain for more time. Try writing a script that seeks to negotiate for reducing the size, scope, or requirements of a task; write a script in which you agree to do something for someone, but according to a time schedule you can be comfortable with; write a script that gives some alternatives to the other person making the deadline request.

4. *Take a mental minivacation* for ten minutes.

5. *Clean your tapes.* Carefully examine your thoughts about people or things that have caused you stress over the past week. Write down your negative thoughts and the corrective responses.

Day 17: Monday

1. *Update your rank-ordered list* for the start of the work week.

2. *Practice all your scripts: negotiation, delegation, "No," and "What I Need."* Look for appropriate opportunities to implement the communications this week.

3. *Desensitization via Guided Imagery and Relaxation:* Review Exercise 6, pages 238–41. Thinking ahead to the coming week, identify an event (a meeting, conference, conversation, social event, et cetera) that is causing you stressful anticipation or worry.

Start with a mental minivacation to induce relaxation. When you feel relaxed, and your breathing is slow and rhythmic, begin to imagine the scene of the anticipated stressful event. Be clear and detailed with your imagery. As you see yourself in the scene, try to see exactly what you look like, how you are dressed, what your body language is saying. As you stay with this imagery, try to maintain a state of relaxation. If you feel yourself starting to tighten up or get tense, stop the imagery about the stressful scene. Return to the imagery of your mental minivacation until a state of relaxation returns. Then try imagining the stressful scene again, still maintaining relaxed muscles and breathing.

Practice this exercise for twenty minutes. As you become more and more able to see the scene in your mind and to maintain relaxation at the same time, you will be accomplishing a degree of stress desensitization. You may expect the event itself to be less stressful than feared as a result of this exercise. Try to practice each day until the scheduled or anticipated event, and use the desensitization technique whenever the stress begins to build to unpleasant levels. Remember, this technique may be used as a behavioral tranquilizer.

4. *Do two pleasurable activities*.

Day 18: Tuesday

1. *Update your rank-ordered list*.
2. *Do two pleasurable activities*.
3. *Practice desensitization* with imagery and relaxation for ten minutes.
4. *Focus on the choices you have this week to use any of the scripts that you have written and rehearsed*. Decide to implement the techniques where you see the opportunity to interrupt the Type E stress cycle.

Day 19: Wednesday

1. *Update your rank-ordered list*.
2. *Do two pleasurable activities*.
3. *Practice your "No" and negotiation scripts*. Think about opportunities to use them, and do so when appropriate.
4. *Do an efficiency and time-management analysis* (see pages 252–55). Have your estimates improved in accuracy? Are you more realistic with your time allocations? Have you identified areas of inefficiency that can be improved?
5. *Do* either *ten minutes of desensitization of an anticipated stressful event using imagery and relaxation*, or *take a ten-minute mental minivacation of your choice*.

6. *Clean your tapes*. Check the quality of your thinking about stressful events. Replace your erroneous thoughts with more rational, stress-resistant responses.

Day 20: Thursday

1. *Update your rank-ordered list;* incorporate adjustments from yesterday's time-management analysis.

2. *Do two pleasurable activities*.

3. *Practice delegation and "What I Need" scripts.* Commit yourself to implementing your scripts when necessary. Look for opportunities to exercise control; be aware of your choices. Ask for what you need. Reduce the amount of unnecessary drain on your finite resources by delegating and negotiating.

4. *Do either a minivacation or desensitization exercise* for ten minutes.

Day 21: Friday

1. *Update your rank-ordered list;* integrate weekend requirements.

2. *Do two pleasurable activities*.

3. *Review and practice all scripts* for ten to twenty minutes. Become as comfortable as you can with the words, until they begin to integrate naturally into your normal speech patterns.

4. *Evaluate your implementation of the problem-solving solution* from last Saturday's exercise. Did you implement the solution? If not, why not? Review the problem-solving method. How did it work? Do adjustments or changes need to be made? Problems tend to be fluid, so problem solving involves periodic reassessment and evaluation of your current operative solutions. Revise your problem-solving strategy as necessary.

5. *Clean your tapes.* Replace your cognitive errors with stress-resistant thinking.

6. *Assume your relaxation response.* Lying down and breathing rhythmically, center your concentration on the feelings of increased control over your life that you now have. As you continue to relax for ten minutes, get yourself mentally "primed" for maintaining your progress after the training period is over.

7. *Look through your spiral notebook of the last twenty-one days' work.* Review the skills you've acquired or practiced. Identify the areas you need to work on further, and develop a plan.

Maintenance

On the first day of maintenance, Day 22, rate yourself on the following scales:

1. Rate your level of Type E stress:

   low stress   high stress

   1   2   3   4   5   6   7   8   9   10

2. Rate your mood today:

   depressed,   happy, up,
   low, blue   euphoric

   1   2   3   4   5   6   7   8   9   10

3. Rate the *quantity* of your achievements or accomplishments during the past week:

   low amount   high amount
   achieved   achieved

   1   2   3   4   5   6   7   8   9   10

4. Rate the *quality* of your achievements or accomplishments during the past week:

poor-quality   high-quality
achievements   achievements

1   2   3   4   5   6   7   8   9   10

5. Rate your overall feelings about yourself:

very negative   very positive

1   2   3   4   5   6   7   8   9   10

Evaluate your progress from Day 1 to Day 22. This self-assessment will help you to see concretely how becoming proactive and responding differently to your life stressors has altered your Type E stress.

You now have learned the necessary tools to break your bad Type E stress habit. Applying the techniques from the training program in your daily life will make a big difference in your stress level.

As you proceed through your maintenance period, which should never end, try to tailor the techniques from the training to your situation. Develop a repertoire of coping skills to control the rate and intensity of demands on your time and resources. Use your relaxation and imagery skills regularly to stay in practice, and use them in particular when you are hit with a sudden increase in stress level. You have many skills that will serve you well in your struggle with stress, skills that you can use to talk yourself down, calm yourself down, set priorities, accurately plan, and communicate your needs effectively.

It is good practice to score yourself on the five rating scales once a month. Write a note now on your calendar for the next three monthly interim assessment periods. Compare these ratings with those that you did on the first day of your maintenance period when you were fresh out of training.

On the basis of your follow-up assessments, decide if you need to do some "booster" training. Perhaps your stress level is creeping upward. Have you been delegating effectively, or doing everything yourself? Have you asked for what you need, or negotiated effectively for more time if you needed it?

Periodically, give yourself a refresher course by re-reading Chapter 10 and studying the exercises and their implementations.

Be aware of the necessity to maintain balance among the complex roles you juggle—balance between positive and negative stressors, between mental and physical activities, between giving and receiving, and so on. Remember to include pleasurable activities every day. It is all too easy for Type E women to slip back into old patterns of doing everything for everybody, and not enough for themselves.

Finally, while I have emphasized the importance of your commitment and psychological awareness in the effort to manage stress, if the program is to have its fullest value, it is necessary to get others in your life to cooperate fully with what you are trying to achieve. But remember to be patient. You can start changing others' behavior and expectations by changing your *own* behavior. Delegate, set priorities, negotiate, ask for what you need, and the behavior of those who are connected to you will eventually be altered in turn.

The long-term maintenance of Type E stress control is a matter of daily, continuous practice. The reductions in stress level and symptomatology, as well as the enhancements in quality of life and achievements, are worthy payoffs to your training efforts.

Conclusion

BY now, if you've read this book carefully and followed the 21-Day Mental Workout, you are a changed woman.

This is not to say that you have metamorphosed into a stress-free female with a glazed expression of bovine contentment. Nobody promised you a life without stress. But you now have new insights and awarenesses of your self-defeating stress habits and patterns of thinking that fuel the stress cycle. And you have acquired new and better ways to manage the reality of your stressful and complicated life.

The dilemma of high-achieving women should not be how to "have it all" by doing it all themselves and enduring the stress. Instead, high-achieving women would better frame the choice as how to live their lives to get *most* of what they really want, while maintaining high-quality, stress-resistant lives in the pursuit of their achievement goals.

You now have the tools to be selective and strategic about when, why, and on whom you spend your valuable time and personal resources. You know that trying to be everything to everybody won't work in the long run.

The choice is up to you.

Notes

CHAPTER 1: WANTING IT ALL

1. "Women, Work and Babies: Can America Cope?" NBC White paper. March 16, 1985.
2. Baruch, G., R. Barnett, and C. Rivers. *Lifeprints: New Patterns of Love and Work for Today's Woman.* New York: New American Library, 1985.

CHAPTER 2: TYPE A MEN AND TYPE E WOMEN

1. Friedman, M. T. and R. Rosenman. *Type A Behavior and Your Heart.* New York: Knopf, 1974.

CHAPTER 4: THE DILEMMA

1. Avery-Clark, C. "Sexual dysfunction and disorder patterns of working and non-working wives." *Journal of Sex and Marital Therapy.* Vol. 12, No. 2. Summer 1985.
2. Personal communication with Dr. Avery-Clark. February 19, 1986.
3. Smith, A. "The myth, fable and reality of the working woman." *Esquire.* Vol. 101, No. 6, June 1984, p. 66. Reprinted with permission.

CHAPTER 5: EXCELLENCE ANXIETY

1. Source material for this chapter in O'Leary, V., R. Unger, and B. S. Wallston. *Women, Gender, and Social Psychology.* New Jersey: Lawrence Erlbaum Associates, 1985.

CHAPTER 6: EGO CONFUSION

1. Bem, S. L. "The measurement of psychological androgyny." *Journal of Consulting and Clinical Psychology*. Vol. 42, 1974.

CHAPTER 9: EVERYTHING-TO-EVERYBODY BEHAVIOR

1. Gilligan, C. *In a Different Voice: Psychological Theory and Women's Development*. Cambridge: Harvard University Press, 1982.

CHAPTER 10: EXERCISE AND TACTICS FOR REDUCING TYPE E STRESS AND BUILDING STRESS RESISTANCE

1. Benson, H. *The Relaxation Response*. New York: Morrow, 1975.

Index

A

Abandonment, fear of, 129–33
Achievement criteria, 4–5
Achievement motivation, 77
  excellence anxiety and, 46–49
  process orientation vs. impact orientation to, 54–55
Achievement self-sabotage, 69–73
Actor-observer bias, 94–97
Addictive behavior, 71
Adrenaline, 11–12
  as reinforcer, 197–99
Affiliation needs
  achievement motivation and, 49, 54
  satisfying, 76, 78

Age, 3–4, 34
Alcohol abuse, 5, 16–17
  as self-sabotage, 71
Ambivalent lovers, 97–99
Anger, 11, 15–16
Anxiety. *see* Excellence anxiety.
Approval, 168–69, 180
  affiliation needs and, 48
Arousal
  chronic, 37, 189
  as reinforcer, 197–99
  Type A behavior and, 12, 17
  Type E behavior and, 17
Avery-Clark, Constance, 38

B

Beck, Aaron, 154

282